The Light Seer's Tarot: Meaning of Cards in Love, Relationships, Work, Money, Destiny, Profession, Places, Objects, Advice and Warnings

Alexander Lee and Maria Sova

Published by Alexander Lee, 2023.

Table of Contents

COPYRIGHT

NOTE

Unfortunately, this book does not contain images of the cards. We cannot use them due to copyright, so keep the Light Seer Tarot deck next to you when reading to make it easier for you to study the symbolism of the cards and other meanings.

MAJOR ARCANA

The Fool

0 Major Arcana

Symbolism

1. According to ancient legends, the precious amethyst was a gift from the titaness Rhea to Dionysus, the god of wine, to keep his mind clear and sober at times of celebration. In the same way, the Fool on his life route strives to keep his mind clear and unbiased, moving towards understanding the world in its true light, perceiving all phenomena objectively and without prejudice.

2. The young woman in the picture spreads her arms in a salute to infinity, she gives herself over to the will of fate, jumping backwards rather than forwards, believing in the favorable outcome of her action. The crystal in her hand serves as a symbol of inner orientation, and she also holds a stick in her hand to protect herself from the unpredictability and difficulties of life's path. A person following this arcana is full of optimism and willingness to take risks, daring to jump into the abyss. Clad in a sunny yellow dress maiden symbolizes vitality, craving for new places and experiences, ease of communication and establishing new contacts. A decisive step such as jumping off a cliff requires courage and daring. The Fool possesses both, and is constantly hungry for new discoveries and uncharted horizons. He explores the world with pure-hearted curiosity, like a child, everything beckons and attracts him, he seeks to experience and see what it is like to soar in the air, and what awaits him at the place of landing. His sincere interest in new things knows no bounds, and he holds no ill intentions in his quest for knowledge, discovering the world and people in all their diversity.

1

3. The woman in the image takes a leap backwards, with her eyes closed, surrendering completely to the will of the cosmos. She begins her adventure by throwing herself into the vastness of the unknown. In these endless patterns of the cosmos we recognize the mandala with the lotus with eleven petals, symbolizing the readiness of man to step into a new stage of his life. This is the sign of a new cycle of life, where the decade symbolizes the end of the past stage and the number eleven symbolizes the dawn of a new era.

Total value

The Fool arcana is perceived as a symbol of an endless cycle: it is both the starting point and the final outcome of the soul's great journey within the Elder Arcana of the Tarot. In the role of the Hero, the Fool represents the soul meeting the lessons and challenges presented by each of the Elder Arcana. The Fool represents the beginning of the journey, filled with spontaneity and the quest for knowledge, as well as the end of the journey, where the soul reaches enlightenment and wisdom, symbolized by the arcana of Peace.

The Fool represents childlike spontaneity, our inner child archetype, open-hearted people who are eager to find out what awaits them outside the familiar world. Symbolizing a clean slate, he represents a beginning without previous marks, a new beginning, the arrival of new knowledge, pleasant encounters. Fool does not hold on to the past and easily meets the new. Zero can also symbolize a person with deep wisdom, realizing the futility of all things. Fool reflects the image of a freedom-loving, open to new knowledge of man, thirsty for travel, ready for change and beginnings.

His attitude to life is easy, troubles do not upset him, as he is not attached to strict principles and does not limit himself to the framework. The Fool can act as a spiritual leader, erasing established ideas in the minds of his students, freeing them for new life discoveries. He is the embodiment of vitality, having a wide range of interests and hobbies. Creativity and creativity are also inherent in the Fool, who respects the opinions of others, their culture and point of view.

The card of the Fool can promise surprises in life's journey, cutting off the craving for stability and heralding a period of change and disorder. It indicates a sudden discovery of a new direction, inspiration for a change of lifestyle, a new job, a change of home, the beginning of a different phase in a relationship, a new chapter in the book of life.

Fool denotes the birth of something new, the emergence of favorable opportunities and chances. It symbolizes initiation into uncharted areas, initiation into the secret knowledge. This is the archetype of a wandering soul, tireless traveler and pioneer, full of brilliant ideas. The Fool appears as an impulsive, open, fearless and sometimes risky person. He can be associated with a rebellious artist, a hippie, a wanderer, a wandering musician or a wise philosopher who brings a touch of extravagance and unpredictability to life.

In a negative aspect, this card can reveal personalities with promiscuous, unbridled tendencies, with mental problems. A person associated with this card is inclined to neglect material goods, may wander without purpose and means of livelihood. He may not care about his own future and the potential consequences of his actions. Such people often ignore accepted social norms, violating the personal boundaries of others. May become illegal and a cause of stress for others, may behave inappropriately and distort reality in their perception. Their behavior can be childish and unserious, which in the worst case can lead to social downfall, to living at the bottom of society - this is the dark side of freedom, when a person has nothing left and can end up on the streets. Such irresponsibility and fickleness can lead to serious problems.

RELATIONSHIPS

In this relationship both people feel joy and carefree, as if they were children again, they highly value personal space and independence from each other, there is no jealousy and any signs of possessiveness, they do not embarrass their partner with manifestations of jealousy, they realize that by giving freedom, the partner remains close and begins to value the relationship even higher. This is the relationship of two people with a positive attitude, having a great sense of humor, adoring travel, adventure, together attending various entertainments, like to laugh, enjoy life, behave at ease, in general it is a light and joyful relationship where partners do not create discomfort for each other. It can also be a symbol of love that unexpectedly appears in life. It is possible a new stage in the relationship, the appearance of a child, a new round of relationships, an opportunity to start over.

It can also symbolize unexpected twists and surprises in a relationship. When partners behave in a non-serious manner and do not take the relationship maturely. A relationship that is characterized by frivolity, unexpected breakups and departures. A partner who lacks stability and reliability, longing to experience everything at once with different people. Lack of pickiness in the choice of connections. This may be an indication of a relationship without commitment, loose connections. It may be a description of a traveler, a trucker who has several partners in different places, and it may also reflect the life of a person who loves his freedom, is single and not in a permanent relationship.

Work and finance

A person identified with the card Fool may experience a complete lack of funds. This manifests itself in the inability to manage finances competently: income appears, but immediately spent recklessly, and the person does not understand how to dispose of them correctly. Such a person avoids responsibility, he is afraid of large sums and hastily gets rid of them, trying to avoid obligations. We see rash investments, inattention to financial details and the terms of contracts; everything is done naively and with too much trust, sometimes trusting unsuitable people. Behavior in business is not serious, the financial state remains unstable and shaky. Here actions are spontaneous, a person relies on fortune and the support of the cosmos, counting on the help of others, their experience, without meaningful plans and strategies. However, it can also mean a high potential for creativity, an unconventional approach to tasks, when it is necessary to act unconventionally, and the result can be pleasantly surprising, if you apply creativity to the matter.

The finances predicted by the Fool card can come spontaneously and from a variety of sources, including winnings or unexpected earnings, forming a fickle and variable income. The card reflects a creative approach to work; the Fool requires space for creativity and prefers professional activities without rigid boundaries or limitations. If deadlines are present in work, they are little compatible with the Fool's nature. The Fool values personal freedom and independence, prefers a flexible schedule and autonomy in business. It can be a person engaged in freelancing, who will easily abandon the project if he feels excessive pressure from the client. For such an individual, freedom of choice is more important than financial prospects. The card can also indicate a lack of experience, professional knowledge and skills, lack of responsibility, as well as scattered attention and waste of energy. On the way to earnings, a person is often hindered by a lack of discipline.

Purpose

Teaching inner and outer freedom, giving freedom to others, allowing uniqueness in each person. To avoid excessive attachment, to realize the immateriality of material goods in this world, realizing that at any second everything can collapse into the abyss, and therefore it is essential to maintain inner freedom and not to be attached to objects, individuals, locations. It is important to realize that life is a continuous adventure and a vast arena to explore the unknown. One should not limit oneself to one thing, one should discover new aspects of the world and believe in the cosmos. One should become more agile, thirsty for knowledge, adaptable and open to new things. One should learn to organize one's life in such a way as to be independent and free, not subject to someone else's influences.

Occupation

Creative professions, artists, musicians, travelers, bloggers, pilgrims, IT specialists, internet and technology field. Research, discovery, working with children, in maternity hospitals. Psychiatrists, psychologists, yoga trainers, people engaged in spiritual practices and discoveries, free schedule in work, remote work, standup.

Locations and OBJECTS

Nature, rocks, cliffs, maternity hospital, psychiatric clinic, places where artists and other bohemians gather.

Tip

Analyze the areas where you still feel constrained, discover areas where you lack freedom, where you fear it and cannot fully embrace it. Perhaps it's outdated principles and beliefs that are preventing your freedom and ease in making new decisions. Or it could be a job that keeps you confined within four walls and takes away your desire to explore the world. Ignite your passion for adventure, take unconventional approaches to problem solving. You must learn to let go, don't cling to permanence, don't be afraid to step into the new, embrace change and new beginnings. It is important to be decisive and spontaneous. Open yourself to change, to the world, to traveling, avoid excessively high expectations of a situation or a person, become simpler, easier to communicate, more positive.

Warning

You should not be reckless with current circumstances and should not give in to momentary impulses. Irresponsible behavior can bring undesirable consequences. This is not the right time to give up everything and start from scratch. You need to show a serious attitude and concentration in the current situation, do not avoid taking responsibility.

The Magician

I Major Arcana

Symbolism

1. Lemniscata, elegantly placed on the hood of the Magician, symbolizes the hermetic aphorism: "what is above is identical to what is below". This sign in the form of a horizontal figure eight symbolizes the cyclic flow of energies that has neither beginning nor end.

2. The dominant tool of the Magician is his unwavering Will and clearly expressed desire. By putting his energy into his chosen desire, he initiates a wave of change in the space around him, and then the energy returns to him, taking the form of an embodied intention. Thus, the Magician carries out an energy exchange with the environment. The Magician acts as a Creator, he realizes his Will, actively manages energy flows, he is well aware that energy is not taken from the void, and everything has to be paid for by participating in the processes of energy exchange. In order to attract to himself what he wants, the Magician must offer something in return, and for this purpose it is not necessary to spend his own energy: he skillfully manages the elements, using their power to achieve goals. He is a master of energy management and knows everything about it. He understands what type of energy is needed for a particular task. His hands are involved in the acts of energy management and the act of Creation, indicating that he uses both logical and intuitive approaches. He manipulates both internal and external space.

3. The dark clothes of the Magician and the black hood hiding his face speak of the impenetrability of his thoughts and the

impossibility of predicting his next actions. He possesses secrecy and influences those around him without them even realizing it. His enigmatic image reflects the hidden power and depth of his thinking, making him inaccessible to other people's understanding and predictions.

4. In the flow of energy, which the Magician directs from his hands, there are symbols of the four elements: fire, water, earth and air. These elements represent the unity and integrity of creation, because everything in the world is made up of these basic elements. The magician is the true creator, wielding the powers of all four elements: water, which symbolizes emotion; fire, representing the spirit; air, identified with the mind; and earth, corresponding to corporeality. He also rules all four suits of the minor arcana, making him a skillful manipulator, a virtuoso player, and a dangerous opponent capable of creating a whirlwind of trouble for his enemies. The magician realizes the malleability of reality and that he has the power to shape it into whatever he sees fit.

5. The Metatron symbol on the Magician's shoulder really adds new layers of understanding to the image of this card. The Metatron Cube, which is a geometric figure consisting of 13 spheres connected by 78 lines, is a symbol of sacred geometry and signifies the matrix upon which all things are built. This symbol emphasizes the deep connection of the Magician with the cosmos, and his ability to perceive, use and manipulate the fundamental energies and information flows of the Universe.

6. The whirlpool surrounding the Magician visualizes his ability to immerse others in his inner world, to create events and situations that allow him to carry out his plans and achieve the desired results. It is a powerful allegory of his magnetism and control over the environment and people's destinies.

7. Magician is the arcana of activity, creativity and manifestation of ideas in the material world. It symbolizes the beginning of action, the moment when the mental image begins to take shape in physical reality. Magician has all the necessary resources for a

successful start - energy, knowledge, confidence and will to act. His appearance in the layout often means that a person has everything necessary for the realization of the planned, he just needs to use it.

8. The described characteristics of the Magician emphasize his leadership qualities, his ability to manipulate and control forces at all levels. He is able to influence people and situations using his intuition, reason, will and knowledge. The Magician is able to exert a strong influence on people, his charisma and ability to persuade make him powerful and respected, but also dangerous if his intentions are not pure.

Total value

The Magician represents the celestial father of the Fool and actively expresses creative energy. His image merges the features of the creator, artisan and master, and his masculine energy is filled with creation. Occupying the position of the first arcana, the Magician symbolizes the beginning of the journey, emphasizing the themes of self-identity and deep self-awareness. In it are clearly expressed such qualities as strong will, determination, awareness of their own responsibility, risk-taking, the desire to innovate and the desire to penetrate into the unknown. The magician is able to turn his plans into the material world, creating a universe of elements according to his plan. His aspirations have the character of immutable laws that must take shape and materialize.

This character is the embodiment of a leader, explorer and pioneer, who is characterized by independence, love of freedom and sensitivity to changes in energy flows. He is distinguished by swiftness in decision-making, quick perception and learning. With natural authority, the Magician is confident in himself and his abilities, and this gives him the strength to support and guide others, to patronize them and become an example for them. A person whose share falls on this card, you need to keep faith in yourself and control your inner world, because the Magician has a unique ability to translate thoughts into reality. This person is characterized by impressive self-esteem, wit and charisma, it is easy for him to establish contacts and keep in touch with people.

In his dark side, the Magician may display excessive self-confidence and arrogance, an inability to adequately perceive criticism and a tendency to be superior to others when his self-esteem crosses reasonable boundaries. He may reject the opinions of others, considering his own point of view to be the only correct one, and apply pressure on others to achieve personal goals. Such a person can endow himself with the status of an unrecognized genius, despising the opinion of others, show excessive obsession and insolence in communication, trying to suppress other people's will and subordinate it to his own. In this aspect, the Magician turns into an egoist, suffering from a complex of his own majesty.

Relationship

In his relationships, he is able to manipulate the environment so that the partner acts according to the Magician's wishes. This includes the ability to influence the feelings and behavior of the partner. For example, in a situation where the Magician would prefer the partner to take the initiative in communication after a quarrel, he uses his volitional attitude to control his own emotions, not to give in to the impulse to contact first and thus influence the development of the situation.

The couple depicted on this card is actively working on their well-being and joy of life. They do not leave the outcome of their relationship to chance, but, rejecting the passive "what will be, is good", they strive for a clear understanding of their desires in the relationship and actively act to improve it. For example, when one partner dreams of the sea and the other of mountains, they find ways to have vivid shared experiences, avoiding selfish struggles over personal preferences. They strive to create a shared reality by choosing places where both mountains and sea can be enjoyed, or by splitting the vacation into two parts to satisfy both desires. In this way, they build a "vortex of happiness" that fills their relationships and hearts. And because the Magician symbolizes powerful masculine and sexual energy, there is a sense of intense passion in such a relationship.

This card can also reflect a situation in which one of the partners takes the leading role and dominates, conducting the life of the other. The magician in this case acts as a cunning manipulator who knows perfectly well what buttons to press to achieve his goals. He has a talent for persuasion and attractiveness. In addition, the Magician is not afraid to take the initiative and make the first step towards his partner. The card can also indicate a person who tries to win the attention of another, and conceives various strategies to draw the person into his sphere of influence. This is an indication of a sophisticated and manipulative relationship style.

The Mage has the ability to control his own feelings and emotions, and everything here is entirely determined by his personal desires. If he does not see a future with a person, the Magician is able to free himself from attachment, and if he seeks to maintain a connection, he will look for ways to arouse interest in his partner. In this way, the Magician can symbolize not so much love for another as love for his own person. But also this card can express a sincere interest in the partner and a desire for new experiences.

The magician is able to remain a self-sufficient unit; he is whole and independent. If something does not meet his expectations or desires in a relationship, he will not hesitate to walk away, or, on the contrary, if he passionately desires something, he will persist in pursuing it. The Magician card, which is a combination of all four elements, can reflect deep emotional attachment to a partner (Water element), continuous thinking about him, sometimes even obsessive (Air element), strong attachment (Earth element), as well as fiery passion and strong desire (Fire element).

Work and finance

The magician embodies the image of an independent and purposeful entrepreneur who succeeds in business. He not only knows how to manage finances with extraordinary skill, but also has the ability to attract funds as if from an unknown source, creating them as if from nothing. His financial flows are strong and steady, resembling a funnel that steadily draws wealth into itself. The magician realizes profits through his relentless drive and bold, deliberate business maneuvers. His own wealth he keeps under tight control, because the Magician has knowledge of how to successfully attract finances and competently manage them. He realizes the personal responsibility for his financial well-being and works tirelessly to strengthen it. The magician achieves the conceived financial indicators, realizes dreams in material terms, attracting the necessary monetary resources and opportunities in his life. He sincerely loves his work, strives to improve his skills and achieves notable success in the professional sphere, which undoubtedly contributes to his advancement on the career ladder and financial growth.

The magician shows himself as a true expert in his chosen field, being a master of a high class. His intellectual abilities and practical skills set him apart from others. The Magician is a virtuoso in managing business processes, personnel and complex financial operations. He is able to transform an enterprise, its structure and appearance, find unique ways to connect different business areas and market niches. The Magician is unwavering in his decisions and infuses his business with confidence. His ingenuity and ability to bring creative solutions make the work process more efficient and original; he is an innovator and creator in his industry. The magician is fully focused on work processes, is characterized by sharp mental work, quick reaction to changes in the market situation and is able to flexibly adapt his products and services to new conditions. He has an intuition that tells him what steps would be best for his business to thrive and utilizes a wide variety of methods to achieve his goals. His endeavors are certainly in the nature of successful and promising projects.

Purpose

Persistently believe in your capabilities, develop and strengthen your willpower, and persistently train it with each new day. Nurture a powerful aspiration in yourself, form the conviction that your desire is an indisputable law, and learn to create the reality of your existence based on your personal aspirations. Be above the whirlwind of circumstances, do not drift on the waves of chance, but form with your own hands the whirlwind of events that is necessary for you, be the creator of your destiny. Compose a scenario of your life and diligently translate it into reality, develop magical skills and the ability to translate thoughts into material things.

Occupation

Magician, esotericist, healer. Work with computer and nano-technologies, engineer, scientific researcher. Hypnotist, masseur, doctor, conductor, painter, sculptor, musician, magician, bartender, financial analyst. A marketer, a person who creates excellent funnels for sales, a salesman from God, so will twist the consciousness of a person that he will buy what he needs and does not need. Presenter, media personality, therapist, writer, manager, teacher, scientist. A trainer who works with an audience, influences the masses, a speaker.

PLACES AND FACILITIES

Places in nature, doctor's office, places where rituals are performed. Funnels in water and earth. Mirrors as portals to other worlds. Workshop, library.

Tip

Strengthen your respect for your own personality, increase the level of belief in yourself and in your unlimited possibilities. Unleash your creativity to its full potential. Take the situation under personal control, do not allow it to be formed on the principle of chance. Show activity and determination in business, because the outcome of any enterprise depends directly on you and your decisions. Focus on the goal and go to it, despite the obstacles, overcoming the opposition of circumstances.

Warning

A situation can get out of control if you put the responsibility for it on someone else. You should reconsider your business strategy. You should not impose your will on another person and pressurize them with your opinion. At this point, self-centeredness and the desire for dominance can turn against you. It can also indicate the presence of a dangerous enemy or a partner who knows how to manipulate people to achieve their own goals.

The High Priestess

II Major Arcana

S ymbolism

1. Mannaz represents the symbol of humanity, its unity and the unbroken chain of life and death. The knowledge of the Priestess encompasses the deepest aspects of being, including all aspects of human nature and its mysteries.

2. Lagu is closely associated with the element of water, the mysterious world of dreams, subconscious processes and intuitive knowing. This suggests that the Priestess has a deep understanding of these aspects and can interpret their meanings.

3. Pertho reflects the mysticism of the unknown, those aspects of reality that have not yet manifested themselves in the material world. The priestess acts as a keeper of secrets and knowledge of the hidden side of things.

4. Wunjo is the rune of joy and bliss. Diving into her subconscious, Priestess finds the keys to achieving complete inner harmony and true happiness.

5. The moon crowning the head of the Priestess, symbolizes the permanence of change, transitional states of being and also denotes the gift of insight, the ability to see the hidden, have prophetic dreams and intuitively feel the world, maintaining a strong connection with the subconscious.

6. The Priestess has moon-shaped earrings on her ears, an echo of her ability to listen to and understand subconscious voices and unspoken truths.

7. Brooches with garnet stones on the Priestess' garments symbolize temptation, a challenge to dare to look behind the curtain of

mystery and gain knowledge that remains hidden from the world. Her necklace of pomegranates serves as a link to spiritual forces.

8. On the chest of the Priestess is the Solar Cross, symbolizing perfect balance and harmony. The Priestess demonstrates the ability to be diplomatic, possessing the skills to influence people, mediate conflicts, bring peace and alleviate suffering, while being cautious and prudent.

9. The Priestess's gaze is hidden, deeply immersed in the world of her sensations and subconscious processes. The eyes painted on her eyelids symbolize her ability to see beyond the ordinary, realizing more than may appear at first glance. Her inward-looking gaze reflects a deep understanding of her own self. After all, the eyes are the mirror of the soul; they reveal that your inner perception determines how the world around you reacts to you. By focusing on her inner state, the Priestess suggests that it is the changes within us that can attract the appropriate life circumstances. By doing so, she shares with us her wise understanding of the universe. The Priestess' posture reads a passive but conscious observation of what lies beyond the visible and material world.

10. The frontal chakra of the Priestess is clearly accentuated, which emphasizes her supernatural abilities of intuition and foresight, sharp thinking activity. The person personified by this card, has a rare gift of insight: she is able to see people through the prism of their true motives and intentions. She not only intuitively feels the nuances of the surrounding reality, but also has the ability to foresee future events. Such a person is characterized by a continuous process of learning and accumulation of multifaceted knowledge.

Total value

Priestess represents heavenly motherhood for Fool, personifying the manifestation of the passive feminine. She does not intervene directly in events, preferring to remind of the importance of the inner voice, which is able to show the right path. Occupying a place on the boundary of the infinite Akasha, the Priestess absorbs knowledge that encompasses the entire universe. Diving into the depths of her subconscious, she becomes the recipient of information and runes that reveal to her the secret symbols of the universe.

In the image of the Priestess we find a gentle, feminine energy, full of harmony, wisdom and mystery, sincerely in love with the surrounding nature. Priestess serves as a mirror for situations where processes remain behind the scenes of reality, where there is a lack of clarity and information, as well as where the reverse side of events is hidden, full of secrets and half-truths. She can symbolize a woman in various aspects: whether she is a mother, wife, sister, daughter, secret admirer, rival, esoteric devotee, nun or virgin.

The call of the Priestess is a call to heightened attention, to intuition, premonitions, dreams, and to all the signs that the world around us sends us. The priestess reminds us of the importance of diving into the depths of ourselves to make sense of what is happening. This is the realm of spiritual knowledge, the secret and magical, the realm of teaching. The Priestess believes that all the necessary answers are already embedded in the subconscious of each of us. In Tarot, she is a mentor who teaches how to interpret the symbols and find answers in the depths of one's own soul. With her help, the outer eye learns to recognize Tarot symbols and the inner eye learns to find the key to them. The priestess is aware of the existence of good and evil, light and shadow, realizing that one does not exist without the other, and perceives through herself the energy of the universe, comprehending its mysteries.

The priestess reflects the image of a person immersed in reflection and focused on his inner world and sensations. Such an individual has a subtle ability to sense the world and is able to decipher its signs. His intuition is a powerful tool, he often sees prophetic dreams and has a developed gift of clairvoyance. This person has a good understanding of people, shows himself as an excellent psychologist. He is not in a hurry to share his thoughts and keeps his personal space secret.

For such an individual, it is extremely important to really feel the situation before making important decisions. He thinks over every step and does not rush to conclusions. Such a person is prone to passivity, acts based on illogical, intuitive impulses. He has the gift of silence and the ability to keep secrets reliably and unmistakably.

In a negative manifestation Priestess can reflect a person insincere, who skillfully hides his true feelings and intentions, shows hypocrisy and succumbs to the temptation to lie. Such individuals constantly use masks to conceal their true intentions. They can be indifferent and indifferent to other people's problems. Priestess in a negative way indicates a lazy person who can leave another in distress, refusing to take responsibility, who shows coldness and detachment. It can also symbolize a person who spreads gossip, behaves evasively and uncertain.

Relationship

The card may reflect the platonic nature of ties between people. Emotions that a person diligently hides, often hides under a mask, so that his true feelings remain invisible to the other. Such feelings can be sublime, and sometimes it seems to a person that his partner is a gift of fate, that in his appearance there is some deep meaning to be unraveled. This is a type of relationship where words are superfluous, because understanding between people is achieved at a more subtle, intuitive level. The partners establish a telepathic connection, they have the ability to feel each other at a great distance.

In such relationships there are often elements of mysticism: people can be separated in different directions, but somehow unexpectedly meet or call each other at the same time. This is a relationship in which partners are able to feel each other's thoughts and emotional state. Sometimes the desire to be near a person arises instinctively, without any logical explanation, as if something unknown pulls to him. In the partner, which displays Priestess, there are features of mystery, insight and spirituality. For him it is important not so much the external side of the relationship, as spiritual unity. In the sexual aspect of the partners seek not just physical contact, but also to spiritual fusion, studying and knowing each other at a deeper level, for which they can use tantric practices, turning sex into a special ritual of energy exchange and strengthening their connection.

The priestess can also symbolize loneliness, the image of a person who has moved away from seeking a relationship or maintaining virginity by focusing on the more subtle, intangible aspects of life. The card can indicate an inner confusion of feelings, when a person cannot sort out his emotions on his own and plunges into the depths of his own inner world to explore and understand them. In addition, the Priestess can be an indicator of secret liaisons, the presence of a secret rival or rivaless. She reveals secrets and hidden aspects in a relationship.

Work and finance

This card may indicate non-obvious sources of profit, when a person prefers not to disclose details of his professional activity or the size of his income to others. In such a context, it is possible to sign a confidential agreement where a non-disclosure obligation is established. Such a person may have an intuitive ability to find non-standard solutions to financial issues. It is important to note that the attraction of finances is possible when he is in a state of inner abundance - the ability to properly tune his thoughts and emotions to a positive mood is extremely important for the Priestess.

In addition, the card can signal the presence of implicit aspects to a situation that are hidden from view, thus creating a double bottomed reality. There may be confusing clauses and hidden clauses in contracts and agreements. Priestess reminds us that if the process of development of a situation is not visible now, it is better not to interfere and let it develop on its own, it is a card that symbolizes the need for patience and ease. It is important for the Priestess to constantly enrich her mind and broaden her horizons, which in turn will contribute to the growth of her material well-being. In matters of finance, especially when it comes to receiving a certain amount of money, the Priestess advises to take into account those factors that are usually left out of the picture or ignored, pointing to alternative routes of cash flow, when funds may not come in the most obvious way, but through intermediary channels.

Purpose

To go deep into the development of one's interaction with the surrounding world and the cosmos, to master the art of deciphering its messages. To work on connection with one's own subconsciousness, to learn methods of managing one's life with its help, to learn how to fine-tune it and effectively use the possibilities of interaction with it. Strengthen female energy, intuitive abilities, clairvoyance abilities. To immerse in the study of psychology, to penetrate into the innermost knowledge, to improve in the field of esotericism. Do not stop the process of learning, constantly expand your knowledge. To study the art of living in harmony and to teach this art to others. To learn to trust one's feelings and inner voice, which helps to move through life.

To perceive the world, one's own self or current events as one would like them to be in reality, and the world will begin to reflect these thoughts and visions, turning them into reality, corresponding to the settings of the subconsciousness of the person. As a Magician has the ability to change reality with the help of willpower, so the Priestess fine-tunes the subconscious mind, sending signals to the world about her desires, and the world responds to them, reflecting and materializing the conceived.

Occupation

Creative professions, esotericism, psychology, professions related to the protection or exploration of nature, landscaping, working with women, student, healers, diplomats, gray cardinals.

PLACES AND FACILITIES

Forest, places in nature, place of learning, temple. Hidden, secret places. Libraries, places where rituals are performed.

Tip

Deepen your understanding of your own emotions, establish a strong connection with your subconscious mind, strive to achieve inner balance. Pay increased attention to dreams and symbols. Avoid hasty conclusions and actions, as the situation requires a thorough analysis. It is necessary to dive into the consideration of the problem with special attention, weighing all the pros and cons and follow the solutions that prompts the heart.

Warning

Some events may occur without your knowledge, certain processes may develop secretly, and you may be bypassed. The card also serves as a warning that now is not the time to take a passive position and keep silent. You should not shut yourself off from your loved ones and accumulate secrets. Be vigilant and make sure that nothing important escapes your attention.

The Empress

III Major Arcana

S ymbolism

1. The Empress card symbolizes the essence of motherhood,
   feminine energy, abundance, financial well-being, aesthetic appeal
   and authority coming from a woman. She also symbolizes a deep
   sense of self-love, the desire for a comfortable existence, to create
   and maintain beauty and order both in personal space and in the
   work environment, as well as a preference to surround oneself with
   only quality and attractive things. The most important aspects
   of its influence are manifested in the images of a faithful wife,
   a favorite partner of a man, a mother, giving care and attention
   to her child, as well as in the role of a responsible mistress of
   the house or business lady, who seeks to achieve prosperity and
   maintain perfect order in all areas of his life. Empress on the map
   appears in the image of nature itself, is the embodiment of our
   planet, its creator and protector. The abundance of water elements
   in the image speaks of her deep emotionality and
   impressionability, as well as the richness of fish stocks, indicating
   fertility and prosperity.

2. The bracelet on the arm is a sign of infinity and renewal, created
   from plants, which symbolizes the inexhaustibility of the
   resources with which the Empress is associated. This sign indicates
   that she has the knowledge and ability to be constantly in a state
   of mental and physical abundance, because she knows how to live
   without knowing the need, and possesses the art of maintaining
   this flow of prosperity.

3. The green leaves woven in the hair of the Empress are a reflection

of her prolific thinking, showing that she always has fresh ideas on how to improve her position in life. She is capable of generating many innovative ideas that can greatly expand horizons and open up new opportunities for development.

4. The Empress pays special attention to her appearance; she artfully arranges green leaves in her hair, giving it a beautiful shape. She shows care not only for her appearance to be flawless, but also fills her thoughts with knowledge of how to achieve, maintain and multiply wealth and prosperity in life.

5. The presence of the Moon on the chart, as a satellite of the Earth, hints at periodicity and certain rhythms in life circumstances. The Empress appears as a model of beauty and self-realization, she can symbolize a loving wife, a wise mother, dear to the heart of the lady. She is a model of calmness and self-confidence, the bearer of love and the desire to share it, embellishing the world around them. This is an active, creative personality, full of care and sensuality, which embodies beauty in all its manifestations. Such a person is characterized by generosity, he has a strongly developed maternal instinct, and he seeks to provide care and protection to others. The value for the Empress is the family, to the construction of which she approaches with special trepidation, forming strong family ties.

Total value

The Empress embodies the image of the earthly mother, who is the protector and patroness of the hero. She symbolizes mother nature, filled with feminine and fertile earthly power. The empress is abundant in fruit and personifies the wild and indomitable power of nature. Like nature itself, she follows cycles, realizing the regularity of the cycle of life, the change of seasons and the phases of the moon. She is familiar with the principles of fertility, growth and development, and manages natural cycles.

The Empress predicts rapid and favorable development of the situation under discussion, promises satisfaction and abundant results. It is a card of favorable outcome, portending stability and reliability. It embodies a sense of confidence, support, and earthly firmness underfoot, foreshadowing a stabilized environment with prospects for further prosperity. The Empress is a symbol of the source of life, the very essence of life-giving energy.

The Empress personifies a person capable of taking responsibility, a person with a pronounced sense of her own importance and power. She is an image of an attractive individual with a fine sense of style. Such a person is naturally sought after by others because of his irresistible attractiveness. He is able to easily attract financial resources and various benefits that come to him from many sources, be it bonuses or gifts. This person knows how to love himself, watches his appearance, preferring to wear stylish and high quality clothes. His home is an oasis of beauty, style and luxury, where order and coziness reign. He is known for his generosity and kindness.

In a negative way, the Empress can reveal excessive responsibility of a person, it can also indicate an individual who suppresses others with his excessive tutelage, showing himself overly attentive and even despotic. This can be an image of a person who seeks to dominate, introducing hypercontrol in all spheres - at work, in the family, in personal relationships. Such a person may be overly concerned with material status, judging others by their material achievements. He requires increased attention to his person and special respect, despite the fact whether it is deserved or not. He can also interfere in the personal space of others, seeking to control their lives.

Relationship

The Moon, a satellite of the Earth, symbolizes the deep interdependence of people in love relationships, just as the Moon causes the tides on our planet. It suggests that partners may have a particularly strong emotional bond. The water element associated with emotions may indicate that lovers are strongly attached to each other and are able to greatly influence their partner's emotional state. The likelihood of pregnancy or the appearance of a child in the relationship is also reflected in this symbolism. Relationships in the couple are described as extremely close, tender and full of joy. In its emotional coloring is a deep sense of love and admiration for the partner, the card is a messenger of all-consuming and deep love, filled with sensuality and warm emotions.

Just as water streams caress the shoulders of the Empress, the partner provides his soulmate with a warm, careful attitude, surrounds him with deep and pleasant feelings, which is a sign of a strong emotional bond. The card hints at the possibility of marriage, and speaks of full understanding and harmony in the relationship. It reflects the maturity of the bond, where each partner is aware of their responsibilities and plays an important role, generally foreshadowing favorable prospects for the relationship. In the context of relationships, the card symbolizes loyalty and devotion, displays the image of a beloved woman or wife. Here there is both passion and reliable connection between partners.

It can also reflect a relationship in which the woman takes on the role of a mother, being overprotective of her partner, which can sometimes be depressing because of the overabundance of attention and care. It can also show that the woman's focus is solely on her own benefit from the relationship, that she is focused on what she will personally gain, rather than on the relationship itself and its quality.

Work and finance

The embodiment of prosperity and progress in business is clearly traced through the ability of a person to bring clarity and direction to their endeavors, contributing to their favorable development. Here we are talking about financial blossoming and strengthening of prosperity. The Empress shows a special skill in investing, continuously increasing her economic prospects and accumulations, demonstrating constant financial growth. She has a talent for turning personal interests and skills into profits, and possesses the art of effective management of resources that will bring her economic success.

The Empress cares for the development of her endeavors, and under her reliable guidance every project flourishes, bringing abundant results. This card symbolizes a favorable environment in the team, where each team member is focused on earning and success. It displays the image of a self-confident leader, the owner of her business, occupying a status position. Possessing a practical mind and deep knowledge in the financial sphere, the Empress is also associated with career advancement and business expansion.

However, in the negative aspect, the Empress may indicate a disorderly development of the affair, reflecting its spontaneous, fertile essence. It may be implied that the project lacks a certain organization and a stable foundation. There may be a risk of employee overload due to excessive pressure and over-control by management. The card may also signal a tendency towards wastefulness, a lack of rigor in spending. A person may disproportionately invest in the external decoration and image of his enterprise, without thinking about the need for a more rational and sensible distribution of the budget.

Purpose

The development of femininity, the ability to be flexible and adaptable in communication with the opposite sex are important qualities. It is necessary to learn to become the basis of the family, to build relationships competently, to care for offspring, to be a support for your partner, to be able to manage both business and personal relationships gently and with feminine intuition. It is also important to take care of your own development, to nurture self-love. To be responsible for one's occupations, to devote oneself to one's preferred activity, to improve it and to reap material rewards. Striving for social fulfillment, creating, bringing beauty to the world around us is also important. To love and appreciate material goods. It is important for the Empress to be respectful of masculinity, to be able to trust men and not to take on excessive burdens.

Occupation

Beauty sphere, jeweler, obstetrician, gynecologist, financier, work with women, nature protection, agronomist, products for women, women's practices and courses, development of femininity and female energy, maternity courses, management position, designer, stylist. In general, this is a realized and self-sufficient woman.

PLACES AND FACILITIES

Places in nature, beautiful, dressy places, maternity, beauty salons, jewelry stores, jewelry boxes.

Tip

Remember to take care of personal well-being, set up your affairs in such a way as to derive maximum pleasure from your interests and circumstances. Be the manager of your destiny, organize the care of your family, financial flows, professional activities, and the health of your body. Strive to make life's circumstances evolve and improve under your skillful guidance. Strengthening your ego, revealing your feminine qualities are the key points in this process.

Warning

Loosen your control and allow yourself to be less dominant in trying to control everything around you. Do not give excessive attention and tutelage to those around you, which may provoke their rejection. Excessive self-possession and focusing solely on personal interests in a situation can lead to undesirable results.

The Emperor

IV Major Arcana

S ymbolism

1. His hand bears the ancient Egyptian symbol of the ankh, which represents a sign of protection and the key to eternal life. This emphasizes that the Emperor acts as a reliable protector for all aspects of life, he stands guard over business interests, family foundations.
2. The ram's head in the image symbolizes its association with the zodiac sign of Aries, which emphasizes its leadership qualities and steadfastness in life beliefs. It indicates the importance of using inner strength consciously and warns that unbridled selfishness can lead to dire consequences.
3. The qualities of the Emperor are also reflected through the planet Mars, which is his throne, emphasizing his activity, results-oriented nature, fighting spirit, and tendency to be aggressive in achieving goals.
4. We see a chessboard and a king piece held by the Emperor. This is a symbol of his desire for tactical superiority, his desire for dominance and power. The Emperor is ambitious and aims for complete control, so that all the actions of his entourage were in harmony with his plans and orders. He perceives himself as superior in any situation, taking a key, strong position in it. Such a person is characterized by strong beliefs and conservatism, thinks over his tactics and due to this achieves impressive results. Chess here acts as a symbol of ingenious strategy in any situation.

Total value

The emperor appears as the earthly ancestor and protector of the protagonist. He symbolizes not only structure and order, but also security with responsibility. His distinguishing features are his ability to achieve goals, his unyielding defense of established boundaries and his surroundings. He is the embodiment of the patriarchal image of the father, a reliable protector, always ready to lend a shoulder to the weak and provide protection.

Emperor acts as a reflection of situations in which there is a high degree of order and structure, a guarantee of stability. This arcana - a symbol of ordering chaotic processes, clarity and detail. Its presence guarantees a reliable state of affairs with a solid foundation, serving as a bulwark for growth and progress. The embodiment of control and discipline, the Emperor has an influential power and authority, and his activities cause sincere respect from others. He relies only on and is confident in his own strength, knowing that self-discipline and self-restraint will be the key to achieving what he wants.

Emperor is associated with the embodiment and implementation of the planned, with a powerful and earthy arcana, which symbolizes real opportunities and tangible achievements. He has a well-thought-out strategy for the development of business, methodical and thoughtful approach to any task. The Emperor is able to create fundamental and strong structures, which he skillfully implements to solve various problems and tasks.

The emperor embodies activity and determination in solving any issues, shows courage and bravery. This is a man with an indomitable will. He strictly outlines the boundaries and rules of behavior, sets clear limits - what is acceptable in relations with him, and what is unacceptable, what standards should be observed in work, and what is unacceptable. The Emperor develops his own rules and follows them without deviation. This arcana radiates genuine male energy, being a symbol of the patriarch, protector and patron. He has impressive control over what is happening and his weaknesses, representing the apogee of masculinity. The emperor is able to organize the environment according to his own desires and established rules.

The Emperor guards against chaos and uncertainty, he builds civilization, providing protection from adversity and wildlife. He is concerned with creating comfort, reliability and light in the home, ensuring that all devices function and order is maintained. In his house one can find shelter from any storms, which is filled with the meaning of the expression "my house is my fortress". As a true master, the Emperor personally takes care of the perfect condition of the dwelling, overseeing that repairs are done to the highest level and everything functions like clockwork.

In the negative aspect, the Emperor can be stubborn, despotic or tyrannical. He is able to exert both psychological and physical pressure. Does not tolerate objections and disobedience, becoming a dictator, demanding compliance with his own rules. In case of disobedience, the Emperor tends to punish and punish. He demands unconditional respect and obedience. He is convinced of his own infallibility and looks down on others. His actions may lack mercy and sympathy for others.

Relationship

The relationship has a patriarchal structure, where the man dominates, actively directing family life and leading the union with his companion, taking care of her and providing protection. Such relationships have a touch of conservatism and deep seriousness. Both partners feel confidence in each other, laying the foundation for a strong and reliable union. In such a union there is stability and orderliness, each partner knows his responsibilities: the man, as a rule, acts as a providing party, and the woman - the keeper of the home. In this relationship, the man takes care of the well-being of the family and the preservation of harmony in the union.

A man also places high demands on his companion: he expects her to maintain order and warmth in the house, to be responsible in cooking and to take care of her appearance. He sets clear boundaries in the relationship, believing that it is discipline in the performance of their roles is the key to their inviolability and durability. Between partners there is a strong sexual connection and a rich intimate life, where the Emperor card symbolizes excellent potency and fertility. Emotionally, there may be a strong sexual attraction, great desire and ambition to conquer the partner. In general, the card reflects the stability of family bonds and reliability in the fulfillment of mutual obligations. It may indicate a husband or permanent partner in a long-term relationship.

In the negative aspect, the picture may depict a person with a pronounced stubbornness and a tendency to be unchanging. It may show a partnership with an individual who insists on playing by his own rules and seeks to dominate the relationship. Such a person does not show excessive emotionality and sentimentality, but he is a pillar to rely on: he is reliable and loyal. In the presence of such a partner can feel safe, as if behind a strong wall. He tends to make independent decisions for both of them, keeping his feelings under strict control.

Work and finance

A stable place of work, respected status in the labor collective, prestigious position, deserved authority. Recognition and honor from colleagues and partners. Issues of work and finance are distributed according to a clear scheme, the Emperor keeps his hand on the pulse of all financial flows, nothing escapes his attention. Professional growth, compliance with the official hierarchy. At the expense of perseverance and strict discipline, outstanding successes are achieved. It is important for a person to have developed financial and work plans, as well as clear instructions for their implementation. The need for a business plan, content plan is obvious.

Emperor symbolizes financial stability, he is favorable to all economic endeavors and entrepreneurial projects, portending success in business and promotion. Under the sign of the Emperor attracts significant funds. The Emperor knows perfectly well how to multiply capital, and realizes that he is responsible for his own material well-being. This person will not deflect blame on parents, circumstances, authorities and so on - he takes full responsibility for his own life, he is the helmsman of his destiny. The Emperor has authority and influence in the workplace. He is active and enterprising in solving financial problems. Effective conclusion of contracts, establishing partnerships. A thorough and balanced approach to business activity.

In addition, the card may indicate excessive stubbornness in decision-making. This is a sign that you should rethink your existing methods of earning and promotion. It is important to reconsider your plans and the scenarios you are used to acting according to. Lack of room for creativity, being constrained by too strict limits - all this can hinder development and growth.

Purpose

Training in the art of competent management of personal life, family ties, business processes with respect for the interests of others becomes key. It is necessary to be not only a support, but also a protector. It is important to cultivate masculine energy, to respect representatives of the stronger sex, to value masculinity, to take responsibility, to be characterized by reliability and determination. It is important not only to earn a livelihood, but also to strive for development in one's profession or leadership position. It is necessary to direct aggression to achieve the set goals, and not on others. It is necessary to be the full owner of your life, to maintain order in each of its aspects. It is important to let go of resentments and claims that may arise to representatives of the stronger sex. The task is to develop your own business, to increase its scale, to strive to build your empire.

Occupation

Businessman, athlete, architect, politician, boss of big corporations.

PLACES AND FACILITIES

Large organizations, government agencies, large-scale corporations.

Tip

It is necessary to develop a detailed plan of action and follow it with discipline, avoiding deviations from the set course, following the chosen strategy consistently and with conscious structure. Taking responsibility for one's own decisions, actions and the results of their realization becomes fundamental. It is important to demonstrate iron discipline and strong-willed qualities. A sensible, logically grounded approach is required in activities.

Warning

It is important not to embarrass yourself or your current circumstances with overly strict restrictions. You should not try to solve all problems for others just to demonstrate your power and influence. You should not overburden yourself with excessive obligations, you should learn to effectively distribute tasks among colleagues and employees. You should be able to protect your own interests and boundaries, not allowing anyone to infringe on your right to control your work, projects or other areas of life.

The Hierophant

V Major Arcana

S ymbolism

1. He represents the guardian at the portals of paradise, and the triple cross of the Hierophant is a sign of his domination over the three dimensions of existence: over the celestial sphere, the earthly world and the underworld, as well as over the physical shell, soul impulses and unknown spirit.

2. The ladder is a symbolic representation of the route to the depths of knowledge and enlightenment. Each of its steps symbolizes a separate lesson and experience gained. Hierophant becomes a sign of the educational process, a period in the life of man, when he learns to distinguish between what is good and what is evil, when he formed a moral consciousness and the belief in the divine origin. However, to achieve an enlightened state, it is necessary to go through many stages of a difficult educational process. Hierophant indicates the road of learning, guiding the seeker to the illumination of knowledge.

3. The lotus signifies purity and deep wisdom. Inside the lotus flower is hidden shining light, to which the ladder leads, it symbolizes that a person has a bright future ahead of him and that true wisdom is gained through personal experience. Thus, the card calls for impeccability in actions and thoughts.

4. The triple spiral, like the Hierophant's triple cross, reflects the supreme authority over the physical self, emotional state, and spiritual aspect of a person.

5. The pentagram symbolizes protection and reliability on the way, protection from the Higher Powers protecting the traveler.

6. Rune Dagaz represents the beginning of a new day, the embodiment of light. This is the luminous power that carries the Hierophant, the light of knowledge and enlightenment, which has the power to transform the human essence.
7. The Om sign symbolizes the three aspects of being: the physical body, the emotional soul and the mysterious spirit, and plays a key role in the quest to achieve a state of enlightenment.
8. The triquetrum is a symbol of the sunrise, zenith and sunset, which together represent life, death and eternal rebirth.
9. The heart symbol reminds us that love is the supreme law. The symbol of fish, associated with the image of Jesus Christ, symbolizes aspiration to divinity and purity of soul impulses.

Total value

A Hierophant is a mentor for a hero. Derived from the Greek word, Hierophant means "one who initiates into the mysteries." It is that teacher who not only leads the way, but also guards knowledge from oblivion. Hierophant is associated with a deep feeling such as love. It proclaims that love is the basic principle of life. The Hierophant represents the true source of light. It serves as a link between the celestial sphere and humanity.

The Hierophant embodies the power of knowledge, legality, family, structure, authority and social status. His role is to transmit teachings, disseminate information, teaching, preserving traditions and established rules. The personality associated with this arcana is characterized by a commitment to organization, a desire to learn, and excellent public speaking skills. She honors family customs and lives in accordance with the law. Such a person is a model of responsibility and education. His ability to assimilate, process and share information is admirable. This manifests a courageous, paternal energy. He acts as a mentor, ready to come to the rescue, support and explain all the nuances. This man is appreciated for his authority, and he is highly respected in society. He is constantly striving for new knowledge and discoveries, always ready to learn and has a well-developed logic. In his actions, he is consistent and respects established rules and traditions.

This arcana symbolizes periods of happiness, a sense of satisfaction from accomplishments, the joy of acquiring new knowledge. It reflects moments of spiritual awakening, insights, realization of ambitions and dreams. The card portends a bright future, a worthy reward for labor. It foretells the entry into a new level of spiritual development. In the image of the Hierophant we see a man with high morals and spiritual aspirations. The card may also indicate that a person has begun to seek answers to spiritual questions, to explore various spiritual practices. The Hierophant teaches us consciousness and morality, while in the arcana of the Devil this morality is put to the test, temptations that test its strength. The Devil reveals our weaknesses, while Hierophant symbolizes our spiritual strength and purity.

The Hierophant arcana in tarot is associated with the concepts of traditions and beliefs. It can signify belonging to religious communities, academic institutions, and can also refer to groups and clans with well-defined foundations, rules and traditions. This card is a symbol of a spiritual advisor. It indicates a person whose advice is relied upon and whose opinion is valued, indicating situations where strict adherence to rules is required. It can indicate legal agreements and rituals such as marriage ceremonies.

While the Priestess also absorbs knowledge and is in the process of learning, her mission does not include the dissemination of that knowledge. In contrast, the Hierophant has the role of an educator, obliged to share the highest knowledge and teachings. It symbolizes initiation into a variety of mystical teachings, rituals, religious and philosophical doctrines. Card Hierophant reflects situations in which there is a hierarchy, where there is an authority whose word has weight, where the truth is presented, not subject to doubt. It calls for responsibility and integrity, suggesting that one will share one's experience and knowledge, instructing others based on one's own life's journey.

In a negative context Hierophant can reflect the image of a dogmatist, inclined to impose his opinion and desire to control others. Such a person may refuse further training and self-development, believing that his knowledge is already enough, putting himself above others and offering unsolicited advice. He may limit himself to narrow frames of thinking and hinder his development by having a limited outlook. There may also be rigid adherence to his dogmas, a desire to impose his own view of the world on others, excessive pedantry, inability to forgive the mistakes of others, lack of flexibility in plans and insistence on his superiority over others.

Relationship

This context implies a stable relationship, a legal marriage, and a long, serious connection. It indicates a deepening of the relationship, enjoyment of each other's company. Here there is a transition of relations to a qualitatively different level, they become more significant, and partners begin to behave as real responsible associates. The Hierophant card emphasizes the desire of people to formalize their relationship. This is a relationship filled with pure and powerful love, where the partners can feel that they were meant for each other by the forces above, as if this union is sanctified by the heavens.

In a relationship between partners there may be a common perception of the world, similar vision of life and consistency of spiritual quest. They may have common aspirations, life plans and ambitions. There is loyalty and deep devotion, full respect for the sacred bond of marriage, the vows made to another person. This means there are mutual obligations and a sense of responsibility to the partner, which the person pledges to honor.

The card may also reflect the desire to impose one's own beliefs and point of view on one's partner. It can be the imposition of one's own traditions and canons, which can be an obstacle to the harmonious development of the relationship. It can symbolize restrictive rules in a partnership. One of the partners may try to dominate, considering himself/herself wiser or more experienced.

Work and finance

Hierophant symbolizes personal dominion and authority, but authority of a special kind - it is authority over oneself and surrounding circumstances, as if saying "it is in my power to achieve what I want", that is the essence of the arcana Hierophant. Connection of this card with the zodiacal sign Taurus strengthens this aspect as classically Hierophant corresponds with Jupiter, and its stay in Taurus portends acquisition of authority. At the same time Taurus is associated with material prosperity.

This arcana symbolizes aspiration up the hierarchy of power, professional growth and increase of financial prosperity.

The Hierophant card also opens up the prospect of educational activities such as trainings, workshops, seminars and educational programs. It is associated with recognition and reputation, implying that in business matters one should act strictly according to established norms, relying on time-honored, traditional methods. The Hierophant may indicate a legitimate business, such as the decision to register a sole proprietorship. This indicates a serious and thorough approach to doing business. This arcana may also advise investing in additional education and accumulation of experience for professional growth. According to this card, a person is able not only to earn money, but also to fulfill his purpose, finding his life mission.

Hierophant can also reflect a situation where a person adheres to certain well-established rules in earning money, which can hinder the expansion of their income. There may be a feeling that one must have special knowledge to earn significant sums of money, as Hierophant is associated with constant learning. In this context, an individual may feel that they lack the knowledge to start their own business or develop a project, which leads to the "eternal student" syndrome - when a person does not feel ready to work because they believe they are always lacking in knowledge.

Purpose

Always strive to learn, to acquire new knowledge, as well as to disseminate it among others, to guide people, acting as a teacher, mentor, source of knowledge, including spiritual knowledge. Continuously improve, build the foundation of a strong and stable family, and be sure to officially register family ties. Expanding one's own horizons, teaching others and guiding them through life implies that one must first enrich oneself with knowledge and wisdom. To be not only generous in passing on knowledge and experience, but to do it with joy and without abandon. To seek ways of spiritual enrichment.

Occupation

Teacher, lecturer, mentor, coach, priest, religious scholar, politician, government worker, judge, bailiff, family doctor, civil registrar.

PLACES AND FACILITIES

Temple, church, institute, school, study rooms, libraries, monastery, home, theological seminaries, state institutions, large organizations with their own rules and laws, places where traditions are honored, civil registry offices.

Tip

To strictly follow the established rules in personal relationships, business and other spheres of life. To take full responsibility for one's own decisions and actions, to carry them out with a sense of duty and justice, to be faithful to one's work. To remain faithful to the promises made, proving their reliability. To actively replenish your arsenal of knowledge, to continuously grow and enrich yourself with life experience. To selflessly and enthusiastically share our own discoveries and achievements with others.

Warning

Refuse unquestionable dogmas and show flexibility in their judgments. Avoid the trap of complacency, when the illusion of full understanding of the subject is created, which inevitably leads to stagnation in development. With the selection of assimilate information, preventing the littering of their minds unnecessary data. Carefully rethink habitual rules and traditions, analyzing their relevance and significance for your current life.

The Lovers

VI Major Arcana

S ymbolism

1. After going through the initiation ceremony, the young woman wears the signs and symbols she learned from the wise Hierophant:

2. On her back is depicted the Triple Spiral, symbolizing the dominance of love over the physical being, the emotional sphere and the spiritual component of the personality.

3. The septagram establishes her as the sign of the whole universe, which crystal clear conveys the idea that the universe originated and exists because of love. And the heart symbol stands as a profound truth conveyed to her by the Hierophant, affirming that love is the fundamental law.

4. Hexagram embodies the idea of harmony of masculine and feminine principles united in a single whole.

5. Runa Gebo symbolizes the principle of balance, equal interaction and harmony in relationships, emphasizes the importance of mutual generosity in giving and receiving, and also promotes the establishment of fruitful ties with others and successful communication.

6. Rune Fehu in this context is identified with the richness of love feelings, emphasizing that the individual has an abundance of emotional resources that allow him to be open and generous in emotional relationships with others.

7. Rune Alghiz is considered a symbol of reliable protection in relationships, confidence in feelings, which indicates the presence of trust in a person. It also portends favor and protection of the

higher powers in undertakings and actions.

8. The image of Cupid, which is on her hand, becomes a reflection of her loyalty to her own heart. It indicates a deep sense of love for herself, for her partner, for her chosen cause, and for the world at large.

9. The hair of a girl, waving in the direction of her companion, is a sign of intense attraction, indicating that the person is entirely immersed in thoughts in the current situation or in another person, finding it a deep fascination and strong attraction.

Total value

This is the moment when love appears on the hero's path, and he is confronted with the warm feelings of falling in love, ardent passion, and the joy of finding his beloved. Then he is faced with a difficult choice: whether to follow the call of the heart or to be guided by the voice of reason. People in love are more inclined to listen to their hearts. This card illustrates freedom of choice, the ability to make decisions based on inner wisdom and the voice of one's heart.

In ancient times, in traditional decks, this arcana depicted a scene where a young man is faced with the need to choose between his beloved and his mother. Symbolizes the dilemma: to stay in the familiar environment, filled with comfort and coziness, or bravely get out of it to follow the call of his heart. This is the moment of making a fateful decision, driven by heartfelt passion and love. Arcana also illustrates the moments of testing before a difficult choice, when you have to decide: to act logically and reasonably or to follow the call of the heart and soul? It demonstrates the search for balance between heart and mind, and in a negative aspect can indicate an inner conflict between feelings and reason. Lovers discover a variety of ways to solve the task at hand.

This card is often a sign of new love, deep love, important alliances and partnerships. It can foreshadow the need to join forces with someone, sign an agreement or contract, enter into cooperation, find reliable partners. With the involvement of others, the situation promises to develop more positively and fruitfully.

The card illustrates a personality that lives in harmony with its heart. It forms an image of a holistic person. It reflects a state of bliss and happiness, which the person seeks to share with others. It also symbolizes the union of irreconcilable opposites. In the context of the Lovers, it is important for a person to achieve harmony of his own consciousness, not allowing internal contradictions to tear him from within. It is necessary to accept all aspects of one's personality, both positive and negative, and find agreement between them, learning to find common ground with oneself. This is the desire for balance between the feminine and masculine beginnings within a person. Lovers expose all inner contradictions and discussions, black and white, light and dark, love and disgust, reminding that balance and the ability to coexist peacefully with diverse energies are important everywhere.

The card shows a person who is the soul of the company: he is open, friendly, charismatic and easy to communicate. In addition, he is attractive and has a fine sense of style and taste. Such a person loves to surround himself with people, share with them positive emotions. He is capable of sincere, deep love, ready to open his heart for relationships. He easily finds common language with people, and people are naturally attracted to him.

In front of us is the map of a person who radiates attraction and emotionality, appreciates aesthetics and surrounding beauty in all its manifestations. Such a person accepts himself and others without judgment and conventions. He is excellent at organizing events, has a wide range of contacts and acquaintances. He enjoys social life, celebrations, events. He cares about his own appearance and strives for perfection in everything he does.

The card may also reflect negative aspects of the personality: a person who is prone to excessive attachment, unable to make decisive choices, subject to hesitation and internal contradictions. He may feel constant cognitive dissonance, a disconnect between reason and feelings. Such a person finds it difficult to defend his point of view, dependent on the opinions of others, who is not easy to make an important decision. He may show insecurity, succumb to the influence of others, not able to refuse and protect his personal boundaries. Such a person often has doubts, seeks to please everyone around him and is hard to survive criticism, is not always able to be frank. Wearing "rose-colored glasses" can make him face hard choices and unpleasant life lessons.

Relationship

A person faces a choice: to continue frivolous life, avoiding serious relationships, or to build a strong love, to create strong ties. There is genuine passion in the relationship, partners feel a strong attraction to each other, their connection is full of energy and warmth. They share a deep, true love, striving to create a strong bond, where everyone brings his soul and gives a part of himself, becoming inseparable and can not imagine life without each other.

Feelings arising in this relationship are characterized by mutual affection, sincerity and concentration on their only chosen one. Such fidelity can symbolize a blissful marriage filled with passion and sexual harmony. Partners share common life goals, aspirations and dreams, coinciding in their perception of the world and thoughts. They have no conflicts or disputes, because they have achieved harmony between logic and feelings.

The card can also reflect the idea that the partner reflects the inner world of the person, complementing it, bringing to the relationship what it lacks. If, for example, a person perceives his partner as reliable and responsible, then the partner will behave accordingly to this image, confirming internal expectations.

In such a couple there is no struggle for dominance or contradictions; the energy balance is perfect and everyone behaves according to their natural roles. The woman expresses herself as a woman and the man as a man. Their feelings for each other are freely and openly expressed without any embarrassment.

However, the same card can indicate superficial emotions and impermanent connections if it falls in a negative position. It can be a symbol of doubts about the necessity of a relationship, indecision in choosing between partners, love triangles. It can also reflect the trap of self-deception, where the person idealizes the partner, seeing the relationship through the prism of unrealistic expectations, striving to be loved regardless of who is in front of them. A person may disregard the misbehavior of an unscrupulous partner, seeing him/her not as reality but as a desired reflection of his/her own dreams. Thus, he can lose himself in the relationship, merging with the thoughts and desires of the partner, making endless concessions and forgiving everything in the world.

Work and finance

Financial flows are often formed through active communication and establishing connections with others. It is recommended to establish partnerships, initiate cooperation or launch a common project. This card emphasizes the need to attract the attention of people and clients, for which it is extremely important to create effective and attractive advertising, perhaps with the involvement of qualified professionals in this area. The card may also indicate successful teamwork. It speaks of the magnetism of desires in the attraction of money. When the activity brings joy and pleasure, it can turn into a profitable endeavor, and it also indicates the prospect of earning income through favorable contracts. Sometimes it can also be about gaining finances through a romantic relationship, or a promotion through a relationship with a partner, also in the personal sphere.

At the same time, in a negative aspect, this card can reveal uncertainty in one's own decisions. It indicates a person's tendency to rely too much on the opinions of others, attributing to them an authority he does not see in himself. Such a person may be too generous to the point of inappropriateness, burdening himself with the needs of others. It also indicates possible errors in the choice of business partners and in the process of attracting clientele, which can lead to suboptimal results in business.

Purpose

Become fully acceptable to yourself, learn to appreciate and love yourself without conditions. Be true to your individuality, develop the ability to make decisions without help, learn to make choices independently. It is important to be attentive to your own feelings, strive to bring joy first of all to yourself, not to others. Your own opinion should take precedence over the opinions of others. Follow the chosen path, avoid attempts of other people to distract you from your direction. Engage in building harmonious relationships with yourself, your partner and others, improve your communication skills, learn how to properly build a dialog and clearly express your thoughts. To free oneself from offenses, to learn to forgive, to open one's heart to love, to create strong emotional ties. To be honest both with oneself and with others.

Occupation

Work with people, organizer of holidays, decorator, designer, a person who creates beauty, creative profession, party organizer, host, beauty sphere, sphere of love and relationships, for example, a registry office worker, wedding salon, family psychologist, marriage agency, organization of dates.

PLACES AND FACILITIES

Registry offices, cafes, romantic venues, wedding salons, design and art studios, and bedrooms.

Tip

Act the way you want to act, not the way your environment expects you to act. Make decisions wisely, listen to your inner voice, make choices with your heart, follow what your heart tells you to do. Socialize with people, make new contacts, participate in events, immerse yourself in the environment, share information and impressions with others. Develop your creative abilities, put your energy into creativity, give your creation to the world.

Warning

Don't try to please everyone and be extremely nice or pleasant to others. Refuse to try to conform to other people's expectations or to do things for others. Do not sacrifice yourself completely for a cause or another person, and do not deprive yourself of personal space and time for your own needs.

The Chariot

VII Major Arcana

S ymbolism

1. Black and white horses visually represent duality, the ability to combine disparate qualities and move in a unified direction despite this. It represents harmony in opposition and the ability to effectively manage multiple projects simultaneously.

2. In many interpretations the Chariot symbolizes the person devoted in mystic secrets and possessing magic skills. The card hints at possible initiations and spiritual initiations. The secrecy of his mission is emphasized by the curtain concealing his carriage. No one knows what he is transporting, emphasizing the mysticism of the performance. The curtain, colored red, suggests that personal boundaries and space will be defended with special determination.

3. The lantern, as well as a garland of radiant lanterns, symbolize deep inner understanding, insight and light that guides a person on his life path. He clearly realizes his goal, moves forward with confidence, because the light of wisdom reliably illuminates his road, pointing the direction.

4. The color purple predominates on the card, which symbolically refers to themes of power, as well as the desire to own something. It also indicates the impulsive nature and passion of the person who owns the card or the situation it is associated with.

5. Energy ribbons of light and shadow, proceeding from boundless cosmic space, control movement of the Chariot. Power of will of the driver allows him to direct these streams. Thanks to his aspiration and directed energy he can quickly reach the set goals,

directing the efforts and intentions for achievement of result.

Total value

Having made a decision on the card Lovers, the hero realizes, where it should be directed, and getting in the Chariot, promptly leaves the habitual environment, heading from the past to the future. The Chariot symbolizes fighting spirit, energy of active actions and perseverance in achievement of the purposes, taking a position of the leader and desire to gain the top. In it there is a powerful masculine energy.

The appearance of the Chariot portends that the situation is gaining momentum, means the beginning of rapid and rapid development of events. This card opens new ways and opportunities, forcing a person to move rapidly and with confidence to the desired. It symbolizes a significant breakthrough in the area to which the eye is directed, marks the road to success, where obstacles are eliminated, and if someone is trying to get in the way, the driver of the Chariot mercilessly sweep it away. This card emphasizes that the process is already started, changes are in full swing.

Studying this card, you can see that a person does not hesitate in choosing the direction of movement, he has clearly defined the goal and steadily moves towards it at full speed. This is a manifestation of determination and initiative, according to this map a person firmly takes power into his own hands, persistently strives for the desired, sets all new tasks and achieves them. This is an image of success and victory. Usually the Chariot is associated with a warrior, symbolizes battles, wars, triumph over opponents. It means a breakthrough and exit from stagnation, transition from one state to another, includes traveling and changes of residence.

Using this card as a guide, it is extremely important to keep control over unfolding events, as well as it is important to be able to control the Chariot, rushing on all pairs. The owner of the card needs to show managerial qualities to keep the situation under control. The card hints at necessity of display of self-discipline, willful efforts and concentration of attention for full control over circumstances.

In the spirit of this card a person does not turn to the past, he bravely accepts risk and enthusiastically pushes his way into the future. He confidently controls the Chariot, directing his gaze forward, that can symbolize spiritual revelation or breakthrough.

The Chariot symbolizes a victory and success which are consequence of the considered decision made on the card of Lovers. If on the map of Lovers there was freedom in a choice of a way, the Chariot represents freedom of action. Here is presented the person who has full freedom in realization of the desires and plans. The Chariot is associated with number 7 which symbolizes cosmic movement of planets, implying changes both in small, and in significant aspects of life.

The card Chariot depicts the person-winner, which confidently directs to achievement of the ambitious purposes, irrespective of circumstances. Reflects a personality bold, active and full of determination. Such a person is characterized by strict discipline, has considerable willpower and persistence. He does not tolerate inaction and static, he is alien to monotony and stagnation. Such an individual strives for personal growth, is able to work effectively on various projects. He enjoys traveling, driving and is fond of extreme sports, be it cycling or skiing. He is a self-sufficient and resilient nature who knows how to focus on the task at hand, always ready for new endeavors, energetic and optimistic in his endeavors.

In the negative aspect of the Chariot can portend conflicts, violent clarification of relations, physical clashes and inability to control their emotions. Can denote an aggressive personality, prone to conflict and disputes, whose ambitiousness is sometimes accompanied by recklessness and willingness to go head over heels for the sake of their interests. Such a person is often drawn into disputes, shows aggression and the desire to gain the upper hand, to prove their point of view to others. The card can also indicate excessive effort without the possibility of rest, which leads to emotional explosions. In such a situation, a person risks being busy without visible progress, superficially jumping from one thing to another and not having a clear understanding of their true goals.

Relationship

The card can symbolize a relationship that is maintained at a distance. Often it concerns the person, deepened in own self-improvement and achievement of personal purposes for which at the moment romantic communications are not a priority. The chariot, having rolled, leaves a noticeable trace - hence, past relationships may have left a significant imprint on a person's heart, which, in turn, affects the way he builds new relationships. This card can also reflect new acquaintances that happened on the road, during service in the army, in travel or on vacation, as well as romantic adventures.

In the emotional aspect, this card reflects an unwavering desire to achieve the desired at all costs, speaking of complete concentration on the object of lust and the application of maximum effort to conquer it. In the context of relationships, the card denotes dynamic events, joint trips, the desire to achieve common goals; it concerns people who are active and self-sufficient in nature. They are continuously busy with something and striving for their goals. Two partners, as if in one yoke, walk along the path of life side by side, sharing common aspirations, able to find compromises for the sake of harmony in the relationship. It is easier for them to overcome life's obstacles together, like two horses pulling a cart together.

This card can indicate a significant breakthrough in the development of relationships, their transition to a new stage. If earlier partners were closed and did not open to each other, the Chariot can foreshadow a period of active development of relations, when lovers begin to establish communication, accept and forgive each other's shortcomings, minimizing the emerging contradictions.

The card can also signal possible scandals and disputes in the relationship, the possibility of a breakup or the desire of one of the partners to leave the relationship. It can reflect competitive moments in a couple, when two strong personalities clash and do not find common ground. Partners may engage in conflicts, make accusations, try to prove their case, make claims and feel the desire to bend the other to their will. In such cases, the card may reflect dominance or tyranny on the part of one of the partners.

Work and finance

A person occupying a status position has an extensive list of responsibilities, finding himself in a leadership position. His professional activities may indicate rapid career growth. There is a rapid promotion and advancement of projects. This card symbolizes dominance and control over finances, indicating that the man is the complete master of his material well-being. He realizes exactly what steps he has to take, is aware of his income and expenses, knows where it is advisable to invest, skillfully manages his budget, rather than allowing money to dictate its terms. It is a triumph over plans and competitors. The card also symbolizes effective teamwork, in which each participant acts in a coordinated and purposeful manner, directing efforts to the overall success and elevation of the case, project. It may portend significant changes in the sphere of labor activity.

When the movement stops and there comes a period of stagnation, finances begin to disappear inexorably, slipping away like a stream of water through the fingers. According to the meaning of the card, it is important to maintain constant activity, especially in financial matters, it is necessary to continuously invest funds, invest them in their further development and advancement. The card may indicate the possibility of changing the place of work or professional sphere. In the negative aspect, it can reflect the excessive fixation of a person on the achievement of the goal, while he becomes blind to details, does not pay attention to what is happening around. Such a person does not dive into the essence of the matter, stubbornly considers himself the only right and ignores the opinions of colleagues, partners, clients.

Purpose

Set clear goals for yourself, show determination and self-confidence, do not avoid difficult challenges and do not deviate from the chosen course. Be active, do not sink into a cozy comfort zone, keep your life dynamic, engage in regular physical activity, explore the world through travel. Avoid stagnation, take a leadership position, seeking to inspire others to achieve common goals. Be a motivating leader, direct your fighting spirit and energy to the realization of ambitions, but avoid conflicts, strive for a harmonious way to achieve the desired.

Occupation

Military occupations, businessman, trucker, freight forwarder, driver, guide, logistician, machinist, stewardess, pilot, sailor, cab driver, stuntman, athlete, cab driver, soccer player.

PLACES AND FACILITIES

Roads, highways, transportation facilities, train stations, airports, military base

Tip

Stubbornly pursue your goal, overcoming your reluctance to act and passivity. Be more active and impetuous, because the card indicates the need to accelerate processes, because the situation requires immediate action. Take control of the situation so that it does not slip out of your control. Focus on your goals and move consistently towards their fulfillment.

Warning

Don't rush headlong into achieving your goals. You need to rethink your priorities and goals. Act thoughtfully, avoid impulsiveness and aggressiveness in your actions. Think first, then act. Be careful, especially if you are on the road, as there are dangers along your route.

Strength

VIII Major Arcana

S ymbolism

1. The lion on this card symbolizes our innate instincts, indomitable aggression, and the animal passions bubbling in the depths of our being. Observe how the woman keeps her wild essence in check, not allowing it to dominate and threaten the peaceful life of the lamb. The image on the card demonstrates how the girl copes with her lion by maintaining strict control over her wild, unruly nature.

2. A girl dressed in an innocent white dress is the embodiment of the highest spirituality and pure love. It is these qualities that help her to subdue the flaring passions inherent in human nature. Her image reflects the purity and light that can transform and subdue the most powerful instincts.

3. The constellation of Leo in astrology is associated with the characteristics of this zodiac sign, emphasizing such traits as generosity of soul, haughtiness, nobility of spirit, high self-esteem and strong self-confidence, as well as a tendency to self-centeredness.

4. The Lemniscata, towering above the girl's head, is a powerful symbol indicating the importance of the superiority of the higher over the lower. It reminds us of the need to balance and complement the two sides of our being: the rational, human mind and the instinctive, animal mind. However, it is emphasized that the rational mind must have the predominant role in controlling the instincts.

5. The lamb on the card symbolizes perfect innocence, shows meekness, demonstrates deep kindness and human warmth. Here

before us unfolds a real test of human nature, the man-lion: how will he behave in front of a completely helpless creature, whether it will protect him or show aggression? It is also a reflection of man's attitude towards such aspects of his personality as goodness, purity of soul and integrity. Will he reject these qualities as something that might weaken him, thereby denying part of his essence, or will he accept them, recognizing them as an integral part of his self?

Total value

In the Strength Arcana, the hero learns the mastery and guidance of his inner beast, while he does not seek to oppress it, but seeks friendship and peaceful coexistence with this part of his. This represents the acceptance of one's own nature, the wild side of one's character, and the skillful and sensitive management of it. A special feminine strength is represented here, demonstrating that with gentleness and affection even the wildest of creatures can be subdued.

The Arcana of Strength is a symbol of balance between the rational part of our self and our instinctive, irrational impulses, which is symbolized by the lemniscata. It indicates the importance of keeping our inner beast under control, lest it escape and bring a lack of order and confusion into our lives. It is important to dialog with this part of ourselves, not to suppress it or deny it, as it is what brings vitality, passion and joy to our lives with every moment we live. It is discipline over your own impulses, behavior, actions and words.

Strength Arcana emphasizes the need for self-control, control over personal vulnerabilities, demonstration of endurance, willpower and spirit. Implies steadfastness in the face of obstacles, courage in overcoming the challenges that represents the fate. This is the inner fortress that helps a person to remain whole in difficult, critical circumstances and does not allow him to give up. This is a manifestation of inner courage and independence. It is absolute faith in one's own strength. It is endurance and the ability to maintain control over one's actions and circumstances. It is domination over one's weaknesses and habits.

This image also conveys the idea of self-sacrifice for the good of others, because the symbolism of the lamb is closely associated with sacrifice. In the context of Christianity, the lamb, being the lamb of the Last Judgment, is depicted in a state of anger, and this aspect is often perceived as the opposite of the lion image. It symbolizes the dual nature of man: the ability to be both unprotected, seeking protection, and a mighty, indomitable protector.

The Strength card represents the image of a strong-willed, full of passion and energy individual with a pronounced sex appeal and charisma. Such a person is characterized by leadership qualities and the ability to withstand heavy loads. His inner strength and self-confidence help to quickly recover from fatigue, take on several cases at once, successfully cope with them and do not lose energy. He finds practical application of his knowledge, is active in action, is able to protect his interests and the interests of loved ones, to achieve goals with gentleness, without resorting to violence. This person has both physical and spiritual power, finds joy in his favorite activities and behaves in a way to get the most out of life. He also inspires others to be strong and purposeful.

In its negative aspect, such a person can manifest himself as a passive aggressor. Prone to sudden outbursts of anger, may seek to suppress others with his will, resorting to rudeness and physical force, sometimes becoming a despot or tyrant. There may be a manifestation of hypocrisy, when in public he wears a mask of social acceptability, but in reality is a completely different person. Such people can exhaust themselves with excessive labor and excessive physical exertion, it is difficult for them to find time for rest. They are aggressive and intolerant of others, try to impose their own opinions, are often intemperate and impatient, wanting to get everything at once, and sometimes take on too many obligations.

Relationship

This card reflects femininity, indicating that in a relationship you should not try to subjugate your partner, fight for power or engage in conflicts. It is important to be flexible and to be able to find compromises with your partner. The card reminds that rudeness and excessive demands can destroy love, while softness, tenderness and love can work wonders, making relationships strong and long-lasting.

This card symbolizes feminine energy and inner strength, and when it falls to a woman, it speaks of the need to appreciate and respect her unique feminine nature. Rather than becoming a rude rival, one should keep their heart open to the person they love, treating them kindly, gently and caring. Recognizing that this is where the real strength lies can help any relationship withstand the storms of life and persist.

The card indicates the opening of the heart, the power of deep feelings. In a couple, it promises respect and mutual understanding, patient attitude to each other's shortcomings. Embolizes devotion, when a person does not allow his instincts to prevail and get carried away by outside connections, maintaining the strength and steadfastness of the relationship. It can be an omen of pregnancy, an image of a mother with an infant. In couple relationships, passion and bright, intense sexual liaisons are expected, where love is able to overcome any obstacles.

The same card may indicate that a person prefers to hide his true feelings, keeping them from his partner, so that he did not recognize their full depth. It can speak about restraint in the manifestations of emotions, about the desire to avoid unnecessary words and hasty confessions.

In a negative aspect, the card can depict a relationship where there is a victim-aggressor dynamic, rudeness and inability to understand each other. It can mean that in a couple one partner tries to dominate, impose his will, creating pressure and aggressive atmosphere, exhausting and tormenting the mental strength of the other. Such a relationship lacks the possibility of reaching agreement and mutual concessions, the partner may be inclined to impose his or her views and opinions.

Work and finance

This image describes a person dedicated to his profession, who works enthusiastically and tirelessly, putting a lot of effort and passion into his chosen endeavor. Such a person stands out for his ability to work, tirelessly investing his energies in the development of his activities. He often commits to multiple jobs or manages multiple projects in parallel. This leads to high results and efficiency in the professional sphere. Such a person is able to manage his time surprisingly effectively, skillfully find a balance between work and rest, and also shows the ability to control his finances and accumulate funds. In work, he shows dynamism and high activity.

This image reflects either the presence of support and encouragement from management or the individual's own role as a mentor to others. There is an unconventional and creative approach to task fulfillment. It is accompanied by a significant intrinsic motivation to work and earn, with the individual being able to provide not only for themselves, but also to be a supportive pillar for others. It may also signal the importance of cooperation and partnership. To do a job successfully, one must be extremely focused and put in a tremendous amount of effort.

It may indicate excessive pressure related to financial matters, when a person is forced to work to the limit of his capabilities, which can lead to physical and emotional exhaustion. Under such conditions, he may become unnecessarily irritable and unfair to his loved ones. Constant work without adequate time for rest leads to lack of recuperation, lack of responsibility and mismanagement of one's finances and overall financial situation.

Purpose

Control your emotions, passions, expressions and instinctive impulses. To improve the inner strength and depth of feelings. To choose the path to higher values, achieving goals with delicacy, gentleness and loving energy. Realize that cruelty brings only destruction, while kindness can do wonders, and it is important to learn how to use this power to benefit yourself and others. Cultivate your abilities, discover new facets of yourself. Direct your own energy to create new things, open your heart to radiate sincere love, strive for equal communication and mutual understanding with other people, establishing contact without coercion and pressure.

Occupation

Athlete, coach, instructor, extreme sport, rescuer, esotericist, energy work, trainer, circus worker, actor, businessman, show business, politics, producer, philanthropist.

PLACES AND FACILITIES

Theater (reincarnations), carnival (masks), farm, zoo, places related to power and control, law enforcement, security agencies, also places of entertainment, clubs, concerts.

Tip

To feel confident in oneself, in every decision made and every activity undertaken. Cultivate and strengthen internal supports. To take responsibility for one's own life and the well-being of loved ones. Protect yourself and your family, defend your personal position, your endeavors, projects, and protect what is of special value to you. Demonstrate firmness of will and courage. Achieve the goals set for yourself with gentleness and openness of heart, keep your feelings and natural impulses under control.

Warning

Avoid excessive burden on oneself, get rid of excessive responsibility that presses. Do not suppress your own aspirations, opinions for fear of offending others. Do not restrain energy, power and passion. Interact with others without coercion and dictate, also do not allow others to impose their beliefs and will on you.

The Hermit

IX Major Arcana

S ymbolism

1. The hermit continues his journey, illuminated by the light he carries within him. This light is the light of knowledge of truth, the light he has discovered in the depths of his own soul, the light of wisdom that serves as a reliable torch on his path.

2. The figure on the card image no longer needs an external lantern - the light of inner truth and knowledge shines brightly, chasing away the darkness of the unknown before him. The girl depicted on the card wears a white garment, which symbolizes purity of intentions, aspiration to deep self-knowledge and spiritual awakening.

3. The ladder on the map of the Hermit appears as a metaphor of his life route - it is a symbol of ascent to his own "I", the search for personal enlightenment and spiritual ascent. It represents the path to higher knowledge, overcoming material attachments and striving for higher truth.

4. In the image, the character sits among stone blocks, which reminds us that the path of every traveler is not simple and full of obstacles. In order to achieve the cherished goal of enlightenment and wisdom, he will have to pass through a series of difficult trials and hardships.

Total value

In the card of the Hermit we see the completion of the path of development of individual consciousness, the achieved peak of wisdom. At this stage, the person distances himself from external teachings and accumulated knowledge, finding the path of his personal reasoning, meeting face to face with his essence. In moments of silence and solitude, he begins true self-discovery, revealing to himself the pictures of the true personality. This card symbolizes the image of a wise elder who has accumulated extensive life experience and now seeks to know himself, alone with his thoughts.

The hermit represents the ideal of asceticism, when an individual rejects worldly goods and removed from public life, the purpose of which is to achieve spiritual enlightenment. The card symbolizes the state of seclusion, conscious withdrawal from everyday life, deep introspection, search for personal purpose in this world, time for reflection, approaching the age of wisdom and comprehension of life's truths.

The main message of the card Hermit is the call to follow the voice of one's own soul, the importance of distinguishing it among many others. The hermit is in a state of deep self-sufficiency, it is difficult to put him out of balance or to change his mind, because he is confident in his views and appreciates only individually found truth.

This arcana can symbolize a spiritual teacher, as well as an individual who seeks to find such a teacher. It is also associated with a journey of a spiritual nature, when a person rushes into a solitary multi-kilometer journey to learn the truth and find harmony with himself. When interacting with the Hermit, changes are extremely leisurely, and people are often immersed in a deep state from which it is difficult to get out. This arcana indicates a period when a person can reach significant spiritual heights, realize the limitations of the habitual environment and a narrow circle of communication, which allows her to realize her development, let go of outdated ties and move away from the familiar environment.

Opens before us the image of a self-sufficient individual, inclined to introversion and asceticism. This person delves into spiritual practices, meditates, and searches for enlightenment within himself. Such people are most often not characterized by sociability and talkativeness. They are secretive and distance themselves from the social bustle. Such a person keeps his secrets and does not reveal them to others, guarding his personal space from outsiders. This introvert prefers to avoid other people's attention in order to maintain his privacy and focus. He possesses calmness and discretion. This arcana is not about social connections, but about a period of solitude and inner revelations. It is a profound arcana associated with philosophers and sages. It reflects a look into the past, may indicate a very old origin of a person or a problem rooted in the deep past, even beyond a few generations, and suggests the possibility of gaining access to the knowledge of antiquity.

This arcana reflects wisdom, the desire for knowledge, passion for research, the desire to penetrate into the past and explore the mysteries of the past. It can represent the image of a historian, thoughtfully studying the ancient chronicles, or archaeologist, carefully examining the layers of time in his excavations. Such a person often surrounds himself with a circle of close friends and like-minded people, and treats strangers with apprehension and suspicion. Such people experience many things internally, they are constant in their attachments, whether to a place or a person. They are characterized by responsibility and extraordinary attention to detail, love nature, animals, enjoy being outdoors.

In the negative aspect, the card can represent isolation, anguish of loneliness, deep depression, complete loneliness, when a person has absolutely no one to share his feelings and thoughts with, no opportunity for communication, which emphasizes the lack of social interaction. It can indicate a socially maladapted personality. Also, the arcana can symbolize illness and aging, when a person repels others, shows excessive caution and pickiness. Closure in himself, excessive suspicion and caution become his characteristic features. While in a positive context the Hermit gains wisdom, finds the truth and like-minded people, in a negative context he becomes a symbol of inaction and loneliness, spends his life in vain. Old stubbornness of thought, hidden inside accumulated negativity, hidden resentments become his companions.

Relationship

This card may reflect a particularly deep reverence and respect between partners. There may be an ancient wisdom embedded in their relationship, with the couple strengthening their bond through religious rituals or communicating on a spiritual level, such as following biblical principles or Vedic teachings, basing their lives on ancient precepts. This card can also reflect the sincere and deep feelings of one partner for the other, such as love and affection, indicating a long-term bond that often lasts a lifetime and is characterized by devotion to one chosen one. In some cases, this card can predict pregnancy, during which the woman becomes more private and immersed in her personal inner world.

This card may reveal a picture of a significant age difference between partners, as well as a relationship with a person who is significantly older. It can be associated with a relationship with a philosopher, a lonely traveler, a person devoted to religious pursuits, who are characterized by isolation and rich intellectual potential. The card suggests a person's tendency to loneliness, to a long study of a potential partner before starting a serious relationship. It can also signal slowness in matters of starting a relationship and late marriage. In such partners there is often difficulty in expressing their own emotions, their affection has a little verbal character. In relationships defined by this card, there are no passionate emotional outbursts and an active sex life.

Partners shown by this card may show a certain closedness and indifference to each other. It can signal the cooling of feelings in the relationship, when people turn away from each other, each absorbed in their own thoughts and experiences. In such a couple there is a clear lack of communication and mutual understanding. Secrets and unknown aspects may shroud their union. The card also hints at the emotional and physical estrangement of partners from each other, when one of them evades meetings and avoids open dialog. It gives the impression of an unbridgeable gulf between the partners and may indicate a significant distance between them.

Work and finance

In professional activities, it is recommended to choose work formats where interaction with others is minimized. This can be in the form of remote work or work via the Internet, where there is no need for face-to-face meetings with colleagues or clients. The choice of an individual project or consulting a single client is suitable, but it is important to aim for a long and fruitful cooperation, and not for frequent changes of customers. This card also emphasizes the importance of in-depth study of the subject of work, improving one's skills and raising the level of qualification.

This card is not associated with material prosperity, it indicates more the need to lead a frugal lifestyle and reduce expenses. It portends a period when a person has to be frugal and practice asceticism. It refers to such areas as esotericism, education, philosophy and scientific work, in which professional growth occurs unnoticed by others and may be accompanied by a lack of a wide range of clients or recognition.

The card may also reflect the lifestyle of a person who finds himself in a difficult situation with finding a job, and these circumstances may drag on for a long time. Such a person may face a lack of livelihood and will be forced to live a life of extreme minimalism. He may be uncomfortable in society and therefore avoid active socialization and work. A life of isolation and unwillingness to change anything about his own situation leads to a lack of incentive to earn money. The situation may be accompanied by layoffs, leaving work on one's own and the inability to find a clientele or a market.

Purpose

Develop your connection with the Higher Powers even more actively. Learn to trust yourself, to explore your personality more deeply, to discover the wisdom and truth embedded in yourself, to study the secrets of your own soul. Strive to bring the light of this wisdom to the people around you, not to reject them, but strive to form a solid circle of like-minded people. Stay true to your beliefs, listen carefully to yourself and steadily follow the chosen road. Without fear to open up to new knowledge, actively seek the truth and devote themselves to spiritual growth. To be generous in sharing one's own life experience with others.

Occupation

Historian, archaeologist, teacher, philosopher, writer, researcher, laboratory worker, esotericist, psychologist, pharmacist, medical worker, pilgrim, monk, scientist, detective who by the light of his lantern, finds the hidden, investigator.

PLACES AND FACILITIES

Caves, cells, hermit dwellings, places in nature, uninhabited places, islands, mountains, seas, away from people, monastery, desert.

Tip

It's time to get away from the daily hustle and bustle, to reduce the circle of socialization, to look deep inside yourself to understand what it is you want, not what others expect from you. Invariably follow your chosen direction, hold a personal point of view, stay committed to your principles. Actively immerse yourself in acquiring new knowledge and strive to improve your professional competence.

Warning

You should not completely isolate yourself from those close to you, go too deep into yourself and withdraw from society, because there is a risk of losing touch with those around you, and eventually loneliness can become an unbearable burden. There is a danger of being completely alone when facing your own problems.

The Wheel

X Major Arcana

Symbolism

1. The Wheel card portends a significant change in life or an area of special interest. The girl perched on top of the wheel represents the need to center within herself, to recognize the constancy of change in life, and to realize that the only person we have to walk the journey of life with is ourselves. She is balancing her body while standing on one leg and trying to maintain her balance to stay on top.

2. The dice on the card symbolize the inclination to risk, the inclination to luck and the favor of fortune. The creators of this deck put into the image of the girl on the wheel willingness to take risks, throwing the dice from the jewelry around her neck. She weighs them in the palms of her hands and makes the roll, relying on the favor of fate and hoping that her desire to remain at the peak of the Wheel will be rewarded.

3. The card depicts four elements of nature and the same number of wheels. In a traditional deck, each of the elements is represented by the signs of the zodiac of the fixed cross: Water is represented by the Eagle symbolizing Scorpio, Air is depicted as Man representing Aquarius, Fire is associated with Leo, and Earth with Taurus. This symbolizes the permanence of spiritual truths regardless of changes in life.

4. The eight arrows of disorder on the map hint at the many opportunities that may present themselves. The eight directions of these arrows symbolize the most important eight points in the annual calendar. These include the vernal and autumnal

equinoxes, the summer and winter solstices, and four important Celtic holidays: Beltane, celebrated on May 1, Lughnasadh on August 1, Samhain, which falls between October 31 and November 1, and Imbolc, celebrated on February 1. These dates symbolize the eternal renewal and cyclical nature.

5. There is an inscription on the Tarot card that has ancient Egyptian roots meaning "the way of the Pharaohs" as well as the Hebrew meaning "Holy Law. Torah." Occultist Paul Foster Keyes has suggested that from an anagram of the words "ROTA" (wheel), "TARO", "ORAT" (says), "TORA" (law) and "ATOR" (goddess) the expression "The Tarot Wheel proclaims the law of initiation" can be made up. This is a symbol of connecting with the Higher Powers and understanding one's true purpose in this world.

Total value

Having found in the card of the Hermit a reflection of himself, the character wonders about his purpose in this world, he begins to look more closely for the answer to the question of his main life mission. The Wheel card symbolizes significant changes in life, when there are sudden and unexpected changes in the paths that a person can choose. It represents unforeseen turns of circumstances, when the next chapter in the book of fate is turned over, opening a new stage of existence. This is the turning point when a chance is given to make an important choice, to take significant steps to radically rewrite the direction of one's life road.

These moments in an individual's life can be significant and defining, they include major events and milestones. They are times filled with joy and change. The card can also indicate a cyclical repetition of events, a farewell or reunion with people. This is the time when it is time to take responsibility for your life path and decide on the direction forward, so that the Wheel does not throw you from side to side. Ten is the first step into the world of two-digit numbers, marking the end of one life cycle and the beginning of another.

The card can also signal the presence of circumstances over which one has no power. It illustrates the cyclical nature of life, showing that everything new is only the well-forgotten old. It can reflect large-scale changes in the destiny of not only individuals, but of humanity as a whole. Some argue that fate is predetermined, while others believe that we write it ourselves, and therefore a person can either submit to circumstances or take the initiative and actively influence the changes. This wheel of time tells us that life is cyclical, and everything has its time: time to be born and die, time to be reborn again. The card prophesies great happiness and success, it is a symbol of luck and prosperity, especially when a person reaches the peak of success.

And also the card reminds us that there is no place for coincidence in life: consciously choosing this or that road of development of events, we either attract good luck or open the door to failure. It is like a huge wheel of karma, the rotation of which is difficult to keep track of. The map emphasizes that in the face of some life phenomena man is powerless: birth and death, the cyclical nature, the change of seasons - all these are cosmic rhythms, before which we involuntarily bow our heads. This is the greatest chronometer of our existence, which unmistakably counts down to a new period in the life of each of us. Arcana tells us that there is nothing eternal under the moon. Everything has the property of coming and going, changing in an endless cycle of existence.

This card symbolizes activity and constant change in life, it hints at a period filled with bright events and changes, like colorful images in a kaleidoscope. It may also foreshadow various trips, moving from one place to another. The card encourages the person to pay special attention to those aspects of his life that require rethinking and adjustment, indicates the need to restore the energy balance and areas where it is important to find harmony. It also reminds that those who are at the top can quickly find themselves at the bottom, and vice versa, those who are at the bottom can suddenly find themselves at the top.

The Wheel card reveals to us the image of a person who is prone to risk and excitement, who is characterized by good luck and ease in rising. This is an optimist who boldly meets new challenges in life, a person with a great sense of humor and ease in achieving goals. His life is a series of fortunate events, he relies on the favor of fate, is a true adventurer who values travel and communication. Such a person is completely immersed in the turbulent flow of existence, his life is full of events that unfold with amazing speed, he has a rich range of interests and hobbies. In his life there comes a moment when all paths are open before him. He is a responsive and socially-minded individual who prefers to be part of a collective and work effectively in a team.

In a negative aspect, the Wheel can reveal that the individual is lost in search of his true path and purpose in this world. Such a person trusts neither himself nor the surrounding reality, lives in a state of unstable inspiration: sometimes full of energy for labor and creativity, sometimes falls into apathy, rejects all the cases and plunges into inaction, as if moving in a vicious circle of constant repetition. Having deviated from the right path, a person inclines to the downward spiral of life. He lacks clear guidelines for navigation in life, he behaves like a tumbleweed, follows other people's calls, not realizing his true desires. His actions can be chaotic: he starts one thing, then throws it and takes up another, superficially approaching everything he does, performs many tasks, but with little result, his labor is fruitless. Such a person expects someone else to make decisions for him, because he is unable to take life into his own hands, shifting responsibility for his fate to circumstances, karmic laws or other people.

Relationship

The Tarot card portends changes in personal relationships, which can often be quite unforeseen. Sometimes it seems that the situation is unfolding according to the principle of "if it weren't for luck, misfortune would have helped". So, for example, two people can not come to a consensus on whether they want to stay together, balancing on the edge of separation, and suddenly there is a disaster or shock that forces them to look at the world in a new way, to reevaluate their relationship. As a result, they realize that it is difficult for them to live apart and that they are destined to build their future together. Sometimes this realization comes through a happy coincidence of circumstances.

This arcana reflects the idea that life can lead us on the most unexpected roads, so that eventually everything worked out in the best way, as you know, the ways of God is inexplicable. It predicts joyful moments in the relationship of the couple, favorable changes. A new stage in the relationship begins, for example, love partners decide to start a joint life, formalize marriage or go on a long-awaited trip together. They may have the confidence that they are destined to be together by fate. People are sure that they have found their destiny and ideal couple in the person of each other, and this relationship becomes fateful. In such a relationship, partners have a profound influence on each other's life paths.

It is also common for people to come and go again and again, moving in a vicious circle. It can also reflect such an impermanent relationship, where there is no clear stability, everything is immersed in uncertainty and constant excitement. The card may indicate the unwillingness of one of the partners to take responsibility, the desire for freedom and refusal of serious relationships, unwillingness to get attached to someone. Such relationships can be easy and relaxed. They are like a ride on a roller coaster, where feelings are constantly oscillating between ups and downs, creating emotional swings.

Work and finance

Fortune is favorable in the financial sphere. Receipt of impressive sums, sometimes unexpected financial receipts. Successful completion of projects and deals, luck leads the way in business. Sudden transition to a higher level, a significant upsurge in career. Fast and effective advancement in the chosen direction. Money as if striving in the palm of your hand. The effectiveness of teamwork, fruitful partnership is revealed. New horizons and excellent opportunities for growth are opening up. Rapid development of business endeavors, projects and entrepreneurial activities.

May indicate that a person follows the call of his or her destiny, finds his or her true calling and is fully realized in it. Changes in the work environment, transformations in business processes, project modifications, implementation of significant improvements in business strategy. Salary supplements, bonus payments, winnings and valuable gifts. Can mean the presence of many work tasks, extremely intensive rhythm of work, when the individual seeks to meet tight deadlines. Continuous flow of clients, endless cash flow.

In a negative context, it indicates that the person loses control over financial affairs and the business situation. Sometimes it seems that the whirlwind of events puts an overwhelming pressure on the person. Vanity around finances, instability of income: sometimes they are abundant, sometimes depleted. A frivolous attitude toward the work process and finances. Can be expressed in the belief of a person that his efforts do not play a role, in the expectation that clients or money will appear by themselves, without his active actions to improve the financial situation.

Purpose

Developing faith in oneself, in the forces of nature and the universe is an important life principle. Developing an intuitive approach, listening to the deep impulses of the soul. Gaining independence, refusal to blindly imitate others, conscious management of one's own life. Avoiding stagnation: there should be constant progress, new images, change of impressions. The need to use the opportunities that generously offers fate. Sincere enjoyment of the path of life, gratitude for its gifts, whether they are trifles or significant events. It is important to strive to travel, to constantly strive forward, because life is an endless movement.

Occupation

Athlete, tourist, traveler, casino worker, esotericist, person who can predict the fate of a person, psychologist, organizer, animator, worker of amusement parks, centers, mass media, marketing, person working on means of transportation.

PLACES AND FACILITIES

Casinos, transportation facilities, amusement parks, moon parks, slides.

Tip

Every chance that comes in life must be seized. Treat the opportunities with respect and appreciation. Take full responsibility for your existence, for the current situation, do not leave your life without attention and control. To actively participate in the scripting of one's life, to guide it along a course that corresponds to one's personal desires and needs.

Warning

Encountering chaos, unexpected plot twists and turns is an inevitability. A sudden element can throw off the usual path and lead to loss of control over what is happening. Possible loss of life guidelines, the Wheel can dizzy, dramatically change the usual course of life, lead to difficulties, from which it will be difficult to get out. In the face of a fateful upheaval is important to remain calm and not to resist, so that the events did not turn out to be overwhelming, and on the contrary, to be able to master the new circumstances and turn them in their favor.

Justice

XI Major Arcana

S ymbolism

1. Her eyelids are down - she allows no bias, she embodies responsibility and the principles of integrity. Her integrity and dedication to her duty are beyond question.

2. However, in her reflection, her eyes are open, indicating that she is able to see everything around her: her gaze is wide and alert, and nothing escapes her. It can also symbolize a loss of neutrality, implying that one is capable of unjust actions, guided by personal interests.

3. She and her reflection hold the same sword firmly, which emphasizes that decisions are not made under the influence of emotion, but on the basis of objectivity and clear understanding. It is the personification of just retribution when life is filled with balance and harmony. The picture also illustrates the situation in an unvarnished way. It also reflects the balance between justice and injustice, as in the case of the scales: light in one and darkness in the other. This is the balance of forces in nature: creation and destruction, chaos and order, good and evil. Justice takes care of maintaining this balance, not allowing it to be disturbed.

Total value

Justice is a certain kind of experience that a person acquires in the course of his existence, for which he is obliged to take full responsibility. In this context, it becomes clear to the individual that he or she will have to answer for each of his or her deeds. It is not just a balance and equilibrium of energies, it is also a reward or punishment for all good and bad deeds.

Justice is a karmic law, according to which each retribution is assigned strictly justly according to merit. Sometimes justice can manifest itself in more cruel forms than even malice itself, because it is devoid of any emotional component.

Justice is the process of restoring the lost balance. If a person has behaved with true dignity, the principle of Justice guarantees him the return of deserved respect from his environment. On the contrary, unworthy actions will result in a corresponding attitude towards him. It is up to each of us to choose how much to contribute to the overall weight of our actions, but inevitably the balance must be restored. Thus, we return to the original state of balance, receiving back the same force or quality that was sent out into the world, and this is the essence of the law of balance.

Relationship

Relationships based on stability, honesty, integrity and responsibility are relationships where each partner interacts with the other as he or she would like to be treated. It is a predictable bond, transparent, without deception or secret agendas. This mutual respect, sincerity and integrity in behavior towards each other is valued above all else. Both honor their marriage vows and respect their partner's personal boundaries. There may not be an overabundance of tenderness and fervent passion in this relationship, but both partners realize how much effort it takes to maintain a strong bond. They work together as a team, supporting and helping each other in everything. They are like a rock for each other. It can also signify marriage as a formalization and affirmation of their relationship.

In negative aspect, a marriage is possible, concluded on the basis of material gain rather than true feelings. If one of the partners remembers once spoken hurtful words and holds a grudge, it can lead to revenge or to a complete breakdown of the relationship. Relationships can be permeated with cruelty and emotional coldness, partners are able to take revenge on each other for the slightest transgressions or without any reason, there may be betrayals, breakdown of ties, divorce. Pervaded by callousness and alienation, these relationships resemble a wall, elevated between people, an insurmountable boundary that no one wants to cross. Such relationships can only be sustained by a sense of obligation. Justice in this context is a cold and impersonal card, lacking emotion and warmth.

Work and finance

In the financial sphere, everything goes as usual: he manages his funds carefully, analyzes his income and expenses in detail. He strives for harmony between time spent in labor and moments of rest, as well as between spending and saving money. Living in accordance with available opportunities is his motto. He treats financial matters with great responsibility, thinking over every item of expenditure. At work, it is fundamental for him to consolidate agreements through formal contracts, paying attention to documentation. He knows how to distribute tasks and delegate authority. Investments bring him income, and the map hints that efforts and honest labor will be rewarded handsomely. Issues related to debts and loans are solved successfully, a person finds a way to pay debts and return to financial balance. He is able to competently distribute the budget and prioritize expenses. The appearance of this card signals a professional who approaches things as responsibly as possible and does his work qualitatively, as for himself.

When the card falls into a negative position, it reflects the violation of agreements, the desire of one person to dominate the rest, creating a tense and unpleasant environment in the team. There are problems associated with inspections of regulatory bodies: sanitary services, tax inspection, judicial instances and other legal interactions. There is a lack of attention when signing documents, which can lead to unforeseen consequences. The lack of balance between the ability to earn and the tendency to spend more than one's finances allow indicates a life beyond one's real means.

Purpose

Learning to recognize the underlying causes of events and analyze the consequences of what happens. To develop the ability to learn from one's own missteps and life experiences. To learn to accept different opinions, recognizing that each person has every right to their unique point of view, and to develop a personal understanding of fairness. Strive to behave toward others so that you are treated with respect. To build positive karma through helping others and reliable fulfillment of promises. To achieve harmony within oneself and to promote the same in others. To study the universal laws of the universe, the principles of karma, the law of balance and harmony, teaching it to others. To strive rigorously for balance and

Temperance, to show responsibility and reliability in fulfillment of obligations, to avoid debts and unfulfilled promises.

Occupation

Law and order structures, lawyers, judges, tax, military, economists, accountants, esotericists, people working with karma. Business, power, politics.

PLACES AND FACILITIES

Places of power, government offices, prison, court, notary offices.

Tip

It is important to understand what you are putting on one of the scales and what you expect in return. According to the values of this card, you can count on a return exactly in the amount that was made a contribution, so if you want to achieve something, you should invest the appropriate efforts. It is necessary to carefully balance your commitments and the allocation of personal time.

Warning

Avoid excessive rigidity and unreasonable harshness in relation to people around you. Do not create insurmountable obstacles. This card warns that karmic consequences will not wait, and a person will certainly face what he deserves. It signals the imminent restoration of lost balance. It can also signal the likelihood of a meeting with the judicial system or the law.

The Hanged Man

XII Major Arcana

S ymbolism

1. The girl depicted on the map stretches out her hands towards the ancient runes, which, like magical symbols, begin their mystical movement from the golden sun, rotating in her direction in a clockwise direction. It is an illumination, the light of knowledge, gradually filling her as she step by step passes her path of self-discovery and exploration of the mysteries of the universe. Around the face of the Hanged Man plays an aura of solar luminescence, symbolizing spiritual enlightenment. He is in a state of inverted world, which allows him to look at the everyday from a completely different angle, to discover hidden meanings, to grasp the essence and come to their own insights. His perspective is unique, insightful and filled with creative ideas. The card symbolizes people who are capable of predicting fate, fortune telling, those who are associated with esotericism. He is able to penetrate into the essence of any issue, to get to the roots of the problem.

2. The very first in the direction of the Sun follows rune Gebo, a symbol of gifts, sacrifices and harmony between giving and receiving. It hints at the need to give up something to gain something valuable. In the same context, the Sun is associated with the human ego, sometimes turning into selfishness, and in this case mentioned the need to sacrifice it is their selfish aspirations.

3. After Gebo is located rune Hagall, which represents the idea of destruction, outdated for the subsequent rebirth and renewal. Man is called to give up something in his being, for example, from

73

the negative qualities of character or internal barriers, for the sake of liberation from them and obtaining new freedom.

4. Next is the rune Othala, which embodies the memory of the family and the transfer of experience of many generations. It calls to appreciate and learn from the accumulated human experience, so as not to repeat the mistakes of ancestors and be able to build their lives more consciously. One, the leading of the Scandinavian gods, is considered the patron saint of this rune.

5. Rune Raido, symbolizing the path and movement, emphasizes that, based on the experience of previous generations (which is implied by Othala), it is possible to follow a more considered and safer path. This path promises to lead to spiritual discoveries and wisdom.

6. And finally, rune Pertho, which is a symbol of mystical and unknown, suggests the ability to penetrate the most secret corners of the universe, to see what is hidden from the eyes of most. Here a person is immersed in the secret depths of his subconscious, looking for and comprehending knowledge, inaccessible within the framework of ordinary consciousness.

7. Rune Turizas is a gate, symbolizing the transition, it is an arch, connecting different levels of consciousness, different ways of perceiving reality, it is the gate of initiation. Through this gate a person can pass, leaving behind the threshold of his former self and step into a new world, renewed, transformed beyond recognition. These gates open when an individual plunges into the depths of his subconscious, as indicated by its predecessor rune Pertho.

8. Rune Mannaz - is a symbol of self-knowledge, reflecting the idea of realizing himself as a person, comprehending his inner strength and hidden capabilities. In this symbol is the idea that a person must explore their essence to understand their unique qualities and talents that he can develop and improve.

9. Teiwaz - rune warrior, symbolizing the qualities of determination and the ability to abandon selfish aspirations for the sake of greater goals. It indicates the need to be willing to sacrifice

personal interests and aspirations for the good of others or to achieve a significant goal, putting the highest ideals above their own self.

10. Runa Gebo reappears in the sequence before rune Dagaz, a symbol of transformation. If previously rune Gebo represented the beginning of the journey, the first step to self-sacrifice of the ego, now it appears in anticipation of the end of this journey as a gift, as a sign of what a person deserves thanks to his sacrifices. At this stage, he is ready to accept as a gift the results of his inner development and is ready to move on to the next rune - a symbol of a new beginning.

11. Completing this cycle, a person comes to rune Dagaz, which symbolizes a radical transformation, the transition from the old to the new. In this symbol lies the idea of a radical change in outlook, the discovery of a new dimension of being and self-identity. Here there is a complete metamorphosis of personality, similar to the transformation of a chrysalis into a butterfly, when a person realizes himself renewed, comprehending the new horizons of his "I".

12. Thus, we see a spiral of rebirth, where the stage of transformation from chrysalis to butterfly has a deep meaning. The picture of the Hanged Man in the Tarot closely echoes the moment when the caterpillar is in a state of immobile transformation, waiting for the moment when it will open its wings to soar into a new existence.

Total value

In the card of the Hanged Man, the hero finds himself in a critical situation, as if in a trap, which he created by his own decisions, choosing a path that leads to a dead end. Finding himself in a difficult situation, the person decided not to take risks and not to go forward, as a result of which his life path went in the opposite direction. The card of the Hanged Man symbolizes the moment when you are on the edge, on the thin border between life and death, and it is at such moments often comes understanding and insight, opening your eyes to the deepest truths.

The card of the Hanged Man represents the idea of self-sacrifice, indicating that in order to achieve something new, something valuable, it is necessary to part with the outdated. It can be a rejection of previous beliefs, a change of views on the world around you, or even a change of social circle, all in the name of spiritual awakening and enlightenment. Such ascetic practices, limitations and self-restraint can be a kind of path to spiritual development, as illustrated in the ancient myth of the god Odin. In search of wisdom, Odin traveled to the source of all knowledge, and Mimir, the giant guarding the spring, demanded of Odin his right eye in exchange for a sip of the water of wisdom. Odin agreed, uttering the wise words, "The wise will see more with one eye than the fool with two," thereby sacrificing his eye for the sake of acquiring deeper knowledge. But this act of self-sacrifice was only the beginning of his long journey to the truth. Odin learned of the existence of runes - sacred symbols that carry the great power of words, and to comprehend them, he had to go through the test of self-sacrifice.

The god Odin was tormented hanging upside down on the world tree Yggdrasil, pierced by his own spear. For nine long days he was in this position, until the giant Belthorn came to him, who quenched his thirst with honey and gave him the desired runes, which became a symbol of wisdom and knowledge. For those who are immersed in esotericism and spirituality, the map of the Hanged Man can be a symbol of a significant turning point in life or a certain situation, also implying service to people and society.

The Hanged Man offers a unique view of problems and situations, calling to look at them from a different angle and to change one's attitude to what is happening. A person who corresponds with this card usually differs from others not only in appearance, but also in his special way of thinking. This is a person with deep knowledge and wisdom, who is not afraid to think unconventionally. The Hanged Man calls for a deep dive into the essence of the issue, to thoughtful and comprehensive analysis before making a decision. It may seem that the whole world of man turned upside down, and this becomes a push to rethink life and reorganize the worldview. The Hanged Man card carries the energy of knowledge and wisdom, motivates learning and spiritual enlightenment, emphasizing the presence of strong intuition and the gift of foresight.

Depicts an extremely kind and responsive person who has genuine compassion and serves society by doing good, for example, through discoveries important to humanity, through which the lives of many are improved. This person possesses not only a creative streak but also a mystical view of the world, making him an innovator with a well-developed imagination. His self-discipline and altruism are impressive. He is able to understand and help others, generously sharing his love. Distinguished by spiritual development and the desire to acquire new knowledge. He generates original ideas and actively participates in charitable activities. He is an inventor and a seeker in one person.

In the negative aspect, it is a personality who continuously experiences suffering, alternating between the roles of victim and savior, attracting aggressors and despots who make him experience painful moments. Feels despair and powerlessness before circumstances, fear of changes in life and inner transformations. Such a person freezes in a daze, afraid to move to a new stage, fearing any change, and gets stuck at the crossroads of life. The Hanged Man is on the threshold of a profound change, being just one step away from the end of the former self and the birth of something new, but it is followed by the arcana Death, symbolizing this inevitable transition.

It is about scenarios when a person, afraid of change, takes a step back and prefers to leave. Moments of life shocks, a state of uncertainty, when a person as if floating in the air, without the ability to move in any direction, and this situation can drag on for an indefinitely long time. Hanged Man's Arcana usually symbolizes long periods of time. It can be a life crisis, a mid-life crisis, or a crisis in a particular area of focus. The person loses control over what is happening. The card may indicate stagnation in some situation that cannot be solved and seems immovable.

Relationship

The individual has the ability to unconditionally shoulder his companion, to show empathy and is able to make many sacrifices for the good of his other half. He is capable of doing deeds for his partner without any expectation in return. His heart is filled with selfless love and this shows his sincere and deep affection. A huge loving heart beats in unison with the needs of the beloved, ready to throw himself behind his partner to any challenge, be it fire or water.

77

The personality can manifest itself in a way that elicits sympathy from others, especially the life partner. Sometimes this leads to manipulation based on evoked pity, attempts to make oneself look like a victim so that the partner feels guilt. A prolonged period of crisis in a relationship leads to stagnation before it finally fades. There comes a point when the couple is no longer able to stay together, but still cannot make a decisive move to break the bonds. It is an attachment that is very hard to part with. People sacrifice personal interests and their freedom for the sake of preserving the relationship, often unilaterally investing in it without getting proper interaction.

One of the persons in the relationship may strive hard to earn the love of the partner, to humiliate themselves to requests, to influence sympathy, to make concessions, being in complete submission to the desires of the other. This can lead to a situation in which a person is the victim of an unscrupulous partner who is able to deceive and even issue a loan in the name of the other, and then disappear. Relationships in which there is discomfort, become like a cage without comfort, where one of the partners feels victimized, as if all the strength and energy is squeezed out of him. On the part of the partner may feel pressure due to jealousy. In such relationships there is routine and monotony, they seem suffocating and agonizing because of the impossibility of change.

Work and finance

An enthusiastic devotee of his craft gives all his time and energy to his chosen endeavor, showing tremendous passion and dedication to it. He serves his art, devoting himself wholeheartedly to it, even if it requires considerable sacrifice. His work is a blend of creativity and innovation, a true sacrifice on the altar of art. As an example of this dedication and creativity, I would like to tell you about a famous experiment by a famous artist:

"Famous artist Marina Abramovich, who is known for her performances, conducted an experiment: she stood motionless in one of the exhibition centers, and next to her lay a variety of objects - from a hammer and gun to watercolor paints. People were allowed to take any of these objects and do whatever they wanted with Marina.

At first the spectators were shy, only looking at her, giving her roses, kissing her. But then she was stripped, painted and even cut. Someone turned her on her axis. Someone lifted her arms up. One man used a blade to make an incision in her neck. Onlookers changed the position of the artist's body. Some attached various objects to her. Some men undressed and groped her. They accompanied their actions with laughter. The performance was stopped by building security when one of the visitors drew a gun. In the third hour all her clothes were cut off with blades. On the fourth hour, the same blades were used to examine her skin. She was subjected to all kinds of harassment. Someone forced her to point a gun at herself. She was so focused on the performance, she wouldn't have resisted anything.

In her performances Abramović revealed the facets and abilities of the human being. In the last of this performance she said that: "This work reveals something terrible about humanity. It shows how quickly a person can hurt you under the right circumstances. It shows how easy it is to depersonalize a person who doesn't fight back, who doesn't defend themselves. She shows that, given the right circumstances, most 'normal' people can obviously become very violent." (Article from the internet).

This incident also illustrates that if the Hanged Man does not stand up for himself and set personal boundaries, there will always be those who will not miss an opportunity to cause him suffering. This situation reflects the dark side of the Hanged Man Tarot card in its negative aspect, where the inability to protect oneself leads to detrimental consequences.

Getting stuck in financial difficulties and professional difficulties, noticeable stagnation in business, no financial income, goods are not bought, projects are not progressing, everything stands still. The situation of having to sell possessions to survive, finding extra work to stay afloat becomes commonplace. The job requires excessive effort and commitments are a heavy burden. To keep a job, a person often sacrifices personal time, hobbies, personal relationships, and sometimes even health. He becomes a slave to his labor rhythm. In such conditions, the risk of becoming a victim of fraud, unfavorable contracts increases, unnecessary obligations, loans may be imposed, as well as dependence on other people, which a person pulls on himself because of a sense of responsibility.

A difficult financial situation in which a person may find themselves mired in debt and loans. Money may be indefinitely delayed, transfers may not reach their destination, accounts are subject to freezing, and payments experience constant delays. In this condition, a person may work excessively hard without pay, allowing himself to be taken advantage of by others, afraid to set an adequate price for his services, or demand payment for fear of raising prices. He may undervalue himself and his labor, fail to see the true value in the services he provides, and experience imposter syndrome, which exacerbates the financial and professional crisis.

Purpose

It is important to be a pioneer, to contribute fresh and original ideas. To leave the position of hopelessness, not to be influenced by others, and instead to create and develop in favor of society, to be a pioneer, to offer unique solutions. It is necessary to value yourself, to give love generously to those around you, to protect your interests, to set personal boundaries and not allow anyone to overstep them. It is important to let go of grudges. It is necessary to support those around you, participate in charity. You should develop your intuition, spiritual aspects of life, connection with the Higher Powers.

Occupation

Yoga, gymnastics, athletics, service industries, social workers, volunteers, esotericists, creative people, inventors, scientists, researchers, innovators.

PLACES AND FACILITIES

Yoga centers, social institutions, hanging shelves, chandeliers, hangers.

Tip

It is important to change perspective on the current circumstances, to look at them from a new angle, to change your own reaction. Consider the situation from different angles, take into account alternative points of view. It is necessary to approach the issue with creativity, to show originality of thinking, unconventionality. It is important to be more adaptive, open to new things, unselfish and sincere in your actions and intentions.

Warning

There is a risk of being stuck in a certain emotional or life state for a long time, and circumstances may not change. If you continue to solve the problem with the old methods, the result will remain the same. Therefore, it is crucial to change your methods of dealing with it. It is unacceptable to allow oneself to be manipulated or to give up in the face of difficulties, because if one gives in to the feeling of helplessness, it can linger for a very long time. It can also symbolize the need for some kind of sacrifice in order to achieve a goal.

Death

The 13th Major Arcana

Symbolism

1. Hidden in the image of the hood on the Death card is the symbol of a star, which represents the desire for freedom. Such a star, distant and mesmerizing, reminds us of the importance of not becoming infinitely attached to any aspect of existence, be it places, people or material objects. In its light lies the admonition to be devoted to oneself all the way to the end of life's journey and beyond. It urges one not to compromise one's conscience and beliefs for the benefit of someone else's desires or material well-being. After all, the essence of our "I" - our soul, is like a star, and it should be guarded, not letting it fade and fall into oblivion. The star also indicates that, having overcome inner fears, a person is able to be reborn anew, and beyond the border of Death awaits something absolutely pure and undiscovered. Stars symbolize new horizons, promising discoveries to those who are ready to leave the established patterns of life and dare to take risks.

2. The forest that spreads beyond the border of Death appears as a metaphor for rebirth and the beginning of a new stage of life. It illustrates the idea that the end of one period inevitably heralds the dawn of something new. It is not just a forest, but a mysterious forest in the silence of night, emphasizing that even if the ending of one story is clear, what happens next remains a mystery, impenetrable and mysterious.

3. The hood on the card carries the meaning of disguise and secrecy. It hints at the fact that a person may be the owner of deep secrets, which he is not in a hurry to disclose to others, preferring to keep

them secret.

4. The scythe depicted on the card is a harbinger of risky changes and unpredictable events, warning of potentially abrupt and painful reversals in a situation. It is a symbol that we can expect trials that can cause pain, but at the same time they have the power to free us from outdated ties and limitations.

5. The red color on the card speaks of the heartbeat of a new endeavor that is emerging beyond Death. This color shows that with the departure of the habitual state something completely different enters into life, a new era of existence, full of life and energy.

Total value

In the arcana of Death is the removal of outdated elements from human life, which have lost their relevance and influence. This arcana symbolizes the end of a certain stage, when some extended and exhausting situation, previously reflected in the arcana of the Hanged Man, loses its impact and ends. With the arcana Death comes figurative cutting off this situation, like a scythe, and its removal from the life path of a person.

This is the process of parting with the past - whether it be relationships, loneliness, health or illness, experiences or even life itself, as well as with established habits or outdated view of the world. Arcana Death emphasizes the importance of releasing the outdated, to make room for newness, to allow the old self to go, so that there is a new self. Death represents a profound transformation, the transition from one state of being to another, symbolizes the end of the chrysalis stage and the birth of the butterfly. The path from the arcana Death to the arcana Moon is a path of night cards, where Death symbolizes the descent into the underworld, meeting with fears and temptations, and in the arcana Sun, which is the 19th, dawn comes, the day begins, and darkness gives way to light. Death is a transforming force that allows you to be reborn in a new reality, to meet a new day, in the arcana of the Sun.

Death represents the natural end of some process and the transition into a new phase of being. Change enters life, replacing the previous stability. This arcana symbolizes relief that comes with changes in circumstances and letting go of the outdated. He is the embodiment of rebirth and radical transformation of the situation, reflecting the transition from one phase to another. Sometimes the arcana can indicate communication on the Internet, associated with the blue light of the screen, which in practice means the monitor or Internet connections.

The card denotes critical moments, encourages not to be afraid to take risks and to be ready for radical changes. It depicts a person who is not afraid of risk and death, he is courageous and welcomes new changes. Such an individual may change his life frequently, saying goodbye to the old and entering a new phase of existence. He often experiences deep inner transformations. This is a purposeful person who is not afraid to stop the old, knows how to let go of the past and is reborn like a Phoenix. He is not attached to material things, is able to see the hidden and has the gift of foresight.

In its negative aspect the card may represent an aggressive person, prone to provocations and unreasonable risks. He may be too unappealing and straightforward with others. It is difficult for such a person to let go of something that is leaving his life, he will stubbornly hold on to it until the last moment, until life itself forces him to let go. Perhaps he has a deep fear of death, often worried about himself and his loved ones. May be reckless with his health and life, unreliable in affairs, not bringing them to an end. This is a cold person who does not value the lives of others. The card can also indicate periods of crisis, when a person feels an inner emptiness. The painful state can be both physical and mental.

Relationship

In this context, the arcana can reflect significant changes in personal ties between people. For example, if earlier in their relationship there was no special closeness, then now there may come a moment when the old ties are broken, a certain boundary is overcome. Relationships are transformed, acquiring new facets of feelings and intimacy with a partner. Or the connection is in a state of uncertainty, when it is unclear what the future will bring, and this arcana can indicate the possible end of this period of uncertainty or the transition from distance and coolness in the relationship to their revival and warmth, when alienation is replaced by a revival of passion and feelings, when outdated emotional ties die and a new stage in the relationship is born.

There may also come events like divorce or farewell, which symbolize the complete disappearance of former feelings, when the relationship is exhausted and there is no trace left of it. At such times, people often feel a complete lack of mutual attraction and become indifferent, like the earth on the grave. Card Death can symbolize deep heartache from failed relationships, broken heart, a state of despair and hopelessness. Such a feeling often comes after betrayal or other cruel blows of fate or from a loved one, when it seems that life is divided into before and after, and from a person as if cut off the most important part of his life. This card can also reflect a relationship permeated with aggression, where words become tools in the struggle, causing pain and wounds, the relationship is filled with heaviness and fatigue. Sometimes this card conveys the idea that if the end has come, it's time to accept it: "The horse is dead, it's time to get off.

Work and finance

This card is favorable to those who are not afraid of entrepreneurial risks. It indicates that investments in projects and their active promotion can bring significant benefits, so you should be bolder in financial endeavors. In addition, the belonging of the card to the eighth astrological house often predicts the receipt of large sums of money, which, as a rule, are the result of risky investments and fearless business. For brave and courageous entrepreneurs, fate often smiles, providing opportunities for major changes in business structures, transformation of projects, successful completion of endeavors and transition to a new stage of professional development, implying changes in the format of work processes.

People may spend their money unwisely, investing in projects with a high degree of uncertainty and financial risks. The card may signal a crisis in the financial sector and employment, the possibility of losing a job, the need to look for a new job, or a reduction in income. It can also indicate the presence of credit obligations and debts that are difficult to repay. In addition, the card can reveal insolvent projects and businesses that are operating on the brink of survival and may be shut down. Financial resources in such situations are often not easy to obtain, accompanied by financial losses, exhausting labor, strained relationships in the team and conflicts with business partners.

Purpose

We should not be afraid of change and novelty, we should not be afraid of things that have become established, of things that are gradually disappearing from our lives. It is important to be steadfast, to be able to move quickly from one state to another, without dragging the useless weight of bygone days behind you. It is worth avoiding unnecessary and dangerous risks. The process of internal change should be based on learning and accepting new ideas that contribute to this change, and in the same way transform the thinking of others. Our mission is to be initiators of change in other people's lives, pointing the way to new horizons, supporting people in freeing themselves from outdated attitudes, useless weights.

Occupation

Workers in cemeteries, ritual services, surgeons, rescue workers, military. Professions associated with risk and death. Plastic surgeon, as a person who changes the appearance of a person. Esotericist. Entrepreneur, as a person who is not afraid of risk.

PLACES AND FACILITIES

Cemeteries, intensive care units, places of transition: doors, windows. Mirrors, monitors.

Tip

It is important to allow the situation to come to an end, to let it go. Risk and adventure in life should not be avoided. Sometimes it is necessary to make a share of shaking to awaken yourself from everyday life. An era of decisive action and momentous changes is coming. Do not be afraid to say goodbye to what is leaving us, because in return will come something new and worthwhile. Now is the time to transform and make changes in the current situation.

Warning

Visible risks to life, health and the area you are now focusing on. The risk may lead to severe and irreparable consequences. The situation can be traumatizing. Now is not the best time for radical changes and abandonment of the usual course of action. You should not rush to make decisions and put the final point. There is no need to destroy what already exists and has value.

Temperance

The 14th Major Arcana

S ymbolism

1. The alchemical symbol of gold represents the gold of the soul, the embodiment of great spiritual transformation, following the middle path on which one achieves harmony and harmony of inner peace.

2. The merger of two triangles symbolizes the unity of opposites: feminine and masculine, the elements of fire and water. It indicates the ability to combine the incompatible, the desire for a golden balance between extremes.

3. Angel's wings reflect the desire for freedom and power of the spirit, as well as creative upsurge. They also symbolize the protection of circumstances and personality, indicating the presence of protection and patronage from the Higher Powers. It is the embodiment of the inner voice that brings relief and resolution of inner conflicts, pointing the way to harmony and Temperance. The card of Temperance calls to rise above the current situation, to rethink it, to move away from a narrow-minded and subjective perception to a more objective and comprehensive one. It is suggested to look at the problem from the outside, to isolate yourself from the bustle, to listen to the answers coming from the depths of the soul in peace and quiet.

Total value

Near the majestic throne of the Most High, there are two light messengers: on the right side majestically sits the angel Michael, representing fire and solar energy, on the left side - Gabriel, symbolizing water and lunar energy. In the image on the map, these two powerful forces are in harmonious balance thanks to the supreme angelic being, which holds in balance both fiery solar power and changeable lunar flows. This symbolizes the synthesis of severity, strength, irascibility and burning passion with tenderness, affection and heartfelt kindness.

Androgyny on the card represents the union of male and female principles, showing the ideal of balance and fusion of seemingly irreconcilable opposites. After the separation of beginnings, symbolized by the card of Death, comes Temperance, seeking to find the golden mean. The Sun and Moon, held in the hands, demonstrates the ability to balance between polarities. This figure also depicts the spiritual guide embodied in the Christian canon by the Archangel Michael, who, standing in front of the Hall of Trials, prevents evil spirits from interfering with the balance of the mental scales.

The guide represented on the map symbolizes that part of the inner "I" that acts as a reference point and a guiding thread, like Ariadne, leading to one's own harmony and integrity of the soul. He manages a person, helping him to overcome the trials and temptations. In the context of the 13th arcana, Death symbolizes total renunciation and the Devil symbolizes unrestrained immersion in pleasures such as excessive alcohol consumption or excessive entertainment. Temperance, positioned between these extremes, reminds of the need to find a balance, suggesting not to give up life's pleasures, but also calling to remember the sense of proportion.

This card reflects conscious self-restraint and the ability not to harm oneself. It symbolizes alchemical transformation, energy exchange, capable of reuniting and reviving what was separated by the deadly blow of the scythe of Death. The card of Temperance also speaks of the inevitable transition of times, the eternal change of eras and moments of life, emphasizing the close connection of the past, present and future. It symbolizes the ability to combine earthly aspirations with the highest spiritual ideals, realizing their inseparability.

It represents the arcana of healing, replenishment of vital energy, restoration of health. It embodies the ideals of beauty, creativity, inner and outer harmony. The card of Temperance is like a beacon of light at the end of a dark tunnel, an angel-guide, pointing to the light of truth. It promises a favorable, albeit slow, development of events, focusing on time. It can indicate ideal timing for undertakings or important deeds.

The card also reminds us of the cyclical nature of time, that sometimes it is advisable to simply wait and refrain from action. Any decision made should restore balance to life. If the decision leads to imbalance, it should be postponed, and if it promotes harmony and happiness, it is time for active action. The card promises stability in affairs, the possibility of finding compromises and restoring harmony. A favorable resolution of the situation is promised, but without haste. According to the card of Temperance, it is often necessary to wait a certain period to let circumstances settle.

This card reflects the period in a person's life, when everything goes its way, life is filled with calmness and harmony, and a person feels his integrity and deep connection with the world around him. Everything in life is formed in a measured and smooth way. A person derives pleasure from every moment lived, is able to delicately find a common language with others, shows diplomacy, the ability to find compromises and solutions even in difficult circumstances. Such a person has fine taste and sensitivity of soul, which can manifest itself in the ability to heal and help others.

This person has generosity and compassion, is characterized by boundless kindness and is always ready to provide support, to help restore inner balance and calmness in others. Easily finds beauty in the world and shares this discovery with others. He adores art in all its manifestations - music, fine arts, a variety of creative directions. Able to create works of art that can amaze and inspire people to the core. This man is shrouded in an aura of nobility, in his society is always cozy and pleasant, he has unsurpassed tactfulness, friendliness and diplomacy. Always knows when to stop, is a model of wisdom and spirituality. He is no stranger to the subtleties of psychology, and it is fascinating to immerse himself in the study of human souls, whether as a psychologist, spiritual counselor or historian, through the prism of creativity. He is drawn to the world of traveling and meeting new people. He possesses not only outer beauty but inner beauty as well, recognizing the importance of balance and proportion in all things. He avoids junk food, alcohol and other bad habits, preferring a healthy lifestyle. He is a self-sufficient individual who clearly understands his desires and aspirations in life. He is incredibly empathetic and has a well-developed empathy and is characterized by a shrewd intuition.

In the negative aspect it can be mental anguish and increased sensitivity to offenses. There may be a tendency for a person to have a hard time defending his own beliefs; he would prefer to keep silent, trying to show that he is above the situation and will not stoop to conflicts, although inside he accumulates resentments that can overflow if he does not give them a way out. The so-called "excellent student" syndrome manifests itself, when a person can lose himself, his opinion and his desires, trying to meet the expectations of others, forgetting about his own needs. Lack of ability to find the golden mean, loss of a sense of proportion can become his problem. Self-abuse and resentment may also manifest. In addition, patience can turn into a heavy burden when it is necessary to restrain one's desires, denying oneself pleasures, which becomes intolerable. Situations can experience severe inhibition, and there may come a time when nothing comes together properly.

Relationship

Companions and like-minded people find a common language, their life is filled with harmony, they cleverly find compromises and quickly settle disagreements. In their relationship is dominated by deep mutual understanding and unwavering support for each other. They are very gentle and attentive to the experiences and feelings of the partner, paying attention to his inner world. For them it is extremely important to maintain spiritual closeness and unity of souls. Harmonious relationship, where opposites do not just coexist, but mutually enrich each other, is the basis of their long-term and reliable union, in which there is no room for disagreement. Partners have the ability to subtly feel each other and communicate at ease. Tolerance for each other's shortcomings and the ability to empathize, getting into the partner's situation, distinguish their relationship. In benevolence and unassuming toward each other lies their special harmony, which is also reflected in the energy exchange in sexual intimacy.

Nevertheless, in a negative context, the same cards can reveal routine, monotony in the relationship, where partners, in fact, just tear each other down, and the relationship no longer brings joy. They stay together because of habit and obligations, fear of hurting the partner or the desire to avoid destroying the usual way of life and loss of stability. Partners can make mutual concessions, sometimes overreacting in an attempt to please each other. There may be a situation when one of the partners is constantly in the role of peacemaker and unconditionally forgives the partner all misdeeds. This indicates a willingness to play the role of guardian angel, even when in fact it is necessary to stop forgiveness and set boundaries so that the partner realizes the consequences of his or her actions.

Work and finance

Based on this card, the individual has enough money to meet his personal needs, he has no financial obligations and no significant gaps in his budget. He is able to provide for himself so that he can feel cozy and comfortable without lack of money. Finances are there, but they are in Temperance, without excesses. A person lives in accordance with his possibilities, maintaining a balance between income and expenses. In the context of the card analogy with the 8th house, this card can also foretell a significant income, which should be used wisely: not to spend spontaneously, but to invest and invest wisely. Displays cooperation, where the ability to find common ground, tact and diplomacy are valued. It is important to be able to make concessions and accept the points of view of partners, colleagues, customers. The card symbolizes effective management of personnel, projects, work and finances. The person to whom this card falls may be able to unite various projects and activities.

This card can also signal that a person will have to limit his expenses and learn to save money, adhere to a strict budget. There may come a time when one will have to endure a period of financial constraints, when there will not be enough money for all desired purchases and needs, and it will be necessary to distribute available financial resources more carefully and thoughtfully. The card may also indicate a misallocation of financial priorities and budgets. In some cases, it may reflect a person's tendency to sacrifice his own interests for the sake of others, even if it is to his detriment, to show excessive generosity, not knowing how to refuse and take on other people's obligations.

Purpose

To devote one's time to the creative process, to strive to bring one's own experiences and feelings into a state of complete peace, and through this creative process to spread harmony to others. To give beauty to the world, contributing to the healing of souls. To become a light that will show the way to a bright future for others. To deepen the connection with one's own soul, to follow its call. To develop the ability to forgive, to find the perfect balance. To learn to perceive harmony and dimension in all aspects of life. To get in deep contact with nature and its infinite rhythms.

Occupation

Creative professions, cultural worker, historian, chemist, psychologist, esotericist, person who works with the human soul, nutritionist, healer, pharmacist, teacher.

PLACES AND FACILITIES

Churches, laboratories, places where something is mixed, combined. Icons, galleries, art exhibitions, music concerts, esoteric festivals.

Tip

It is important to learn to see the world through the eyes of another person, the ability to find a common language, to show more diplomacy and tact. It is necessary to be more flexible, adapt to circumstances. Support others, while maintaining a sense of proportion, show Temperance. Gather strength, strive for inner peace and harmony, strengthening your state of mind.

Warning

You should not suppress your voice in yourself and force yourself to be silent, you should not constantly limit your feelings, you should not be overly generous to your own detriment. Do not allow others to exploit your kindness and take advantage of your good intentions without compensation.

The Devil

XV Major Arcana

Symbolism

1. The submitted hand symbolizes the temptation on the part of the Devil to offer a person to take part in a risky game, without hiding its dangers, because the palm is opened and submitted with the left hand. It symbolizes the importance for a person to accept himself completely, including all his weaknesses and shortcomings. It hints at the need to realize and accept one's dark sides, acknowledging them, but not allowing them to control oneself. Here lies the Devil's trick: he offers a tempting opportunity to plunge into the seductive darkness, to get lost in it. You should keep all your aspects under control, but do not suppress them, because they are an integral part of our essence. After all, if you constantly suppress them, there may come a moment when they will break out and drag you into the vortex of darkness. Recognizing and accepting the different aspects of the personality contributes to its integration and harmony.

2. The invisible threads emanating from the person symbolize the path that he himself laid before he was trapped in this game, having created it by his own thoughts and actions that led him to excessive temptation. The ephemeral threads, the ghostly figure of a person suggest that any addiction is nothing more than an illusion, and if one takes a broader view and courageously faces one's fears, one can understand the true cause of addiction and free oneself from it.

3. An individual who covers his ears is trying to isolate himself from external information, and his gesture of holding his ears indicates

that his thoughts are stuck in a vacuum, which also prevents adequate perception of reality. Thus, the person shows his closedness from the outside world, which indicates distrust in the surrounding and lack of faith in positive changes. He refuses to recognize shadow aspects in himself, is afraid to look at them directly, is afraid to see in himself what he tries so hard to hide even from himself.

4. The image of a ram tattoo symbolizes the tendency of a man to give in to his basic instincts, to obey the animal side of his nature, ignoring the voice of reason and giving in to impulsive actions. The presence of a chain around the top of the ram's skull emphasizes the difficulty of freeing oneself from any form of dependence and submission. If we allow our instincts to dominate our lives, we become vulnerable to manipulation and capable of developing addictions, especially if we refuse to listen to our inner rational voice and act unconsciously.

5. What the Devil hides in his right hand remains beyond our perception. What consequences await the person who reaches out to him? It is the concealment of one's inner vices when the individual believes himself to be blameless, good and righteous. The individual is fueled by a sense of pride, seeks superiority in all endeavors, displays arrogance and disdain, and demonstrates his dominance over others. In such a state, egoism increases and the person begins to think that he is the center of the universe.

6. The sign on the chest is a unicursal hexagram, conveying the thought: "as above, so below". This symbol depicts the continuous movement and connection of our consciousness with the subconscious, the combination of the light and dark sides. It reflects all that we expose and conceal within ourselves, emphasizing the inseparability of the fundamental aspects of life. Only against the background of light can we see our shadow and distinguish good from evil, which emphasizes the indivisibility of the most important principles of existence.

Total value

The character encounters the darkest part of his journey, where he faces his own darkness. This is the realm of shadows, the abode of hidden fears, repressed desires, those personality traits we try to avoid recognizing. It is here that we feel shame and rejection. In these depths of consciousness lies the unconscious potential, those aspects of self that we are afraid to shine a light on and show others. Here lies our inner shadow, the elusive companion of our existence.

The Devil symbolizes the card of social attraction and human desire for social self-realization, the desire to surround oneself with a variety of achievements and worldly pleasures. Through this card, the Devil can realize his goals by involving others in his affairs. He has a passion for easy and large financial means. The Devil incarnate is a combination of charisma, attraction, visual brilliance and sexual energy.

The Devil card represents the test of a person's strength in the face of temptation: whether he can ignore his own conscience and sacrifice values, or resist temptation and keep what is dear to him. What beckons and seduces, often disguised in the guise of irresistible attractiveness, like the Devil himself appears before us. However, behind this enticing facade lies a danger that can lead to harmful consequences. This can manifest itself in the form of addictions - be it alcohol, sweets, irresponsible sex, unwise risks, and so on.

Relationship

Intense libido, intensity of intimate life, passionate relationship between partners. A person can find sustenance from the resources of his partner. There is a strong desire to possess the partner at any cost. Animal instincts, sexual deviance, BDSM practices dominate their bond. The partners seem to be absorbed in their relationship, where the real world recedes into the background, their desires become dominant, they are as if in the trap of their passions, becoming dependent on this madness. They are very much attached to each other, have an emotional dependence that deepens excessively. This is a fatal relationship that can completely turn a person's life upside down, when constant quarrels and reconciliations do not give peace, when it is difficult to be together, and separation seems unbearable.

Sexual anomalies and behavioral pathologies. Departure from generally accepted norms. Strong dependence on their partner, pathological attachment. Violence in relationships, psychological pressure. Manipulation, deceptions, cheating, betrayals, violent quarrels, scandalous situations, alcohol use, drug addictions in the couple. Aggressiveness and hostility in the relationship. One of the partners can exploit the other, maintain the relationship for the sake of their own benefits, monetary interests, improving their social status. Pathological jealousy in the couple, reaching absurd manifestations, violent actions caused by jealousy, quarrels, humiliation. Dominance of one partner over the other, suppression of the will, imposition of one's own opinion. A person becomes a pawn in the game of the partner.

Work and finance

Excellent position in the professional field, high level of income, excellent opportunities for profit. The ability to influence in the work environment, in business, the ability to convince clients and colleagues, to force them to make concessions, to sign contracts on favorable terms. Obsession with achievements in work, irresistible desire for power and fame. Excellent financial results, brilliant ideas to increase profits, quick earnings. Spending money to maintain social status, a luxurious life. In the context of business map suggests the need to create a spectacular packaging of goods, to form attractive advertising offers, to apply methods of psychological influence on consumers, to master marketing strategies. The importance of attracting a professional who has the skills of successful sales and knows how to influence the decisions of buyers. Active involvement of potential customers in a dialog, offering trial samples or services for free to arouse interest and create a sense of commitment in the consumer.

Purpose

Strive to develop your will to such an extent that it becomes unshakable even in the face of your own shortcomings. Learn the art of influencing others, managing them consciously and for their benefit. Illuminate for people their vulnerable sides, so that they have the opportunity to make them stronger. Learn to accept your shadow side, fully embrace yourself, and treat others in the same way, striving to harmonize your own personality. Actively work on your addictions, try to identify the root of the problem to be able to finally get rid of it.

Occupation

Esotericist, magician, psychologist, good salesman and marketer. Work with finances, power, politics, representatives of the oldest profession, models, drug dealers, alcohol, casino owners, killers, swindlers.

PLACES AND FACILITIES

Modeling agencies, television, escort agencies, drug cartels, liquor stores, casinos, places of worship.

Tip

In this situation, show guile, courage, your own charisma and attraction. Act in a convoluted way, do not reveal all your cards at once. Do not hesitate to express your desires, be bolder in self-expression, allow yourself more than usual. Strive to get the most out of life and the situation in which you find yourself.

Warning

The situation can be confusing, and you may have individuals with questionable reputations in your midst. There may be hidden dangers behind the appearance of attractive offers. Before taking any action, you should think carefully about the possible consequences and consider what it might entail in order to avoid undesirable outcomes.

The Tower

XVI Major Arcana

S ymbolism

1. The squirrel was storing acorns, accumulating supplies in a secluded corner of his dwelling, but one unexpected lightning strike destroyed it all. The squirrel is a symbol of caution and foresight, but even the most prudent creature can not prevent the interference of random elements in their well-thought-out plans. In Christian parabolas, the squirrel acts as a symbol of divine Providence, which is associated with its custom of using its own tail as a shelter from rain.

2. Acorns are traditionally honored as sacred gifts of Thor, the god of thunder and lightning. They themselves have become an emblem of strength and fortitude, and on the map, even after a crushing lightning strike, they remain unharmed. This suggests that overcoming difficulties requires not only strength, but also endurance and a resilient spirit.

3. The butterfly is a symbol of re-creation and metamorphosis, implying man's ability to rebirth after experiencing upheaval and radically change his way of life. Lightning destroys outdated things, shattering what has become a vacuum of life, providing a path to freedom from confinement. It breaks old structures and habits, destroying the comfort zone and pushing us beyond it.

4. Lightning represents an act of divine will, a manifestation of the power of the Supreme Forces influencing fate. It also hints at the possibility of a person acquiring previously unexplored abilities in moments of extreme situations, gives deep spiritual insight, purification. Although lightning is dangerous, but it brightens

the night sky and cuts through the impenetrable darkness. It is a sharp break from the past, immediate and unpredictable. It turns everything into ruins, leaving only the open sky overhead. The expansive celestial space replaces the pressurizing ceiling of the tower, providing release. The four walls surrounding man are crumbling away, and he is now forced to erect his way of being anew. This is liberation from limited worldviews, expansion of consciousness, spiritual awakening.

Total value

When the event symbolized by the card Tower occurs, we are faced with the destruction of the established order and the movement from darkness to light, to enlightenment. The destruction of the enclosed space, which is the tower, is accompanied by a powerful impact - fire from heaven, which is the embodiment of divine lightning. This is an expression of the anger of the gods, the consequence for not passing the exam before the temptations faced by man in the arcana Devil, labeled number 15. In ancient times, the arcana Tower had the name "House of God", which emphasized its sacred origin and power.

Arcana Tower, designated by the number 16, symbolically represents the place for the royal cards in the Tarot, as their number is also equal to 16. This arcana is the embodiment of the myth of the Tower of Babel, where a single language speaking people in their desire to build a structure to the heavens faced an angry God. As a result of their excessive pride and confidence in their own infallibility, God punished them by forcing them to speak different languages, which ultimately prevented them from communicating and completing the tower. Similarly, the four suits of the Tarot also "speak" different "languages" - Cups in the language of emotions, Wands in the language of aspirations, Swords in the language of the mind and Pentacles in the language of bodily sensations. It is this archetype that indicates that any overzealous construction will collapse under the weight of its weight.

In astrological context, the Arcana Tower is associated with the tenth house, which symbolizes the individual's desire to achieve social heights and career growth. It points to governmental organizations, centers of power and control. The tower depicts the process of tearing a person out of his habitual frames and limitations, removing obstacles to success, breaking down established barriers, breaking through the "financial ceiling", destroying the usual way of life in order to make room for new beginnings, new positions and opportunities. The card reflects a strict structure, in which there are both leading and subordinate links, demonstrating the existing hierarchy.

The collapse of everyday existence, the disintegration of stale guises, outdated beliefs and habitual patterns of thought processes. The habitual support of life collapses, entailing a chaotic state where a person has to re-shape himself. Falling away from inner barriers, confusion, removing fetters, freeing oneself from what has been holding back and causing painful knots in the soul, preventing one from being more purposeful and asserting oneself more vividly. This is the exit from the darkness of ignorance. Transition to spiritual rebirth.

Manifests reconstructive changes, cardinal repair works, change of the habitual structure of being. Entering a new system, adopting statutes and orders. It can be following new religious teachings, receiving deep spiritual revelations. Opening new horizons in spirituality, achieving a higher level of connection with the Divine Essences. Initiation ceremonies, spiritual initiations, integration into energetic communities. Immersion in a new system of values. Moments of illumination, when it becomes clear to a person that his habitual way of life does not satisfy him, and he realizes the need for immediate change.

Displays a personality that is a drive for change and has a knack for causing amazement in others. This is a courageous and energetic person. The unforeseen insurgent stands before us. A leader who is bent on creating his own system of values and rules. Such a person is open to the new, strives for self-realization and spiritual enlightenment. He is abundant in energy, capable of opening new horizons for others, guiding them to enlightenment, releasing them from the traps of deception. He is an innovator, determined, prone to extreme activities, a lover of thrills and adrenaline rushes.

In the negative aspect the card demonstrates stunning circumstances, indicates that a person experiences a powerful shock, his inner world is shaken by an unexpected event. This is the limit of extreme, stressful situations. The fury of emotions that have been accumulating for a long time bursts out. Life is experiencing a crisis, like a thunderous blow in the middle of a clear sky. May indicate danger, agonizing destruction of values, objects or certain spheres of existence. It is a failure of plans and sudden changeable circumstances. Destruction of stability in life. Disasters and devastating events, accidents, collapse, incarceration. It is the violation of personal boundaries, invasion of private space. Traumas and crises. The card may indicate an obsessive person whose excessive attention is annoying and disturbing. This is an explosive and aggressive individual. A scandalous nature that enjoys getting into conflicts and quarrels. Tyrant, unable to restrain his emotions, can rudely express himself and destroy relations with others. Moral and spiritual decline. Such a person is inclined to impose his opinion on others, make spontaneous and rash decisions.

Relationship

The card can reflect the difference in the social position of two people, one at the top, the other at the bottom. An indicator of hierarchy within family relationships. Describes the moment of release of long-restrained emotions and sexual desires, when a person suddenly spills on the partner all the power of his passion, honesty, falls on him a flood of his feelings, a real storm of emotions and desires. This leads to changes in the perception of each other in the couple. The relationship is extracted from stagnation, from a bleak confinement where both only assumed what the partner's true feelings were. Then suddenly the walls of delusion crumble and the clear light of truth flashes into the relationship. Such truth can either delight or be a disappointment. It is a release of the mental and emotional heaviness that has accumulated within. Confessions of love, which seem to knock the ground out from under the feet, lead to shock and leave a person in such a state of joyful shock that he loses sleep for many nights. If this card appears in the layout for loneliness, it predicts the imminent end of loneliness, the destruction of the prison of solitude, where the individual was isolated.

In negative aspect, this card indicates relationship ruptures, conflicts, loud scandals, physical confrontations, bitter arguments and divorces, as well as shocking revelations that can cause pain. A person may suddenly announce their departure, leaving their partner in a state of shock comparable to a cold shower or a hammer blow to the head. In a moment of anger, harsh and hurtful words may be said that destroy the relationship and provoke heated conflict. The cracks in the relationship become obvious. This is reminiscent of the story of the Tower of Babel, where one seeks to suppress the other, seeking to dominate because of pride and vanity, putting themselves above their partner. As a result, people lose the ability to understand each other and negotiate as if they were speaking different languages. When one tries to erect a kind of tower of domination over his partner, the other cannot withstand this pressure, and the relationship deteriorates. Also, when one tries to hold the other captive to jealousy and possessive feelings, the outcome becomes obvious: the partner is no longer tolerant, and this leads to a sharp confrontation or the final breakdown of the relationship.

Work and finance

The Tower card foretells the urgent need to create a clear hierarchy, an orderly system in professional activities, as well as the establishment of a certain order. This is a moment of epiphany, when you get valuable insights on how to improve the situation, how to act in the most reasonable way. Embolizes a way out of a predicament, the discovery of a non-standard solution to a problem. If previously it was difficult to understand how to move the case forward, how to remove it from the stagnation, and everything was repeated in an endless cycle, then with the appearance of the card Tower comes the destruction of this vicious circle, getting rid of the prison of a narrow view, where a person could not cover with his eyes all the diversity of his case and the actual state of things. Where he had been imprisoned among his inconspicuous projects, now he finds insight and understands how to free himself and show his ideas to the world, to realize his potential.

The card also indicates the potential for dismissal, departure from the current place of work, may portend a financial crisis, loss of money. It symbolizes the collapse of a personal empire, the collapse of business structures, the destruction of dreams of material well-being, undermines the foundations of financial stability. Loss of control over the workflow, business, some aspects of activity out of control. Shocking changes in the professional sphere, which make you immediately change approaches and methods of work. Change of workplace, transition to a new one, various difficulties and obstacles to professional development.

Purpose

To follow the path of spiritual awakening means to destroy old mental attitudes, long-established patterns of thinking. To direct your indomitable energy and power to positive transformations, to break the limiting frameworks, monotony, misconceptions and deception. To discover in people the spark of divinity, to bring knowledge and freedom of spirit, to remove the veil of ignorance from human eyes, to learn to see reality as it really is - without unnecessary embellishments, to be open to new things, not to hold on to material wealth and to instill similar principles in others.

Occupation

Translator, linguist, nutritionist, psychologist, trainer, rehabilitator, builder, repairman, military. Business, work in government agencies, large companies, large structures, participation in business systems, cryptocurrencies, work in corporations.

PLACES AND FACILITIES

Skyscrapers, mountains, tall buildings, ruins, places of fires and lightning strikes, large companies and corporations, government offices.

Tip

It is necessary to radically transform circumstances. This is the era of radical change, when it is essential to leave the usual comfort zone. It is necessary to break non-functioning systems, scenarios that hinder development and progress. It is important to change the entrenched structure of business and activity.

Warning

There is a possibility of collapse, breakdown of routine and stability of life scenarios. Events may unexpectedly push you out of your comfort zone, leading to the need to face dangerous and risky changes in the environment. Situations can spiral out of control, leading to a significant crisis.

The Star

XVII Major Arcana

Symbolism

1. The Star card symbolizes aspirations, hopes, dreams and strategies, it is a beacon pointing towards the future. It is a path to the bright periods of life, to the resolution of difficulties. The card encourages that the chosen route is correct, that the road ahead promises great horizons and wonderful chances. This is the realization of goals, the realization of cherished desires. This is a blessing from the Higher Powers, the onset of a favorable moment for the implementation of plans. Belonging to the 11th house, the Star tells about the future, opens the eyes of unusual projects, art, futuristic constructions and design, advanced nanotechnology. This is the ability to foresight, contact with higher energies, it is the study of uncharted space and the search for extraterrestrial civilizations. It is a movement towards perfection, an aspiration to improve existence, to raise the quality of life of mankind.

2. The star is the embodiment of wisdom and intuitive knowledge. It is associated with femininity, charming beauty and eternal youth. In iconography, the Star is depicted as a young woman, generously endowing the earth with healing moisture, providing all those who are thirsty to drink from the source of pure living water. She embodies youth, purity, delightful attractiveness, the magic charm of femininity, flawlessness, the ideal. It is a state of deep meditation, it is openness and purity of soul. Development, growth, a state of peace and harmony of soul and mind.

3. Creative impulse and conviction in a favorable outcome, working through far-reaching plans and ambitions, all this indicates a

period stretched in time. Here the key is purity of thought and established connection with the depths of your own soul, with that spark that flickers within everyone. Develop yourself, learn to recognize the symbols and signs that are rich in the world around you. The star promises that inclement weather will go away, the sky will clear up and there will be times filled with light and purity. It is a symbol of renewal, a ray of light that inspires confidence and helps to choose the right direction. It is a reliable life principle and a boundless stream of inspiration, as well as a tendency to supernatural perception.

Total value

After the devastating events in the Tower Card, in the Star Card man emerges from the rubble and moves to the limits of his world, tempted by renewed ambitions and aspirations. He finds again his lost connection to the celestial by remembering his origins. The man connects with his own inner light and reaches the place where living water flows, the symbol of true life. After the Tower, he is liberated from the limiting framework of former perception and achieves true freedom of spirit.

In this place a person gains a clear vision of his horizons, his future, this epiphany pushes him to the paths previously unexplored, which are to be thoroughly studied and cognized. There is a desire to overcome routine, to move away from the usual activities. A new angle of view on life circumstances and tasks opens up, when a person begins to live, create, work and love differently. He rises to a supernatural, transcendent level of being, discovering unexplored facets of the world. Astonishing horizons of unprecedented existence, unseen and brilliant creatures open before him. Man changes his perspective to a full one, he looks from a bird's-eye view, as if he is soaring above earthly problems, gaining spaciousness of thought and liberation from the narrowness of former views.

The star appears to us as a symbol of a man creating something special, a man who seems alien. There is something sublime in his works, beyond the ordinary. Such a person impeccably strives for perfection, and his projects and works often balance on the edge of something magically tantalizing. Card Star also symbolizes the desire for fame, indicating the potential of a person to become a real star, to stand out with his extraordinary talent. This is a bright and extraordinary personality, with a well-developed imagination and perseverance in achieving goals. Such an individual loves to be in the center of attention, shows himself in the world of art, likes to attend exhibitions and concerts. Optimism does not leave him, he believes in a bright future. This is a skillfully expressing his feelings of the artist, hungry for recognition, high position and success.

In the negative interpretation of the card Star can mean obstacles on the way to the realization of plans, difficulties in initiating actions and in achieving goals, when a person lives dreams and plans, not realizing them in life. It may indicate the unreality of some ambitions, when a person strives for the unattainable, trying to jump above his head. Star disease manifests itself, when conceit and arrogance lead to a bad reputation and disgrace. A person may not really evaluate their abilities and talents, be cold and unfeeling, obsessed with the idea of their own genius and despise others for their ordinariness.

Relationship

It is an expression of deep fascination with one's partner when he or she is perceived subconsciously as a role model. People in a relationship sometimes put each other on a pedestal, considering their life partner to be flawless. This can also symbolize the rekindling of feelings and the beginning of a new phase in the relationship. Interaction between two sensitive, creative individuals who are a source of mutual inspiration. A love that can be felt as a gift of destiny, as a heavenly blessing. In such a relationship, happiness and peace reign, and mutual devotion and loyalty are achieved through deep trust. It is a transition to a deeper and more open level of relationship.

An abundant sex life that abounds in exquisite, sensual fulfillment and is full of tenderness. An ideal compatibility portrait of two people in love. Mutual attraction that is accompanied by a sense of irresistible charm and seduction in the relationship. Describes the state when from the overflow of emotions it seems that the earth slips from under the feet, the feeling of falling in love and as if a person gains wings. This is also the moment of the soul's arrival in the material world, the first meeting with parents, the moment of conception of a child. All-consuming femininity and external attractiveness of the partner. Intertwining of common aspirations, plans and dreams when a couple makes long-term joint plans.

It can also be an indication of communication via the Internet, when relationships develop at a distance. Individuals sometimes create idealized images of their favorite persons, fall in love with popular actors or musicians. It is possible when a person sets himself unrealizable criteria, dreaming of unattainable models, not recognizing that real people differ significantly from their images on the covers of magazines or in films. Some may avoid creating relationships for long periods of time, believing that there are no suitable candidates in their environment and feeding on dreams of an unattainable ideal. Attachment to an idealized image rather than a real person can lead to a person valuing their partner highly, seeing them through the prism of their illusions. It can also manifest itself in the fact that a person retains feelings for someone he or she has never met in life, creating an idealized image of him or her and living in his or her imaginary world.

Work and finance

An approach that eliminates mediocrity is required in the execution of assignments. The pursuit of excellence should be at the core of all project and work initiatives. This attitude reflects a desire for greatness and increased influence in the professional and business world, as well as the ability to make your business recognizable and appealing to a wide audience. Quality developed proposals and projects invariably encounter approval and interest. Growth in the professional hierarchy becomes a natural consequence. Achievement of set goals and aspirations, receiving a deserved return on invested efforts. Signals the prospects for improving the financial situation, although this usually takes time. Financial recovery becomes achievable, excellent prospects for professional growth and opportunities for expansion are opening up. Creativity in business is emphasized. It is noted that the individual has found his true purpose in life and is successfully realizing it, moving up the career ladder. The person personifying this card is a master of his business, who achieves exceptional results and full realization of his talents.

However, in a negative way, the card can indicate a tendency to put things off until later, reluctance to start work and a tendency to endless dreaming and planning without real action. A person may set himself overly ambitious goals, dream of immediate enrichment, but lack the skills to gradually achieve what he wants. This creates a stupor, because the distance between him and his ambitious goal seems insurmountable without dividing it into smaller and more feasible steps. There may be a tendency to meet deadlines. There may also be a tendency to plan too many tasks for a limited period of time, which inevitably leads to failure to accomplish what is planned. In addition, the individual may lead a lifestyle that exceeds his or her financial capacity, spending a significant portion of income to give the impression of a luxurious and successful life.

Purpose

The desire to achieve fame and recognition can be an inspiration to many people, lighting the way for them. This drive includes the desire to showcase one's unique talents, to strive for excellence, and to realize one's original, big ideas. It is necessary to discover and deepen one's creative potential by creating new things, and to encourage others to discover and develop their talents. It is important to develop intuitive abilities, to establish a connection with the Higher Powers, as well as to confidently believe in yourself, your abilities and natural giftedness.

Occupation

Artist, painter, designer, musician, esotericist, astrologer, tarologist, numerologist, astronomer, ufologist, space explorer, model, fashion photographer, actor.

PLACES AND FACILITIES

Stage, concert, exhibitions, observatories, planetariums, outdoor LOCATIONS AND OBJECTS under the night sky, parks, fountains, theaters, cinemas.

Tip

It is important to take a fresh look at the current circumstances, to assess them from a new, higher perspective, as if looking at them from a bird's eye view. It is necessary to set correct and thoughtful goals for oneself from the very beginning, to have clear life guidelines. It is important to fully realize the inherent potential and talents, following the call of your heart and soul. One should approach any situation with creative uniqueness, correctly formulating one's desires and aspirations.

Warning

Do not get too carried away with dreaming of future successes, neglecting the present and avoiding actions that could lead to real results. You should not sugarcoat reality or put individuals on a pedestal. The approach to achieving goals should be pragmatic, you should not dwell on long thoughts and unfeasible plans. Perhaps the wrong benchmarks were chosen earlier, which requires reassessment and adjustment.

The Moon

XVIII Major Arcana

S ymbolism

1. Behind the backs of wolves stretches the forest, where one can easily get lost and find no way out. Wolves symbolize the instincts and dangers that are encountered on the life path of man. They indicate that in moments of mental repression, the personality is capable of generating within himself terrifying creatures of his own consciousness, capable of destroying him from within. The white wolf represents intuition, while the black wolf embodies all fears. The white is the protector and the black is the adversary. And in the pale light of the moon, the girl loses the ability to tell them apart.

2. In her gripped terror, she slips and falls into the water, losing her awareness of where the bottom is and where the surface of the water is. However, the moment she stops her panic and stops struggling frantically, she manages to see the light of the moon, which becomes her saving reference point in the darkness.

3. The luminary of the night touches the surface of the water, it is a symbol of diving into the depths of one's feelings. The image of a girl immersed in water shows us her left side, symbolizing the feminine, subconscious. The reflection of the bottom on her body symbolizes a deep unity with the subconscious, feeling its closeness, as if touching its skin, and possessing secret knowledge. This ability to influence yourself and the world around you with the power of the subconscious mind requires an irrational approach. The card speaks of the impermanence of circumstances and changeability of situations. Reflects events related to water

and calming the mind and soul with the help of water procedures. The card depicts the Full Moon, the time when the tides are strongest, this symbolizes a period of high emotional sensitivity when emotions flood a person and become difficult to control. The Full Moon falls on the fifteenth lunar day, which is associated with deception and illusion, which harmonizes with the overall message of the arcana.

Total value

Before the protagonist opens a difficult route to return to his native land, passing through the mysterious arcana Moon. This path is a search for a way out of the shaky labyrinth of illusions, emerging under the deceptive glitter of the Moonlight. Immersion in this world means a descent into the unconscious depths of consciousness, where a person can lose the reference points of reality and find himself face to face with shadow projections of his inner world, which can lead to a loss of reality and even to a state bordering on madness.

When an individual begins to sink deeper and deeper into the vortex of his anxieties, pulling to the surface of consciousness the most sinister images from the bottomless wells of the subconscious, his fears take on gigantic proportions. At this point, he loses the ability to control his thoughts, looking at the world around him with the distorted gaze of his own fears, severing ties with reality. The sensations become so powerful that the person begins to dream that everything around him is obeying exactly the scenario whispered by his hidden terrors.

Relationship

Since the Moon is a reflection of the Sun's rays, there is a mirror effect in the relationship between partners: one partner's behavior becomes a mirror image of the other's behavior. As a rule, the influence one partner has on the other determines how the response will be shaped. It is important to treat your partner in such a way that the attitude you want to see in return is exactly how you show it. The perception of your partner and your attitude toward him or her will undoubtedly be reflected in reality. Similarly, one's attitude towards oneself will be reflected by one's partner: if you respect and love yourself, your partner will show you love and show you how valuable you are to them. There is often a strong attraction in a relationship, which can act as a powerful magnet, attracting partners to each other. Mutual daydreaming and a sense of mystical attraction, as well as a compulsive obsession with each other, deep affection and following their base instincts also characterize this relationship, making it a rich sexual experience.

On the negative side, the Moon can reveal insincerity, ulterior motives, secrets, and even the possibility of infidelity, as its light is cold and can indicate a cooling of feelings in a relationship. Difficulties arise when relationships become entangled to the point where partners no longer understand what their roles and relationship status are - whether there is one at all, or whether it is an illusion. Such relationships may involve long distance, correspondence or connection with those who are often away from home, such as sailors or truckers. In this context, there may be fears and painful jealousy, obsessive thoughts about the partner, and a tendency to impose the worst possible scenarios on oneself from the subconscious mind. Through the prism of their fears, a person can perceive the relationship in a distorted way and screw themselves up, leading to instability in the relationship. Partners may only make assumptions about each other's feelings for each other, lacking clarity about their emotions. It can also lead to manic attachment and pursuit of the object of their attraction. Since the Moon is inconstant, it can also show emotional fluctuations as people move closer and farther apart.

Work and finance

Progress in creative and esoteric pursuits is predictable. The Moon has the power to attract financial resources like a magnet, and if there are Pentacles in the neighborhood, the probability of this increases significantly. There may be temporary vacancies, irregular earnings and, as a consequence, an unstable financial state where income is erratic and the financial base is quite shaky.

Incorrect understanding and evaluation of personal finances often leads to misconceptions about work. There are cases of deception, loss of money, which may result in theft. Fears regarding finances are heightened; a person may be afraid of earning or owning large sums of money because of possible risks to personal safety. Financial instability accompanies him constantly, the monetary situation fluctuates: sometimes there are funds, and sometimes they suddenly do not become. In contracts a lot of room for deception, the details are often hidden. In professional life there are many non-obvious obstacles, and the prospects in the workplace and in business seem unclear and confusing. There is a fear of going to work, expressing oneself and earning, because financial success is perceived as a potential threat.

Purpose

Practicing control over one's own thoughts, conscious acceptance and management of personal fears becomes an important skill. Immersing oneself in the realm of creativity, developing abilities in acting, visual arts, and music can become a life calling. Moon-inspired personalities are often focused on practicing magic, it is important to direct these pursuits for the benefit of others. It is necessary to actively help those around them to discover their creative ambitions, support them in overcoming fears, and improve visualization techniques to attract positive changes in their lives.

Occupation

Creative professions, artist, actor, painter, musician, psychologist, physician, esotericist, magician, person who studies dreams, designer, photographer, videographer. Show business, as the Moon is a luminary, like the arcana Star and Sun, so a person can be popular, in front of many people. Navigator, illusionist.

PLACES AND FACILITIES

Water bodies, rivers, seas, marshes, photo studios, mirrored terrains, cinemas, creative circles, psychologist's office, places of rituals.

Tip

It is important to connect with your subconscious, to learn to trust your inner self. You should learn to face your own anxieties face to face without fear. To approach the solution of problems unconventionally, to show ingenuity, artificially creating indirect ways to the goal, without revealing all their intentions. Develop critical thinking, strive for clarity and awareness of one's thoughts, avoid the influence of negative attitudes.

Warning

The current situation can be confusing and hide potential dangers, which requires careful analysis of all details and circumstances. Fears and doubts become an obstacle to progress, they can deter from necessary actions. There is a possibility that there are unseen factors in the situation, deception and misrepresentation are possible. One should be extremely careful to avoid mistakes due to distorted or incomplete information.

The Sun

The nineteenth Major Arcana

S ymbolism

1. The mandala glistening under the rays of the Sun is like an earthly paradise, newly found by man. Having overcome many obstacles, he achieves harmony and wholeness. The purification of body and mind leads to renewed strength, abundant energy, and sincere love. All this leads to the budding of life, the explosion of its colors, memorable and joyful moments, to the noble generosity and greatness of the peaks reached.

2. The map presents rune Sowuli, symbolizing the Sun, which is a sign of integration, omnipotence, inexhaustible power, clear understanding and prosperity. It stands for the fullness of being and harmony of existence.

3. The girl, stretching her arms towards the bright Sun, absorbs its warmth and the endless flow of joy coming from above. Her necklace also stretches towards the sun's rays, symbolizing the infinity and cyclical nature of life processes, emphasizing the aspiration of all living things to growth and development. This image conveys the idea of man's relentless pursuit of personal and spiritual perfection.

Total value

In this Arcana, the character overcame all the trials, passing through a great initiation, and returned renewed, as if he had found a new youth. The darkness that had enveloped him before had dissipated, and the world was filled with the light of the sun. Traveler, once naive and inexperienced, now, under the rays of the Sun Arcana, understands the importance of each stage of his journey. All previously hidden truths and secrets are now revealed, and he reaches wisdom and maturity.

Under the rays of the Sun, everything becomes extremely clear and unraveled, fears and false ideas disappear, doubts and uncertainty dissipate. The Sun symbolizes great luck, the triumph of life, its bright moments. It helps to overcome obstacles at any level, illuminating the path of man and his whole life light. This Arcanum is associated with creativity, activity, vitality, eternal youth, personal growth, excellent health. It indicates authority, power, well-being in society, success in professional and personal relationships. The Sun is also a sign of divine presence, spiritual insight. Arcana symbolizes transformation and rebirth in both spiritual and physical aspects.

This is a manifestation of masculine energy, the embodiment of rationality and concrete action. Here there is a deep life experience and purity of thought, which opens the possibility to realize one's advantages and disadvantages, skillfully strengthen good traits and overcome weaknesses. It is about resolving karmic debts. This state of enlightenment is combined with active action. Good mood, sustained optimism and the desire for life, self-development and giving light to others prevail. Leadership qualities, a dynamic approach to life and high, inspiring goals are inherent. Marked for such a trait as openness, along with sincerity. These are often the moments when the truth comes to the surface.

Here we have before us a person with a bright personality, being in the center of attention, possessing artistry, energy and optimism, able to instantly improve the atmosphere in any company. He has a significant impact on others and is focused on self-expression and self-realization. He is distinguished by powerful energy and the ability to heal. Such a person is frank and open to the world, generous in the distribution of his resources, knowledge and enlightenment of others. He likes communication and active participation in collective and public initiatives. Such a leader is able to inspire and enthuse people. A person who seeks to create, contribute to the dissemination of knowledge and has a responsive soul. He is full of self-confidence and is characterized by high self-esteem.

In the negative aspect, the card reveals the image of an overconfident and self-centered person, who is too fond of his own person and selfishness.

It can indicate infantilization, when an adult acts like an unrestrained, capricious child, believing that the world should revolve around him. Such a person is capable of imposing his will on others, demonstrating arrogance, haughtiness and overconfidence. He may try to attract the attention of others at any cost, trying to always remain in the epicenter of attention, but his methods are often rude and intrusive.

Relationship

The blossoming of harmony in a couple, a sense of deep love, warmth, emotional connection and mutual comfort. Positive prospects in the development of relationships. Frankness and honesty underlying the communication of partners. They are mutually inspiring and have a beneficial effect on each other. Relationships are filled with happiness and joy. Renewal of harmony after misunderstandings, partners feel a deeper connection, their relationship gains more brightness and warmth, emotional content becomes more passionate. Synchronization in the relationship, a lively sex life. Partners generously give each other attention, exchange love and care. They joyfully share their feelings. The union of two mature and harmonious personalities, in which both feel the fullness of unity. It is all-consuming love and boundless bliss. In the context of the layout may indicate marriage and the birth of a new member of the family.

In the negative perspective, there is a desire for dominance and control in the relationship. One of the partners may show immaturity, avoid responsibility, behave inappropriately for their age, show capriciousness and spoiling, cause conflicts and demand excessive attention. A tendency to put one's own interests above those of one's partner. Selfish behavior, when the partner constantly thinks only about himself, without taking into account the needs and desires of the other half.

Work and finance

Wealth and stability in the financial sphere. Holding a prestigious position with the ability to influence decision-making in the workplace. Assignment of status of an important person, gaining authority and well-deserved respect. Increased interest and recognition from others in personal affairs, business or organization. Excellent presentation of one's own work, attracting clients and consumers to the services and goods offered, just as plants seek the light of the Sun. Provision of solid income, prosperity, abundance, complete luck in money matters. Realization of oneself as a person, active participation in social events, teamwork. Launch of new projects and successful advancement up the career ladder.

Insufficiently developed financial management skills, when a person spends money received instantly. Spending money on personal whims, frivolous and careless attitude to finances. Possibility of impulsive spending of significant amounts of money without thinking about the consequences beforehand. Tendency to excessive generosity, which can harm their own interests. Attempts to maintain a certain social status by any means, which leads to indiscriminate spending. Using money as a means to gain the loyalty and sympathy of others.

Purpose

Striving for leadership requires lighting the way for others without showing pressure and desire to dominate. It is important to aim for social activism and recognition of one's own achievements. Showing generosity through charity and altruistic deeds becomes key. The need to inspire and support the development of those around you, channeling their energy into new creation, artistic expression and improvement. It is important to work on self-esteem, thereby increasing self-confidence. It is necessary to provide assistance in healing soul wounds and discovering the inner light in others. Support them in getting rid of negativity, inner limitations, and help them to discover their creative abilities.

Occupation

Creative and educational work, politics, spheres of power and influence, show business, television work, agriculture, working with children, organizing events.

PLACES AND FACILITIES

Hot places, warm countries, tanning salons, beautiful places, beautifully furnished homes, educational institutions where people are educated en masse, government offices, city halls, regional administrations, television, lamps.

Tip

It is necessary to act with confidence, following one's own desires and tastes. The ability to take care of oneself - a healthy egoism - is especially valued. It is important to believe in your abilities and possibilities.

Courageously demonstrate your individuality, actively express your own thoughts and feelings. The importance of showing your talents and skills, readiness to generously share resources, as well as openness to receive them. Do not forget to please yourself, to organize small holidays for the soul.

Warning

Excessive egocentrism can turn against you, because if your interests are solely concerned with personal gain, it can alienate others. It is important to abandon the childish perception of cases and learn to approach them more balanced. You should be serious and reduce the time allocated to hobbies and whims. Perhaps some circumstance or a certain person is taking up too much of your attention, distracting you from really important matters.

Judgement

XX Major Arcana

S ymbolism

1. The image presented here shows us a soul absorbed in dance. Take, for example, a girl who as a child was suppressed by her parents, who were not allowed to do what she loved, even though her soul yearned for it. She dreamed of dancing, to be the center of attention on stage, but her parents did not support this passion and directed her to study mathematics, slowly preparing her for a career as an economist. But here comes the day of epiphany, when a person sees all the truth accumulated in the soul, as if on an X-ray. This is the moment of explosion, when, for example, he quits his unloved job and rushes to sign up for dancing, and at that moment his soul starts dancing by itself. He is freed from the narrow framework, where he was driven, his soul sings and rejoices, the man finds unity with his own essence. According to the meaning of this card, a person feels the call - the call of a higher power, the call of his soul, the call to awaken and open his eyes. This is an awakening, after which one can see one's true nature.

Total value

In the arcana of Judgment there is a process of healing, symbolizing the rise from the darkness of death, resurrection. The rays of the Sun illuminate the physical, tangible world, while the Judgment opens for us the secrets of the invisible, spiritual dimension. Having experienced purification in the arcana Sun and Judgment, cleansed both outside and inside, we find complete inner harmony and harmony, and eventually this leads us to the arcana Peace, where we achieve merging with the world around us and with ourselves.

The collision with the arcana Judgment can be likened to a meeting with a huge wave: if you are able to hold it, you will be able to submit to it, if not - it will inevitably cover you. The meaning here is that if a person honestly fulfilled the tasks assigned to him, passed his way of life with dignity and justly overcame all the obstacles without hiding many vices in his soul, he should not fear the approaching judgment. If everything was otherwise, the Judgment may become his destruction. This card proclaims the necessity to live as if tomorrow you will have to face the judgment of life.

Arcana Judgment means liberation from narrow boundaries, outmoded habits and hackneyed patterns, from everything that prevented free to breathe, create and be truly yourself. It symbolizes the release of long-buried ambitions and aspirations, their revival, and they find their way into the real world to find embodiment. Also, emotions that a person had previously suppressed find an outlet. It is a relief, a release from an outdated, undemanding burden. This transformation is freedom and deliverance from fetters. It is a widening of horizons, revision of habitual ideas about oneself and the universe.

During this period of life, all burdensome factors are removed and one is relieved of the feeling of being squeezed into a tight framework. Goodbye, adversity and hardship; it is a time of freedom and full deep breaths. There is an era of relief when massive changes in life take place, when ways out of difficulties are found and the general state of affairs improves. Farewell to ailments, to poverty, to loneliness, to sadness and despondency. A sense of happiness is re-injected into the human soul, life is filled with content, the pleasure of each day lived becomes evident. This is the moment when one can exhale deeply and think with relief: "That's it, the difficulties are over.

Judgment is a symbol of a final and irreversible decision, marking a radical change in life. It portends a serious choice that will change the course of life. This is an awakening of consciousness, spiritual enlightenment, a call to higher self-consciousness, to connect with the unknown. This card symbolizes reincarnation, transmigration of souls, karmic ties and resolution, ancestral memory and connection with them. It speaks of healing of the spirit and connection to the beyond. It brings faith in good changes, in the help of the Higher Powers and spiritual discoveries that come from the depths of the heart. The card means rethinking established values, looking at familiar things from a different angle. It represents the moment when a person sheds outdated masks and is reborn, transforming into a new self. It is also a flow of information, an information field, which includes the dissemination of knowledge through television, radio, and this is the information that can cause public resonance. This is an opportunity for a person to make himself known, to succeed. And also the card predicts favorable changes in family life, support of relatives and the joy of new lives.

The Judgement will reveal the image of an individual endowed with psychic gifts, the ability to see the future, contact with the world of ancestors, the connection with which is transmitted from generation to generation, with the family. Such a person attaches great importance to his origin and loved ones, and his relationship with them is strong and meaningful. It is as if he balances on the edge between material existence and spiritual space. This is a person who has a deep awareness of the universal laws, able to penetrate into the most intimate aspects of existence, solve riddles and find hidden truths. He has a philosophical view of existence and the end of life's journey. Such a person has a high level of spiritual development, listens to the voice of his soul and follows its call, ignoring the opinions of others. He refuses to limit himself to any conventions, preferring to follow the path destined to him by fate. Realizing his great mission, he seeks to announce it to a wide range of people. He is a spiritual leader and teacher.

In the negative perspective, the Judgment card symbolizes retribution for past deeds, the coming of the time of justice, when a person will have to face the consequences of his actions. In the face of this card are powerful shocks and metamorphoses, radically changing the inner world of the individual. This is a period of atonement for sins and correction of wrong actions. Can symbolize litigation and proceedings. The meaning can also go in the direction of detachment of the soul from the earthly existence and its transition to another world. Troubles related to family and ancestral ties are also reflected in this card. A period saturated with difficulties and dangers. A person under the influence of the map can show exorbitant criticality, the desire to dominate and impose their vision of truth on others.

Relationship

This moment can symbolize the union of two close souls, an unexpected meeting, which seems to be a gift of fate, like the flight of Cupid's arrow, sudden love, joy that raises a person to the heights of the seventh heaven. Reflection of warm family relations, husband and wife, joy at the appearance of children. The opportunity to revive and transform relationships that seemed lifeless when people separated and stopped communicating, and here comes the moment of rebirth and restoration. People begin to look at each other in a new way, evaluate and build relationships from a different perspective. There are significant changes in personal connections, forgiveness and mutual healing. Feelings are ignited with a new intensity. A lonely individual following this sign is freed from the chains of loneliness and finds love. It can be a vivid marriage proposal, emotional and resounding, making the heart beat more often. People generously share the most valuable things - themselves and their feelings.

The individual may be reluctant to share details of their personal life, drawing others into their relationships. Freeing oneself from the bonds of personal ties can lead to deep relief when the partner is freed from them and feels relieved. There are relationships that require a person to give their whole soul, sometimes transcending themselves. The person may devote themselves too much to the partner, losing their own boundaries. Decisive changes may occur, such as divorce or a final breakup with a partner. Secrets that one has tried to hide may suddenly become public.

Work and finance

The card may reflect a family business or a long-standing skill that is traditionally passed down from older to younger family members. It can also signify labor in which a person is pushing certain boundaries, including the boundaries of accepted norms, or is engaged in doing business with foreign colleagues and companies. It can speak to the recognition and prominence of a person's business endeavors, where many are aware of their products or projects and they are good at promoting them. The vision may signal a change of jobs, revival of forgotten records, updating of outdated methods and systems, and breathing life into old projects. The card may portend an increase in earnings, overcoming financial limitations, achieving a higher level of income. It can also be a symbol of gaining a new social status or position, advancing in one's career and realizing a long-planned project.

On the negative side, there may be difficulties in delivering information to the target audience, difficulties in self-promotion and promotion of one's own services in the market. Negative aspects include the loss of a job or the need to change it. Possible legal disputes and litigation related to work or financial issues. The card may also warn of upcoming inspections by the tax service and sanitary supervision authorities.

Purpose

Strengthening the connection with one's own ancestry is important, it includes forgiving ancestors and praying for them, as well as developing ancestral scripts and cleansing the karma of the family. To strive for harmony in relationships with family, to respect and pass on family values from generation to generation, and to strive to create a cohesive and strong family structure. It is important to devote time to gatherings of the whole clan, mutual help and support of each other. Become more attuned to your soul and interaction with the Higher Powers, strive to improve your intuitive abilities, clairvoyance, develop psychic talents. Choose a profession that helps to heal people's souls, for example, to be a psychologist or esotericist, or simply to carry useful healing information to the world.

Occupation

Resuscitator, pathologist, medical worker, teacher, educating people's minds. Work with dissemination of information: on television, in newspapers, radio, blogger. Obstetrician, work in maternity hospitals (where new souls are born). Esotericist, psychic, psychologist. People working with ancestral problems, regressologists, people working with ancestry, with immersion in past lives. Judges, lawyers. Creative professions that make the soul sing and dance: painting, dancing, music, movies and so on.

PLACES AND FACILITIES

Churches, monasteries, cemeteries, resuscitations, television, broadcasters, dance studio.

Tip

It is important to transcend established patterns of thinking, to free oneself from limiting beliefs that hinder development. This requires a complete rethinking of your life path and following the clues of intuition. It's a good time to revitalize forgotten projects. It is also the moment of liberation, you need to get rid of everything that restrains, whether it is outdated ideas or vestiges of the past. Your emotions, feelings and talents should be let out, so that they find their true use and expression.

Warning

In this period you should not make sharp turns in life. Radical decisions and radical changes can wait. This card warns: a person may face the need to pay for past deeds, heralding the approaching moment of truth. It symbolizes events that can deeply shake and turn the inner world of a person.

The World

XXI Major Arcana

S ymbolism

1. In a traditional Tarot deck, similar to the Wheel arcana, the image contains the figures of a man, an eagle (sometimes a scorpion), a bull and a lion, arranged in a certain geometric composition. This plot symbolizes the act of creating the universe through the four basic elements, on which, according to ancient teachings, is based on all things, as well as their harmonious unity. This is the unification of different life paths, partnerships, people united by common aspirations. It is a step in the direction of development, merging for the sake of improving circumstances, increasing prospects, comprehensive well-being. The coming together of people, whether individuals or entire communities. Acquiring one's own home, moving to a new place of residence, immigration all emphasize the theme of unity and new beginnings.

2. The rainbow-colored dress in the image symbolizes the fusion of all spheres of the universe: mind, emotions, aspirations, material world, and spiritual dimensions, the unity of all life on the planet. It embodies the idea of a worldwide harmonious combination of all aspects of existence, from the smallest desires of life to the majestic cosmic laws. This outfit as if tells us the importance of a holistic view of the world, when each element of the universe is in balance and synergy with the others.

Total value

In the World card, the character achieves absolute harmony. The destiny is fulfilled and the character has found anew that lost ideal country.

This is a sense of wholeness and harmonious filling of life. Ouroboros, closing the circle of eternity, symbolizes the fullness of existence, its true completion. On the card Fool girl makes a bold leap into uncharted areas of cosmic regularities, and now these spatial forms become her faithful companions, she confidently holds them in her palms. This is the completion of one life path and at the same time the entry into a new one, which leads to the reincarnation of the Fool. The world unites with the Shute arcana, demonstrating the inseparable connection of the end and rebirth.

It is a revival of lost harmony, a return to the primordial basis of existence. This is the achievement of peace, the cessation of strife among people, the restoration of broken ties, the fulfillment of plans, the realization of dreams into reality, the acquisition of cherished completeness, that magnificent state, which was only dreamed of, and at the same time favorable circumstances arrive in life, the world of the individual becomes truly whole. If earlier a person lacked something for complete happiness, if some aspect of life left much to be desired, the World comes to the rescue, correcting and improving all aspects of existence, becoming the last key element, which is folded into a complete mosaic of worldview. This is the realization of all those aspirations and aspirations that we nurture in the depths of our souls.

This is the realization of the deepest connection with the world around us, with nature, understanding and acceptance of its diversity, manifested in a sincere interest and respect for all living forms. Card Peace symbolizes the soul, having passed through numerous tests, through the Great Judgment, freed from the burden of past actions, achieved complete freedom and entered a state of calm and harmony. Here there is a complete harmonization of the inner world with the surrounding reality. The girl performs a dance that symbolizes the continuity, infinity of movement and constant renewal of all things.

It is the successful completion of projects that have been started. It is the realization of plans and their prosperous development in the real world. It is the harvest of labor, reward for diligence and striving. This is a chance to organize the world around you in accordance with personal aspirations and desires. The card also portends the expansion of horizons, majestic plans, traveling, exploration of new countries and cultures.

It is the embodiment of global thinking, a large-scale perspective of world perception. Objectivity in judgment. Interaction via the Internet, exploration of new countries and cultures. A person is imbued with a deep love for the Earth, people, nature, animals, he can be an advocate of ecology, become a supporter of saving fauna, or support certain segments of the population. The man has a wide outlook and a variety of hobbies. The man has found his own place in the world, having determined his path and direction.

This card opens before us the image of a person with a diplomatic mindset, able to establish contacts with different people. He shows high tolerance and respect for other people's views, beliefs and cultural values. This person brings peace and harmony, considering everyone around him as his equals. His aspiration is to reconcile others, to establish friendly relations between them. He acts as a messenger of his ideals and views, influencing vast social strata united by common goals. Initiator of various communities, including hobby clubs, political parties and large-scale online communications. Open to learning new cultures and foreign languages, may be a polyglot. One is also drawn to the natural beauty of the world, to spaces of large size, majestic buildings and wide horizons.

On the negative side, this card may indicate an individual's excessive preoccupation with a single idea or ideal that occupies his or her entire conscious space. The person may find himself as if in an emotional vacuum, where his whole world is centered around one grandiose idea or desire that has reached enormous proportions. He begins to set goals for himself, the scale of which borders on the fantastic, and strives for their realization immediately. Because of the abundance of interests, it is difficult for him to focus on one direction for development and self-realization. In the search for his path, he can lose direction, which eventually leads to a loss of time. He lacks the ability to move toward his ambitious goals in small, consistent steps. While dreaming of realizing a global project, he often lacks the understanding of how to put it into practice. The goal can be so grandiose that a person gets lost without seeing concrete steps to achieve it. Focusing on one's worldview often leads to isolation from the outside world, to deepening into one's own ideas and completely cutting off external influences.

Relationship

Immersion in the world of a loved one. For someone, his or her chosen one becomes the main axis of existence, a real boundless universe, deeply personal and mysterious, which you want to study ceaselessly. He is an important part of life, a source of joy, peace and inspiration. The card can symbolize a partner coming from far away or living in another country.

This is a merger on the most subtle level of being, a solid and reliable alliance. Partners make great plans for the common future, tirelessly discovering unexplored facets in their other halves. They expand each other's horizons, gladly share the experience of traveling, learning, comprehending new and exciting, enriching their existence with the diversity of worldviews, and build together their unique space, their heavenly corner, where they both feel good and happy.

If earlier people experienced disagreements, here there is a harmonization, a reunion. This is a departure from loneliness, a reunion with a partner. Perhaps the conclusion of marriage, the birth of children. Ideal co-partnership of partners in all aspects of life: in aspirations, thoughts, emotions and physical intimacy. They do not emphasize on trifles and weaknesses of each other. A mature relationship where partners feel serenity and confidence in their feelings, remaining faithful and devoted.

On the negative side, it can indicate the end of a relationship or love at a distance. Conducting correspondence. It can also express a person's unwillingness to focus on one partner, the desire to experience the diversity of relationships with several people at once. It may indicate the partner's attempts to limit the person's freedom, to create conditions in which the other becomes the only world for him, isolating him from the rest of the world.

Work and finance

These initiatives are large and influential endeavors that mean large-scale business development, including attracting investment, networking with partners, actively announcing themselves in the market and successfully pushing their product or service. It is about launching a perfectly planned advertising campaign that helps to attract a large number of customers to the products offered. This is a transition to unprecedented heights of success, a qualitatively new level of income, which allows you to satisfy any material desires.

It is about deep satisfaction with the current financial state. Continuous economic growth, active business expansion, achievement of impressive results in the professional sphere. A person's projects gain popularity, his products or services become widely known, attracting the attention of many fans and providing a stable circle of regular customers. It can also mean expansion to the international level, attracting foreign investors and partners, expanding the client base outside the country. Long business trips are possible, or even moving the company's headquarters abroad. A person achieves true professionalism in his business.

In a negative context, a person may be overconfident in his or her idea, believing it to be flawless, and unwilling to make changes or listen to criticism, even when the need for adjustments is obvious and has been pointed out to him or her by experienced professionals. Such a person may be convinced that his or her concept has reached perfection and that he or she has more knowledge of how things should be done than anyone else. Spending may be ill-considered: living only in the present moment, a belief that everything in the world must be tried, resulting in important daily obligations such as paying bills being neglected. Instead, money may be spent on expensive jewelry or other large purchases, with no money left over for key aspects such as advertising and product promotion.

Purpose

Strive to relentlessly expand your horizons, constantly discover new aspects of the world, learn different languages and immerse yourself in unique cultures. Think ambitiously and strive to break stereotypical notions that limit your mind. Team up with people who share your interests to push the boundaries of worldview and consciousness together. Organize yourself to participate in large-scale projects, get involved in activities aimed at peacemaking and saving not only people, but also animals. Take an active part in the protection of nature. The task of these actions is to lead people to spiritual integrity, enlightenment, to the understanding of divinity, to the harmony of the soul with the highest absolute.

Occupation

Tourism, travel, seafarers, truckers. Global organizations, projects to protect nature, people, animals. Translators, linguists, religious scholars, historians, philosophers, diplomats. Internet, IT sphere, mass media, television, bloggers. Esotericists, people who help to find the contact of the soul with the divine. Work in large corporations, foreign campaigns, space exploration.

PLACES AND FACILITIES

Home, a place where one feels in one's own world, at ease. Other countries, outer space. Big buildings, large-scale constructions.

Tip

It is important to use all the chances that life offers, bravely accepting everything new that comes to you. Be ready for change and for learning the unknown. Expand your perspectives, increase your resources. Think and act in a grandiose way, boldly turning to wide opportunities and resolutely realizing your ideas.

Warning

You should be conscious of what you put at the core of your inner world, what you aspire to in your dreams and what your soul lives by. When planning large-scale tasks, don't forget to pay attention to small but important details that can make a difference in the long run.

CUPS

Ace of Cups

ymbolism

1. When used skillfully, singing bowls become a powerful tool for therapy and healing. The human body, being a complete system of living vibrations and waves, responds to the sounds of singing bowls. They not only affect the physiological level, but also help to achieve alternative states of consciousness. Singing bowls take us away from the hustle and bustle of everyday life, helping us to remember who we are. They have a calming effect on the state of mind, reduce inner aggression, relax the mind and allow us to delve deeper into our inner space. Symbolizing the bosom of the divine Mother Earth, they represent emptiness, ready to be filled with anything. These bowls are a kind of starting point from which something new can be born, if the appropriate seeds of thoughts or intentions are put into it. In psychological terms, they remind us of the illusory abyss of the collective unconscious, where the roots of our being go.

2. The emphasis on the lower lip emphasizes sensuality. The foreground view with the character with his back turned to the vast cosmos and his head lost in this unexplored depth speaks of the harmonious connection between man and the higher forces. It is also a symbol of love permeating the entire universe.

3. Blue clothes complement the image, emphasizing the immersion of the man in the world of feelings. He trusts his emotions and intuition, follows the call of his heart, which makes him an open, creative person with a wide consciousness, ready to accept and share new things. The person turns his palms to the heart-bowl, expressing a mystical view of the world and seeing it through the

prism of the flow of love and abundance.

Total value

In this unique deck, the images of the classic Cups are replaced by sounding singing bowls. Those who stop to listen intently to their harmonious sound experience a sense of expanding spaciousness and deep peace. Water is the perfect conductor of these vibrations, and when you strike the bowl, you can feel even the air around you begin to pulsate in synchrony in response to the sound.

The Ace of Cups is a joyful card, symbolizing the fulfillment of desires and bringing variety into everyday life. It also pacifies the soul and brings renewal of feelings. Ace of Cups promotes reconciliation and harmonization of relationships, eliminates anxious thoughts and fears, rejuvenates the heart.

Among the Tarot cards, the Ace of Cups is considered one of the most auspicious. It portends favorable changes in life and fulfillment of desires. This card brings joy, happiness, generosity and altruism. It symbolizes inner satisfaction, mental comfort, good intuition and rich imagination. The Ace of Cups teaches that everything that happens originates from love and that the whole world is permeated with this energy. The emotions it brings can range from inspiring to dramatic to hysterical, as emotions are quite multifaceted.

Relationship

Openness and loyalty in partner relationships. Nobility of soul, manifested not only in emotions, but also in actions. The individual does not spare resources for sharing with the beloved. The emotions of the participants of the relationship are not locked inside, they do not melt in silence. The desire to support the partner lives in them strongly, they are always ready to make efforts for the good of each other. Overflows with the feeling of a new crush, ambition to make happy the object of their attraction. Ace of Cups usually appears when feelings either arise again, or return to a familiar person, but already looking at him in a new way, on the other hand, when emotions erupt with unusual power. This is a state of delight, when there is a thirst for novelty, readiness to reboot the relationship. Ace of Cups symbolizes an intense emotional attraction, the desire for the object of his adoration or a familiar hobby, for example.

The Ace of Cups can be a herald of the imminent beginning of a new love in someone's life, a love that has the potential to become long-lasting and diverse in its emotional palette. The Ace of Cups card is a symbol of a wish come true and emphasizes the importance of trust in the cosmic forces in this context.

Personality characterized by the Ace of Cups, does not hide his feelings that bubble up in him like a waterfall, he can literally plunge his partner into the abyss of his love, so he can be full of emotion. The Ace of Cups speaks of turbulent passion and depth of emotional experience. It is time spent together, filled with mutual interest and such lively interaction that the couple loses track of time in a whirlwind of attraction.

The personality personified by the Ace of Cups is open in his feelings to his partner and is devoted to him entirely, both on the bodily and emotional levels. In his heart there is no room for someone else, the partner feels the complete absence of rivals. Such a person is exceptionally attached to his partner, cherishes him and perceives his union as a source of true bliss. The traditional meaning of the card is associated with the conception of new life and may portend pregnancy. In general, the card reflects the theme of fertility and prosperity.

Such a person is particularly sensitive to any changes in the emotional state of his partner, which is symbolized by the sounding bowl that he holds. The heart inside this bowl symbolizes the ability to catch even the smallest fluctuations in the mood of their soul mate. This means that the partner will not be able to hide any of his experiences or feelings from such a person, because the one, like a sensor, catches them and feels them fully.

Therefore, if, say, his partner comes home tired after work and is in a depressed mood, this may cause a deep response and concern in the soul of such a sensitive person. He may feel strongly empathizing with and adopting his partner's heavy mood. To maintain his inner balance, such a person needs regular affirmations of feelings from his partner, expressed openly and with emotional warmth, for in the absence of these manifestations he may feel depressed and lose vitality.

Work and finance

The Ace of Cups symbolizes customer satisfaction, reflecting success and the long-awaited conclusion of profitable contracts. It can herald the receipt of pleasant gifts or joyful purchases. This card indicates favorable circumstances: a bowl of plenty, wealth in the house, a plump purse and a safe filled with money, which are signs of abundance and prosperity.

According to the Ace of Cups, there can be shopping on an emotional wave - purchases that bring joy and pleasure, including through feelings of happiness and enjoyment from buying desirable goods. In a work environment, projects evoke feelings of joy and fulfillment.

This card is also associated with professions that require enthusiasm, creativity, imagination and inspiration. It portends good luck in business, at work, bonuses and bonus payments. The Ace of Cups is a symbol of success, recognition and satisfaction from your own activities, realization of projects and income from them. The card suggests that the upcoming deals will be particularly successful and profitable, so it is worth taking them seriously and if possible - unequivocally agree. In the sphere of marketing and promotion, the card advises to appeal to the emotions of the target audience (such as desire for possession, anger, rage, love and other powerful feelings).

Occupation

Artist, musician, creative profession, healer, psychologist, fortune teller, as it is possible to associate the bowl with fortune telling on coffee grounds. Organizer of celebrations and holidays, bartender, seller in an alcohol store, writer, presenter, event organizer, catering worker, worker in the medical field, cardiologist.

PLACES AND FACILITIES

Ace of Cups can indicate such places as: rivers, seas, oceans, any bodies of water, fountains, aquariums, oceanariums, musical and esoteric festivals, cafes. Places for dating, romantic places.

Tip

To open our hearts to others, to become a conduit of love and energy, able to heal not only souls but also the hearts of people. To gradually develop in the field of music and art, doing so with an open heart and soul. Also, matching hearts through providing marriage agency services, arranging romantic dates and more. It is important to be open to love and show your emotions without suppressing them, regardless of their nature. Anger, joy, sorrow or love - emotions need to be allowed and lived.

Warning

However, reactions and actions that are based solely on emotion should not be allowed. It is important not to let emotions overpower reason and overshadow logic. Reasonable and rational thinking should always be at the center of decision making. Do not allow yourself to get too caught up in your emotions, as this can lead to rash and irrational actions.

Two of Cups

Symbolism

1. The fact that people hold hands indicates a deep attachment to someone or something. It means that they have happiness and confidence that they have support from this side. There is complete understanding and a powerful attraction in this gesture. It expresses trust and willingness to walk hand in hand, following their partner. However, this gesture can also symbolize holding something or someone back, such as when there are issues of constraints such as: "Will the bosses at work allow more freedom for employees, will they allow them to feel more free in the workplace?" In this case, despite all the positive aspects, the Two of Cups card may indicate that the restrictions will not disappear so soon, and people will continue to hold things back.

2. The rainbow, in turn, represents a bridge that connects people, events, cities and more. It serves as a symbol of connection that helps to bridge distances, both physically and emotionally. The rainbow symbolizes harmony in relationships on all levels: physical, emotional, mental and spiritual.

3. The dark hand is intertwined with the light hand, symbolizing the union of the feminine and masculine. Partners fill each other's missing qualities, burn for each other, have many common interests and are ready to go together hand in hand through life.

4. Bracelets on the hands symbolize fidelity and the desire to be always together. In some cultures, such as in India, bracelets have acquired the status of marriage paraphernalia, representing a symbol of marriage. The closed circle on the bracelet symbolizes the integrity and firmness of marriage. One partner has a rainbow

bracelet, and the other with a purple bead, which means that one carries the whole gamut of feelings and mixes them between the two hearts, and the second, with a purple stone, unites opposites in character and smooths out the corners.

5. The energies of their hands flow into their bowls under their arms, symbolizing the partners' access to the depths of each other's soul. They feel each other subtly and influence each other very strongly on an emotional level. Their relationship is emotional and can signify the beginning of a relationship or a new stage in an existing relationship, reconciliation after a quarrel, as we see the Sunrise in the background.

6. A ring on the middle finger of the right hand of one of the partners means strengthening the relationship with a loved one and indicates the seriousness of the person.

7. The other partner has the ring on the little finger of his left hand, which indicates his romanticism and lightness. Thus, both partners complement each other. The Two of Cups speaks of the potentiality of having a child.

Total value

The Two of Cups represents friendship, gratitude, sincerity of feelings and harmony in all spheres of life. After a stormy emotional experience, represented by the Ace of Cups, there is a bright rainbow - a bridge that connects two people. The Two of Cups symbolizes heartfelt unity and love relationships.

This card reflects the period of falling in love, when people are deeply attracted to each other. It is a time of new, bright acquaintances, when from the very beginning it becomes obvious that your sincere companion is near. It can be the beginning of a romantic relationship, but it can also represent an acquaintance with a person who will become a great friend. This is the moment when people have just met and are excited to share different ideas and interests with each other. They have many common topics to discuss and each can offer advice or support to the other. For example, two people met and immediately decided that they wanted to continue socializing, so they enjoyed each other's company and became good friends or even a couple.

It's also about when you fall in love with something special at first sight. For example, a person attends a concert and hears the sound of a musical instrument that he was not familiar with before. He is so inspired by this sound that he decides to buy the instrument, learn to play it and eventually even perform. That's the moment when a person immediately realizes, "This is my calling."

Two of Cups personifies an individual who is open to others, shows sociability and is ready to help even strangers. For example, if someone on the street asks how to get to some landmark of the city, the person, guided by the spirit of this card, not only gives the direction, but perhaps even lead to the specified place and share interesting facts about it. This person lives by the principle of "treat others the way you want others to treat you."

His benevolence manifests itself not only in answering questions. For example, if a group has plans for a performance, but lacks some decor to make it the way they would like, the person corresponding to the Two of Cups card will look for contacts to get the necessary decor items, organize delivery and contribute to the creation of a positive atmosphere in the team. The Two of Cups is also associated with the atmosphere of dating, marriage proposals, pleasant pastimes, and the conclusion of favorable contracts and mutually beneficial relationships.

Relationship

People fully accept each other with all their peculiarities, talents and shortcomings. They learn from each other, support and respect each other. There is no selfishness, envy and injustice in their couple, and everyone is reverent and caring towards their partner.

There is also a risk of dissolving into the partner and becoming too emotionally dependent on each other. A couple can feel each other so intuitively that they may have the same dreams even when they are at a distance, or one of them may pick up the phone to call their partner but find that their partner has already dialed their number.

Work and finance

Cash comes from collaborating and partnering together. This includes strengthening ties with customers and developing their trust. An important aspect is a successful business partnership, effective collaboration, mutual understanding within the partnership and a shared commitment to a common goal.

It is important to note that partners in business can also have an impact on personal life. This also implies a trusting team relationship where respect and equality are present. Supporting and inspiring each other also plays a meaningful role. Partnership and cooperation imply loyalty and collective participation, as well as the ability to rely on each other. Contracts and agreements, joint ventures and coming together to achieve a common goal are key components. Interest in cooperation and collaboration is important.

At the same time, shared resources and mutually beneficial relationships, where one partner's connections and capital benefit the other, also contribute to material well-being. Successful negotiations, good reception, recognition and respect from partners play an important role in this process. Money comes with support from others, and this can also indicate partner-related expenses.

The Two of Cups is associated with the Second House in astrology, which is responsible for comfort and prosperity. This means that a person will not have to suffer from lack, especially in financial matters. If there were questions about the financial situation in the near future or business prospects, it indicates a good level of income and financial well-being.

Occupation

Diplomat, translator, artist, musician, craftsman, jeweler, forecaster (rainbow), any creative professional. Work is related to the home and garden. Interior design and landscape design are also part of interests.

PLACES AND FACILITIES

Dating locations can include marriage agencies, dating sites, music concerts, romantic venues, and levels of bodies of water and mirrors. The home can also be a place where romantic relationships develop.

Tip

Seeking to improve relationships with someone close, reflecting on the need to leave behind solitude and loneliness. It may be a time to reconcile with someone significant in your life. This is an invitation to be more gentle with others and to express your emotions openly, avoiding insensitivity and coldness.

Warning

Maintaining your uniqueness and personality, even while in a relationship, is essential. It is important to stay true to yourself and not give in to your partner's every word. It is necessary to avoid losing yourself in other people's emotions and not allowing yourself to become completely immersed in them. To look at the situation more deliberately and with restraint. In addition, it may indicate that some circumstances or obstacles are holding a person back, preventing progress in some direction.

Three of Cups

Symbolism

1. The Triple of Cups in this deck can indicate a long-distance relationship, symbolized by distant stars in the sky. This card represents beauty, romantic feelings, mental balance and peace.

2. The lavender fragrance depicted on the card can attract mutual love and emphasize tenderness and softness in relationships. Falling in love and infatuation are also included in the symbolism of lavender.

3. The Triple of Cups indicates family harmony, especially if there are three members in the family. The couple seeks to plan for the future together, with the intention of improving the quality of family life and strengthening their relationship.

4. Spirals on the card emphasize complete trust and mutual respect in the relationship. Each member of the couple makes efforts both for their own good and for the good of their partner. This reflects perfect balance and harmony, support, spiritual rapprochement and mutual respect.

Total value

After combining the energies in the Two of Cups card, something new emerges. And this new phenomenon generates an even stronger vortex of energy and a higher emotional octave. Three, a dynamic number, brings freedom in the manifestation of emotions, which are not suppressed, but interact, creating a whirlwind of passions.

The Three of Cups is associated with the intention to realize one's desires. The Triple of Cups portends a joyful event, a celebration and a good time spent in great company. It also indicates important events such as the birth of a child or a wedding. If the Triple of Cups falls out in divination for the near future, it indicates that events will develop favorably, enveloping the person with emotional happiness, making his experiences brighter and more relaxed.

The stars on the card symbolize the seven sisters of the Pleiades, which means that the people on the card perceive each other as close, ready to support each other. This indicates that their true home is among the stars. The stars on the chart indicate that regardless of the darkness in a person's life, it will soon begin to dissipate and the person will see not just one guiding star, but many stars that will shed their light of hope, illuminate the path and dispel the darkness in the soul and consciousness. This is the time of happiness and fulfillment of desires.

For example, if a person felt sadness because of long loneliness and lack of love, this card portends that his sorrows will soon end, and his soul will be filled with a variety of feelings, giving the desired satisfaction and joy.

This period is filled with the desire to be creative, to initiate new endeavors and projects - it is a time of energetic rise, as evidenced by the stars and the spirals depicted. In these moments, the human soul is overflowing with joy, and he expresses gratitude to the universe for such magnificent times.

Spirals reflect the flow of energy between the inner world, rich in intuition and non-material, and the outer, material world. They symbolize the evolution of both the individual and the whole of humanity, emphasizing the connection of people with nature and the cosmic beginning. Spirals also speak of a person's ability to subtle perception of others. Three spirals on the map is a symbol of the eternal cycle of life, death and rebirth. The triplet of spirals can indicate pregnancy, as each of them corresponds to a three-month period, and, therefore, can symbolize the birth of a new life, as a result of the connection of two energies from the Two of Cups.

The light of the stars is too distant for us to discern the intentions of others in the darkness; here we can only rely on trust. The night is a test of everyone's conscience: what will a person do if he thinks that his actions will remain invisible? Will he oppose humanity or support it? And how will his behavior change when night gives way to day, the stars go out, and the rising sun illuminates the whole truth of his being? In these moments, honesty, humanity, and empathy are tested. The spiral indicating the movement of energy reminds us of the golden rule: do unto others as you would have them do unto you. What will you contribute to this eternal cycle of existence? What messages will you send out into the world? Because the world will respond in kind, multiplied threefold, following the law of the triple helix.

The Three of Cups is a card of humanity. It represents both individuals and communities of people, whether they are small groups or large masses. For some people are just an anonymous crowd, like stars in the night sky, but for others, each person is a unique individual who deserves respect for his or her individuality.

The Triple of Cups also speaks to the diversity of perception of the world and those around them. The differences in the girls' appearance on the card, such as height, hairstyles, and clothing, emphasize the individuality of each person and the importance of accepting these differences. The card indicates a person who respects multiple points of view, allowing others to be themselves without imposing their opinions.

Ultimately, the Triple of Cups reflects how we interact with the world: by being bright, attractive and visible, we attract attention and receive feedback from the world, genuinely enjoying life and human connection.

Relationship

However, if the Triple of Cups is surrounded by less favorable cards, it may indicate that the person is not going to remain faithful to his partner. He may show interest in other possible partners and look for a more suitable option. It is also possible for a third party to interfere in the relationship. This card may indicate that the person is comparing his current partner with others and seeing potential alternatives. He may be striving for the ideal image of the partner he is chasing, which may affect his relationship.

The Triple of Cups can also indicate a person's sense of freedom and choice. The card shows three people and many stars, which may indicate that a person has many potential partners and may seek them endlessly. He may not plan to spend his entire life with one partner, looking for constant improvement and constantly evaluating his relationships. This may include comparing his partner to others and striving for the perfect match, which is emphasized by the stars on the chart.

Work and finance

The Triple of Cups in this context can symbolize the flow of money and the influx of customers. It can also indicate that people may show interest in a product or service, sometimes just "looking in" or asking questions, but not always making a purchase. This card indicates a response to advertising and marketing, but not always a final sale.

Lavender, depicted on the card, symbolizes the attraction of money and portends good income and the arrival of funds. The Triple of Cups indicates a satisfactory result and successful completion of projects, which affects the work aspects. It also indicates a positive atmosphere and enjoyment of work, where every day is a celebration. This card may reflect profits from joint ventures and investments, as well as abundance, prosperity and good income. It heralds the fulfillment of wishes and can be associated with corporate events.

The Triple of Cups often indicates working in a team of like-minded people, where each member strives for a common goal. This card also indicates the possibility of setting high career goals and realizing them successfully. People associated with this card can expect promotions and raises. The Triple of Cups provides boundless opportunities where a person can realize his projects and earn money.

Occupation

Astrologer, astronomer, tarologist, esotericist, herb collector, witch doctor, perfumer (lavender), essential oils (lavender), organization of holidays, weddings, costumer, masseur (back), hairdresser, fisherman, florist, ecologist.

PLACES AND FACILITIES

Near bodies of water, dark place, observatories, planetariums, travel and tourism stores, fields, herb stores, esoteric festivals, large crowds, holidays, concerts.

Tip

Learn to accept people as they are, without hidden masks, and appreciate their uniqueness. Organize a celebration to get away from the daily routine and feel a deep connection with others. Be more human and compassionate in your dealings with others. You may need to support a loved one or ask them for help. Allow yourself to dream and make long-term plans for the future.

Warning

Don't limit yourself in trying to conform to someone else's ideal, also don't try to bring your partner to someone else's standards. Love the person, not the illusory image you have created. Don't count on support from others at this time and be careful about trust. Third party interference may appear, as well as the spread of gossip and negative influences in a team.

Four of Cups

Symbolism

1. With just one singing bowl, one can explore the vast expanse of the subconscious and inner cosmos, delving into practicing and playing with its sounds, which will invariably reveal new facets to the owner. By ignoring the bowl's capabilities, the character in the illustration rejects the vast array of perspectives that could be accessed through the bowl. Instead of diving headlong into a single activity, the man wanders aimlessly down a multitude of paths, trying different things in insufficient depth and without seeking insight or connection to the outside world.

2. The character is nestled on a cushion, which implies he is in a fairly comfortable position to live in, but he doesn't give it much thought. He is cozy and happy in the position he is in at the moment, and has no desire to get out of his comfort zone. There are certain advantages for him to remain in the position he is in now.

3. A tree symbolizes the presence of established roots of a person, his attachment to a certain place. A tree can also be a symbol of home, family ties, heritage. The image shows a mighty, leafy tree, and in general the picture resembles an idyllic scene shortly before the events shown in the Three of Swords, but already filled with life and color. In the Four of Cups, the person does not value his opportunities, nor what he has in the present, which is a reliable rear, roots, connections. He turns his back to the tree, while in the Three of Swords the person experiences the acute pain of loss and begins to appreciate what he had, when the tree in the illustration is already lifeless and devoid of leaves.

Total value

The Four of Cups symbolizes the morning after the raucous revelry depicted in the Three of Cups. It carries a sense of melancholy, unwillingness to look into the future and stay in reflection on the past. A person does not realize the presence of significant moments in his life, in the current circumstances, he is filled with longing, but the reason lies in his inattention. This state is filled with fatigue and indifference, perhaps the person suffers from illness and is immersed in longing.

The Four of Cups reflects the moment when a person is trapped by himself, creating his own world, like an aquarium, filled with gloom and melancholy. This state can be caused by routine, boring everyday life or an excess of something in life. The person is in stagnation, whether in one particular area of his life or in general. It is a period of emotional crisis, apathy and despondency. Nothing pleases or inspires a person. He is absolutely indifferent to the world around him, and the map depicts a real phlegmatic. This is an individual with low self-esteem, who finds it difficult to allow himself to dream and strive for high goals, because he considers himself not worthy of achieving them.

The Four of Cups symbolizes caution, which prevents a person from taking risks and making changes in his life, as he fears unpredictable consequences. He avoids entering into relationships for fear of disappointment and pain, does not dare to change his place of residence for fear of discomfort, and does not give up an unloved job to maintain stability. The Four of Cups symbolizes the comfort zone and resistance to change. This card also indicates fatigue with attention from others, a need for solitude, a vacation or a secluded place. It can also indicate a person who does not accept other people's opinions, believing themselves to be the smartest and refusing to listen and learn from others.

Relationship

Monotony of life is felt, partner's suggestions seem unimportant. Exhaustion from monotony of relations and daily routine is felt. The interests of the partners lie on different planes. One prefers a slow, non-exciting pace of life, while the other seeks change, wants to bring elements of novelty, thrill to life and relationships, but his aspirations remain misunderstood. The proposed cup, radiating scarlet light of energy, activity and adventure, does not attract the protagonist, who is overly cautious and risk-averse.

The card signals a person who has lost perception of the outside world, deepened in his own thoughts and worries, who does not want to even try to get out of his stagnation. The person is in a state of complete apathy, lack of initiative and dissatisfaction, ignores the possibility of achieving his desires. He does not realize how happy he can be.

Similar to the Three of Cups, the Four of Cups can also indicate a person who has created an ideal image in his imagination and does not pay attention to real people. This arcana can be a symbol of undivided love, when a person is immersed in his thoughts about it and refuses to notice or listen to anything but the object of his attraction. The Four of Cups tends to be selective about people, believing that most are not worthy of her attention. A person may also suffer for the object of his feelings, losing interest in life and appetite, refusing to entertain. There is a possibility that such a person will close in herself, isolate herself within the home walls and avoid public places.

One feels unbearable boredom in the relationship, when partners do not go out anywhere, do not visit new places, stay in the confinement of their homes, busy with monotonous daily activities. Such a habit not only does not give development, but also causes rejection. Partners become so bored together that this feeling of indifference passes to other areas of life. They are indifferent to each other, not mutually attracted. There comes a moment when one of the partners is so saturated with the presence of the other that he is no longer able to bear it. This relationship becomes a burden, and love seems to have completely disappeared.

However, this card can also indicate a deep offense to the partner caused by a perceived betrayal on the part of the person. For example, the partner feels that their trust has been violated and they feel deeply resentful. The question arises as to whether the relationship should continue, as the partner is completely preoccupied with their resentment and cannot forgive the person.

Work and finance

The person is dissatisfied with his working conditions, team, salary and other aspects of his job. He performs his duties without much enthusiasm, often immersed in his own thoughts and ignoring what is going on around him. He feels out of place in the work team.

He may be asked to stay at work after hours or to perform tasks that he does not enjoy. He works at one job but dreams of something else. Job offers may come at inconvenient times, and he goes to work gnashing his teeth, solely for financial gain, executing projects by sheer force of will.

He may also be lazy and avoid commitment and responsibility, afraid of earning money. Sometimes he gives the illusion of looking for a job, even attending interviews, but as soon as it comes to the actual job, he has many excuses for rejection. He always feels the lack of money, believing that what he receives and earns is not enough for him.

This chart also shows that he has problems with procrastination. He can set a lot of projects and tasks for himself, but then he gets scared of the amount of work and starts to procrastinate. He is even sick of looking at all these tasks he has set for himself, and he is afraid that he will waste a lot of time and effort, not sure if it is worth the cost.

In this situation, he can be advised to break his tasks into smaller parts in order to achieve quick and inspiring results, and reward himself for each step he passes. It is also important to go towards his goals gradually in order to avoid the despair that will befall him in the future.

According to this card, he has a complete lack of motivation, lack of confidence in his own abilities and frustration. Every new order or task becomes a real torment for him, and he is simply unable to fulfill them, because he is already bored with them.

Financially, the situation is stable, but it is not satisfying because the income may not be high. A person wonders how to make money, but he may have only one way of earning money in his mind. For example, if he is an artist, his only goal may be to sell paintings and he does not consider other sources of income, even if he is offered to invest money in some venture with the promise of profit.

However, this card could also mean that he simply has no new ideas on how to spend his money and has already exhausted all possibilities.

Occupation

Social worker, psychologist, cook, bartender, salesperson, marketer, sales manager, gardener, agronomist, farmer, nutritionist.

PLACES AND FACILITIES

Garden, vegetable garden, places near calm bodies of water, marshes, boarding houses, psychologist's office, sanatoriums, hospitals, canteens, cafes, restaurants, it can also be dressing rooms, bars.

Tip

In order to get out of the state of decadence and apathy, it is necessary to find the brightness of life, to shake oneself up. It is important to open one's eyes and see that the world is much richer and more exciting than the limited "four walls" in which one often locks oneself. These "walls" can be symbolized by a monotonous job, daily routines, or socializing with the same people. The person urgently needs variety and a change of scenery. It is important to find chances and opportunities around you and to immerse oneself in the essence of what is happening.

Warning

There is a risk of remaining despondent and allowing yourself to sink into heavier emotional states. There is also a risk of missing out on favorable opportunities and important people. Due to apathy and lack of faith in yourself, you can miss the best moments and chances. It is important not to refuse offers, as they can be really important and meaningful for our lives.

Five of Cups

S ymbolism

1. This is an energy vampire that can draw energy out of a person, like this funnel on the map that draws the contents from the bowls. The girl is sitting on the sand, and the sand is very shaky, and her condition is on the verge of a breakdown, and in some cases this breakdown has already happened, the sand vortex drags away everything that the girl throws there.

2. Four bowls of opportunity she has already missed. Since the action takes place at night, the girl sees no way out, no light, but at the same time the sky is full of stars, and in the fifth bowl behind her you can also see the glitter of stars, which says that there are still prospects and opportunities, just take them, believe in it. But she is indifferent to the stars in the sky and in the bowl, she does not believe in their brilliance, she considers happiness to be false and shaky, she has lost faith in everything and everyone.

3. She turns the bowl not with her hand, but with her foot in general, which indicates her complete disregard for any chances and opportunities. The person does not value what he has and treats it irresponsibly.

Total value

The Five of Cups speaks of regret over missed chances and opportunities that one has missed in the Four of Cups. The Five of Cups is a state of decline, grief and depression. It is a card of longing, which draws in like a vortex, and it is very hard for a person to fight back this force.

This condition can overwhelm a person to the point where he finds himself simply blind to the possibilities of the world that could get him out of the situation. Its emotional weight is so great that it literally drags him down with it into a bottomless well of sadness. The man is devastated; he has been worn down by some difficult situation. He can't trust anyone and sees no way out. Can lose the meaning of life. This is depression and fatigue with life.

It can also mean a situation when a person is not interested in anything in life, his time is gone, he wastes it. The person turns into an amoeba, degrades. He can be so lazy to do something that this person is ready to quit work and live on pennies, handouts, in order not to achieve anything, not to exert himself in society and at work, to lazily and sluggishly spend time at home.

The person feels bad, lonely, doesn't know how to live, and what to do next, he or she just goes with the flow. The person can also play the role of a victim, constantly complaining about something, being dissatisfied with everything, saying that everyone around him is so happy and lucky, but he is not, and in general life is unfair to him. He will beg for pity for himself in every possible way.

Relationship

A breakdown in the relationship has led to a complete misunderstanding between the partners, and both feel drained by their mutual presence. One of them may have acted as an energy vampire, subconsciously or intentionally draining their partner's vitality. The suffering of unhappy love, where feelings go unanswered, became apparent. Separation has led to suffering and now one or both partners are experiencing deep grief, which can cause one of them to slip into a depressive state. Love failures and loneliness mar their lives, and negative patterns in the relationship are inexorably repeated. The Five of Cups here symbolizes deep sadness, pain, and melancholy, and in the context of relationships can indicate that one feels so depressed that one's vitality is running out.

In a partnership relationship, there can be dominance by one party that drains the other, whether through tyranny or emotional exhaustion. These are instances where one partner oppresses the other who is unable to leave, perhaps due to personal insecurity, habit or other reasons. Such an emotional breakdown can lead to extremely tragic consequences. In addition to this, according to the interpretation of the card, the person may lose interest in his own appearance within the relationship, succumbing to over relaxation or losing inspiration from his partner. Or he may believe that, having accomplished his "mission" - having formalized the relationship, further efforts are not required.

The Five of Cups symbolizes the shattering of illusions concerning a partner, when the hopes and expectations placed on them are finally dispelled. It can also signify the end of a stale but unhappy relationship that preceded the Four of Cups. A person so accustomed to the stability of his previous relationships that any change in them is taken as a shock is now puzzled and does not know how to move forward. It seems to him that his whole life, everything he was used to, has collapsed into the abyss.

Work and finance

Money flows, it is invested incorrectly and spent on unsuccessful projects. A person directs his efforts in the wrong direction, which only brings disappointment and depletion of financial resources. Empty and reckless spending serves as an attempt to dull the inner pain and fill the emotional void. The financial situation is unstable and on the verge of collapse. Money is spent on urgent expenses such as medical treatment or emergency repairs.

You can also consider the presence of debts and loans, when a person finds himself in a debt hole, and money literally flows out of him, and there is no source for repayment of debts on the horizon. Nevertheless, the Five of Cups card shows that options can be found, provided one is proactive and shifts the focus of attention from problems to opportunities. Instead of falling deeper into a hole, a person should start looking for solutions.

In addition, this card can reflect an extremely strained work relationship, where the person is working out of necessity but feels deeply resentful. This may be due to incompatibility with the workplace, superiors or coworkers. This work is draining his sources of energy.

It is also possible that the card reflects an unsuccessful project in which a person has invested his money and efforts, but which has failed. This can cause depression and lead to doubt in one's own abilities.

Occupation

Psychotherapist, psychiatrist, physician, addiction counselor, cemetery worker, funeral services, car washer, dishwasher, janitor, person working with severe human conditions.

PLACES AND FACILITIES

Places near calm bodies of water, swamps, cesspools, latrines, washing places: dishes, cars, cemeteries, mental hospitals, garbage dumps, wells, sinkholes in the ground water, sewers.

Tip

Notice the contents of the bowl - there are twinkling stars, as if falling from the heavens. In the darkness you can see the light that shines at the end of a long and dark tunnel. The Five of Cups reminds us of our ability to find joyful moments even in difficult periods. Often the source of our disappointments lies within ourselves. These challenging times should be seen as a chance for personal growth and self-development. Believe that with time, new ideas and ambitious goals will emerge. Give up the idea of manipulating others by exploiting their sympathy for you.

Warning

Avoid going too deep into gloomy thoughts - you can get lost in them and miss something meaningful. Avoid isolating yourself from the world and building a protective barrier around yourself. Refuse the position of the victim and the constant stay in a state of self-abuse. You should not fold your hands and stubbornly hold on to your worries. Pay special attention to the resources you are losing, to the way the priceless slips from your hands like water slipping through your fingers.

Six of Cups

S ymbolism

1. The dog symbolizes loyalty to oneself, to one's long-standing principles and ideals. It represents loyalty to one's habits and childhood dreams. A person appreciates his past and finds in it a source of inspiration. The dog represents unconditional attachment to past moments of life, bringing pleasant nostalgia.

2. A person has grown up, but has not stopped appreciating those who have been with him throughout his life. We can compare this process to a journey, starting with a little boy and a puppy and ending with a grown man and a big dog.

3. Time has passed, the person has changed, but his love and loyalty remain in his heart. This attachment can manifest itself not only to people, but also to a cause, values, worldview, and so on.

4. The bowls, like this process, seem to grow and gradually increase in size, indicating that the situation will gradually change. Everything has its time, and it is important to act step by step, step by step, approaching the set goals. This is a slow but systematic and stable development in various aspects of life, be it love, finances, success and so on.

Total value

The Six of Cups represents the past, what one has lost or left behind. It is what was lost in the Five of Cups and now comes back with the Six of Cups. There is nostalgia present and the appearance of people from the past. It is the reliving of old events as history repeats itself.

This is the moment when a person lives according to familiar scenarios and patterns, believing that things used to be better. Perhaps, he longs for his past and believes that everything used to be easier. According to this card, old, unfulfilled desires are bursting into his life. The person may feel young and inspired again by reviving old dreams.

Six of Cups can refer to both children and adults, but in any case to naive and infantile personalities. This person can be fond of fairy tales, be very naive and sincere. He is able to support another person, comfort him and return his gaze to more simple and uncomplicated things, as if washing away the seriousness of the problems of this person. The Six of Cups symbolizes sentimental memories and a strong connection to the past. The card points to the inner child in each of us, our most sincere desires and dreams.

Relationship

As time goes on, there is a strengthening of the bond in the love relationship between the partners. One continuously discovers something new and exciting about their life partner. This strong sense of friendship that exists between the partners contributes to their mutual affection and the habit of being close to each other. The devotion that exists between them is incredibly great. The partners have formed shared memories that are filled with warmth and joy. The age difference between the partners does not always matter, and they often raise a child in common. These people show genuine concern for each other.

People address each other with tenderness and special trepidation, they know perfectly well the habits of their other half and try to make unexpected and pleasant surprises, taking into account the hobbies and preferences of each other. Over time, our manner of expression evolves, our energy "sounds" change, which is symbolically represented by singing bowls, arranged in order of increasing tone. In the same way, partners in a relationship adapt to the changes that occur to each of them. This is expressed in the willingness and ability to share all aspects of the joy of love. People in a relationship honor each other's life history and do not reproach their partner for actions taken in the past.

The image of the Dog symbolizes unwavering loyalty and devotion, which speaks of the many years spent together and how the partners have learned to appreciate each other even more. This card also emphasizes the deep emotional connection between people.

This card can be an interpretation of the fact that despite the age-related changes in the appearance of the partner, the person still sees the same youth and beauty in his/her companion. This is a sign of a long and reliable relationship. Based on this card, we can talk about nostalgia for the times spent together with the former partner. The person keeps the memories of his departed love, carefully preserving them. He feels a strong emotional connection and cannot afford to let go of his former partner, perhaps by re-reading past correspondence, looking at photos from the shared past and often delving into memories.

The card can also predict the revival of old feelings, for example, if a couple has been separated for some time and now meet again, finding that their mutual feelings have been renewed. This card can also indicate an unexpected rekindling of a relationship with a past love, with a former partner. It makes you wonder what exactly binds you to the past and why you are still attracted to a certain person, as well as why nostalgia for the past seems more pleasant than planning for the future.

Work and finance

For this individual, mental comfort and pleasure from work are more important than just earning money. When choosing a place of work, he is guided by many factors, where the level of salary is not in the foreground, and much more attention is paid to warm relations with colleagues. He is probably not inclined to change a familiar and already established place of labor. Money is important to him, it gives him satisfaction and makes him happy. Earlier investments of money and effort have brought good results, as the person has developed his business into a profitable occupation, thanks to his dedication, passion for his work and energetic contribution to it.

The Six of Cups indicates the presence of regular clients and emphasizes the importance of cooperation and honesty in business. The Six of Cups indicates the presence of regular clients and emphasizes the importance of cooperation and honesty in business.

In addition, this card can mean that a person resumes old abandoned projects and starts them again. It can also indicate a return to a previous job. This indicates a return to stability after a period of hardship, as indicated by the Five of Cups. The card also indicates an increase in income, similar to the increasing size of the bowls in the card image, which may indicate a gradual increase in the financial status of the individual.

Occupation

Veterinarian, trainer, volunteer, regressologists, worker with children, specialist in karmic connections and past lives, hypnotist who helps to remember the past, retrieve forgotten things from the subconscious, cosmetic rejuvenation specialist, work with children and the elderly, history classes.

PLACES AND FACILITIES

Old, abandoned houses, history rooms, historic landmarks, circus, zoo, veterinary clinics, animal shelters, animal shows, daycare, places with children, beauticians' offices, native places that evoke nostalgia.

Tip

To go into the new, but based on the experience of the past. Spend time with loved ones, visit places that are dear to your heart. Do what you love to do, find a hobby, pay attention to children and animals, help loved ones. Try to realize long-held dreams. Meet with old friends.

Warning

There is no need to reflect deeply, to live in the past, to be overly fond of memories. It is time to look around and start living in the here and now. Strong attachment can be disadvantageous. You should also not absolutely trust a person or promises. The way you knew a person, place or situation previously may now change beyond recognition.

Seven of Cups

Symbolism

1. The wreath is a symbol of the strong temptation to glory, as well as the vanity that often accompanies such aspirations. The castle, meanwhile, reflects the narcissism and hubris that can be experienced by those at the top. The mask represents an exciting choice, full of temptation and opportunity, but its consequences remain vague and unpredictable.

2. The winged dragon symbolizes keen feelings of jealousy and anger. One of the bowls is adorned with a skull, indicating that choices made without due deliberation can have fatal consequences.

3. The snake figuratively expresses gluttony and a tendency toward excesses such as drunkenness. In the Seer's deck, the serpent masterfully lurking among the clouds is particularly prominent. This image tells us that while a person may be engaged in slow reflection, something very significant may be quietly taken away from them or a lucrative opportunity may be missed. This is a clear warning to be vigilant and keep a clear mind in any situation, as potential danger can lurk just around the corner. The snake also suggests that any choice should be made wisely and deliberately, weighing all possible consequences and factors.

4. According to the deck creator's plan, the character on the card hid his lucky talisman under one of the bowls and forgot which one. This leads him to think deeply about whether he really wants to choose another bowl, perhaps the one that holds riches? It is under one of these bowls that the path that will lead him to his desired future is hidden. In this regard, the card's advice is to look deep inside yourself, try to figure out what you really want deep

down, and not let outside stimuli and clutter distract you from that quest.

5. The water, the sea, and the flow of water from the sea overflowing through the bowl, creating a path - all this symbolizes the importance of listening to the voice of your subconscious and following your intuition. They are the ones who can tell you what the right choice is. This emphasizes that understanding one's own path and making the right decision requires deep self-reflection and inner enlightenment.

6. The two ladders leading to the vast heavens symbolize the desire to find even more alternatives and paths to take. The presence of two ladders creates a situation in which a person may be caught in hesitation and uncertainty, unsure of which one to follow in order to achieve their goals.

Total value

Returning from a nostalgic Six of Cups journey, the individual is faced with a moment of choice. This is the time when a panorama of options unfolds before him, each capable of forming a separate path to the future. This point of choice is critical for determining the future direction of life.

The Seven of Cups is associated with the world of deep illusion, the illusory world that each of us creates in our minds. It symbolizes the wealth of possibilities, emphasizes that everyone has the power to influence their own destiny, choosing from a variety of available paths. The card is also a symbol of visualization and attracting what is truly desired into one's life. When an individual begins not just to dream, but to immerse himself completely in his dream, reproducing the desired life in his thoughts and actions, he thus brings the illusion closer to the status of reality according to the principle of attraction of like to like. This is a statement about the greatness of visualization and the ability to attract into one's life those realities that are preferred.

The Seven of Cups also emphasizes the importance of consciously choosing one's own thoughts, rejecting automatic, superficial thinking. It reminds that what a person concentrates his thoughts and attention on, tends to materialize in his life. Therefore, it is extremely important to approach the choice of mental focus with awareness. In addition, the card advises to start not just thinking about your desire, but to really feel it, to live in a state as if the desired has already been achieved, to attract the necessary version of reality through visualization techniques.

In the context of the Seven of Cups, it is possible to be in an altered state of consciousness. The person may immerse himself in various practices that lead to a change in perception of reality, or even resort to the use of substances that modify his view of the world. Potential addictions may lurk here, and the Seven of Cups may indicate the danger of being influenced by bad company.

This card reflects the situation when a person has a wide range of possibilities, but all of them are presented without clear contours, seem blurred and indistinct. Seven of Cups indicates the uncertainty of choice, the lack of clarity in determining what is really desirable for a person.

According to this card, it is necessary to find inner balance and realize what is really important. In this case, illusions and mirages will disappear, and a person will find a clear direction for his life path. However, the Seven of Cups also warns of the possibility of self-deception, the risk of living in a world of illusions and being completely detached from reality. This card indicates a tendency to accept sweet lies and a commitment to a fantasy world. The Seven of Cups speaks of a person's many desires, which do not always correspond to reality and are not always adequate. It also brings inspiration, promotes creative uplift and inspires a lot of creative ideas.

Relationship

A person is fickle, always in search of new partners, does not linger at one, constantly comparing, always in a state of choice. He is going through the options. Constantly on top, imagines himself above the rest and can easily use people and manipulate them. The person is windy and is not characterized by loyalty, prefers to mislead and lie. Uncooperative, often distorts the truth, promises but does not fulfill his obligations. May have several partners.

A person, not knowing what he wants, may impose his ideas on his partner. He may not like the appearance or behavior of his partner and will start to impose his ideal image, determining how his partner should be, how to look, how to behave, how to walk, how to talk and what to do. May seek to control the partner because he is superior. In addition, this is done with ease, as the person is in the clouds, which gives ease to his actions.

Here you can also meet toxic people who have achieved nothing themselves and are trying to destroy their partner's self-esteem by saying that he/she can't do anything, does everything badly, has no talent, no brains and so on. This is done only to elevate themselves above their partner. They create a poisonous fog and put pressure on their partner. Can be very cunning and psychological, their devious intentions are not always immediately apparent.

This is a typical situation in which a person creates an illusion for his or her partner that he or she is disconnected from reality, is unable to understand what is going on, and may even appear to have lost his or her mind. Cynically and persistently distorts reality and confuses the mind of his partner, seeking to indoctrinate him with his vision of who he should be. Masterfully twists circumstances and serves them with a seasoning that benefits only him.

Work and finance

Man is often lost in finding his way. He longs for immediate wealth, but his ideas about how to make money are not clear. He lives in a world of illusions and hopes, dreams a lot but does nothing about it. He often finds many excuses and obstacles to avoid making decisions and acting on financial goals. His vision of his own desires and abilities is vague and far from reality. For now, money is just an object of dreams for him.

For example, a person decides to become a photographer, but instead of starting by buying a camera, undergoing training or practicing skills, he starts developing grandiose, unrealistic projects. He conceives magnificent photo shoots with extravagant outfits for the models, and perhaps even decides to make the dresses himself. He gets carried away with such ideas that it becomes extremely difficult to tear him away from the earth and his real work. His procrastination and deviation from real work can be very noticeable.

A person may have a financial conundrum where he needs to allocate his budget between different urgent needs: buying a new bed, going to the dentist, paying tuition, traveling, and so on. All these obligations are equally important to him and he tries to figure out how to manage his money better.

You can also expect additional income from various sources on this card, although it will not always be significant. Money can come from different directions. Also the Seven of Wands can indicate the possibility of earning in cooperation with a partner, as this card is associated with the seventh house in astrology, which denotes partnership.

However, when relating to customers and selling one's own products or services, it can be difficult for a person to convey information to customers, so it pays to simplify his product line and clearly describe his offerings. People may feel confused and misunderstood about what he offers and how it can help them.

Occupation

Artist, magician, esotericist, painter, musician, hypnotist, anesthesiologist, anesthesiologist, anesthesiologist, anesthesiologist, forecaster, creator of commercials, films, videographer, writer, photographer.

PLACES AND FACILITIES

Above the clouds, on an airplane, in the mountains, on top floors, in bohemian, creative places, exhibitions of paintings, photos and so on.

Tip

It is necessary to develop the ability to grasp different possibilities, to make decisions about one's destiny and to choose a route in life. It is time to give up illusions and stop creating non-existent images. It is necessary to honestly admit to yourself what it is time to get rid of. Think about what you can change in yourself and around you to create fertile ground for future significant changes in your life.

Warning

Don't lose sight of reality and don't let yourself get entangled in the web of many options. Choose one that resonates with your soul, otherwise all opportunities will slip away. The situation is ambiguous and the person may be hiding something important from you. Be careful not to get into a dangerous position due to lack of attention.

Eight of Cups

S ymbolism

1. A tattered garment symbolizes a person's accumulated experience and wisdom gained over the course of life's journey. Footprints in the sand are an ephemeral trace that symbolizes the short-term presence of a person on the edge of their decision to leave. This feeling can be distressing and cause longing, but it will eventually go away.

2. You can also see sand on the shoes, this could symbolize loved ones who are having a hard time accepting the person's departure, or a former boss who can't accept their departure. To put it bluntly, it could be a person or some matter, a feeling that sticks like sand to the shoe. However, sand is a crumbly and unstable substance, something that is associated with time, hence no one will stick on a person for long.

3. The character on the card performed a ritual of burning the cups, in which she destroyed everything unnecessary: bad habits, unhealthy relationships, any negativity. This rite of purification freed her heart and soul, and she realized that she deserved more, that she had surpassed all the possibilities that the Seven of Cups presented to her. She walks away without a backward glance, leaving behind the last burning goblet, realizing that it will disappear into the waters of the past.

4. Traces in the water is an image of submerged cups, containers of passed experience that will remain with the person forever, because water is a symbol of the subconscious, and the accumulated experience strengthened in its depths. In one of the cups there is still a smoldering fire, this may indicate that the

person has left an unfinished situation, a person who loves him, a project that can still be successful. It could symbolize an open gestalt. And this cup, just like the others, will soon sink to the bottom. But the man has put this situation behind him and stepped into a new day.

5. The girl leaves behind the burning goblet, but walks towards more light. Her path lies towards the rising Sun. This emphasizes the idea that despite the crisis and the things one has to leave behind, one has a brighter future and new perspectives ahead.

Total value

In the Eight of Cups card, the character has already made a decision about his future path, which he pondered in the Seven of Cups. Leaving all the cups behind, he chooses a path radically different from the previous ones. The Eight of Cups is a symbol of farewell, the end of relationships, the beginning of new journeys and striving for a new level of existence.

The Eight of Cups shows that a person is going through a stage of parting with the past. This is a time of change, when there is a shift in life goals and priorities. The Eight of Cups reflects the idea of obligatory leaving, often accompanied by sadness and disappointment in the soul.

Relationship

Breakup. A chill in the relationship. A long-distance relationship. The person is finally free from a difficult and toxic relationship that has been dragging them down. The Eight of Cups is a card associated with personal relationships and is often a harbinger of the end of that relationship.

The card depicts a person with his back, which symbolizes his determination and sluggishness. He has already made his choice, perhaps even planning to start a new relationship. He has nothing to go back to the past, and he decides to close this chapter and move forward.

The card also indicates alienation and dissatisfaction in a relationship. It may be a decisive step onto a new path, albeit without much enthusiasm, but with a desire to say goodbye to the past that outweighs the discomfort of change. In some cases it may mean that a person is ending a rambunctious and carefree life, beginning a new phase, perhaps out of a sense of obligation.

The Eight of Cups indicates disappointment, unfulfilled hopes and emotional exhaustion. A person may suppress his feelings in order to avoid acute pain after separation. In marriage, this card may indicate that the couple is connected by a long life together, which is symbolized by the sunken bowls. Deep experiences together have become so embedded in their consciousness (subconscious) that it is difficult for them to free themselves from old patterns of behavior in the relationship. Sometimes this can lead to them transferring these patterns to new partners, seeing them through the lens of past experiences.

Work and finance

Man has climbed out of the swamp and new, bright prospects are opening up before him. He has grown out of his old pants and has set higher standards for himself. It is desirable for him to reach a higher level of earnings and status. This moment symbolizes a change in the work sphere, a new project or a move. Perhaps there is tension at work and the person needs to leave a hopeless situation, leaving a job that has already become small for him. Sometimes it may indicate a mismatch with the team, which was the reason for leaving.

Often this card means traveling and business trips. It can also indicate financial and work crises, urging a person to urgently change his direction in work and earning money, to reconsider his prospects and correctly prioritize.

The Eight of Cups can mean a complete change of the working sphere. For example, earlier a person worked as a programmer, but he was bored with this occupation, and he decides to radically change the sphere of earnings, moving, say, in business with real estate. This card also implies good earnings at a new place, as the Eight of Cups corresponds with the eighth house of astrology, connected with big money.

It can also indicate that a person has gotten rid of something or someone, for example, after a divorce, when all property was left with the former partner, and the person left, leaving the past in the past and taking nothing with him or her into a new life. Similarly, a person can suffer a significant financial loss by giving up something in an energetic sense, for example because of a serious illness. This is a sacrifice made for the sake of new, brighter days and a bright future, not confused by the dark shadows of past difficulties.

Occupation

Remote work, guide, trucker, hiking organizer, cab driver, courier, a person who is constantly on the move. A person can also work in the sphere where people are helped to cope with loss, to open their eyes, to show the way in life. This can be both psychologists and esotericists.

PLACES AND FACILITIES

By bodies of water, open spaces, swimming pools, nature, park, walking areas, beaches.

Tip

To learn to let go of people and things, to realize the concept of giving something away, to sacrifice something, to leave for a new life. Get out of your comfort zone for the sake of personal development. Change your lifestyle and go on vacation to relax.

Warning

This is not the time to abandon the familiar or your intentions and go elsewhere. It may be better to stay where you are and wait for a better time or option to leave. Or to reconsider your intentions about leaving altogether.

Nine of Cups

ymbolism

1. A person powerfully fills the surrounding atmosphere with positivity and happiness. Like the bowls under water, he too is enveloped by this energy, which only enhances his ability to transmit his feelings and energy, because water, like an amplifier, intensifies its effect.

2. From the girl's heart beats the energy of love that fills each of the bowls. In the Seven of Cups, the character believed that the bowls were a gift from the Universe and he should choose one of them. However, now, in the Nine of Cups, the person realizes that all of these bowls are of his own making, and are meant solely for him. He no longer has to make a choice - everything he desires is already his. The Nine of Cups symbolizes deep satisfaction and fulfillment of desires, bringing success in affairs.

3. This card is dominated by the color yellow, which speaks of luck, joy, optimism and happiness. The person on the card seems to be surrounded by this joy and simply enjoys it like the sea. In addition, yellow associated with fertility, maturation and communication, which means that the person is ready to generously share with others what they have in abundance.

4. Blue hair, as the blue color is associated with the Ajna chakra, responsible for intuition and thought process, as well as hair that symbolizes our thoughts, indicates that the person has a very developed intuition and clarity of mind. Such an unconventional hairstyle of the girl indicates his unconventional thinking and view of the world. This card encourages a person to listen to his intuition and follow the path that suggests the heart.

5. The treasure chest is at the bottom of the sea, underwater, which symbolizes that happiness can only be found within oneself, in the depths of one's soul.

Total value

In the Nine of Cups a person has come to that new day, to happiness and fulfillment of his desires, which he was so eagerly waiting for, having started his journey in the Eight of Cups. Since singing bowls emit powerful vibrations in the surrounding world, it indicates that a person has a noticeable energy, able to change not only himself, but also the surrounding space, customizing it to his vibrations.

Relationship

In every communication with his partner, the man strives for complete immersion, he longs to understand the secrets of the beloved's soul, seeking a serious and spiritually enriching relationship. In his partner he sees not only love, but also inspiration, sincerely wishing to discover and support the hidden talents of the other, generously gifting him with the most sincere compliments and emotional support.

When two people meet under the sign of the Nine of Cups, their joint existence is transformed into a magnificent fireworks of happiness and delight. Their mutual understanding becomes the basis for the realization of long-awaited ideas and endeavors, and together they build a road to common dreams and goals. The Nine of Cups symbolizes the intensity of the relationship, which can lead to unnecessary theatricality or even ostentatious behavior, if the partners too zealously demonstrate their feelings in front of each other and others.

Such a union can mark the convergence of two original and creative individuals who mutually nurture each other's new ideas and attraction. In such a relationship, partners can inspire each other's exploits and work together on unique creative projects, finding the basis of attraction in their shared creativity.

The Nine of Cups depicts a person full of admiration for his partner, ready to surround him with endless signs of attention and generous gifts, without missing a chance to show his pride in his chosen person. Such a person may be eager to show their partner to the whole world, actively sharing happy moments on social media and introducing them into their wide social circle.

At the same time, there can be a situation when one party puts all the strength and love into the relationship, as if throwing his soul into an impenetrable wall of water, while the other partner remains unperturbed and impenetrable, creating the feeling of an insurmountable barrier. This aspect is important to analyze, considering other cards of the layout.

Work and finance

Large profits and a constant flow of customers - a man has found a gold mine, and his life is bathed in abundance. Happy owner of abundant resources, he not only enjoys these benefits, but also shares his wealth with others. His generosity knows the limits only when he can help his loved ones and get involved in charity. After all, according to the laws of the universe, money comes to those who are ready to let go and share.

The Nine of Cups also symbolizes selflessness and acts of charity. However, it is important to remember that in this generosity should not lose measure. A person may be tempted to give away too much, giving in to the urge to help everyone and everything, and here you should beware of losing your own resources.

The Nine of Cups can also have an impact on gambling. Under the influence of enthusiastic emotions and joy of victories, a person can risk his money without thinking about the consequences. In such moments it is important to keep a cool mind and control your finances, so as not to lose all the gained good.

Occupation

Artist, creative person, restaurant business, organization of celebrations, wine taster, food industry, toastmaster, dancer, hairdressers, bartender, sommelier, night club worker, organizer of presentations and banquets, participant of charitable organizations.

PLACES AND FACILITIES

Banks, boxes, purses, islands, places by bodies of water, bars, restaurants, concerts, stages, theaters

Tip

Be self-indulgent, but avoid excesses. Fate favors you and promises all sorts of good things, and in fact, you are entering a bright streak in your life.

Money, success in your personal life, career growth and loyal friends. What more could you want?

Warning

People may begin to hate you for your success, any achievements, so you need to close for a while, and all positive events to share only c the closest.

Ten of Cups

Symbolism

1. The Ten of Cups symbolizes the semblance of light at the end of the tunnel, like a rainbow after rain. Rainbow represents the diversity of life, combining solar and water elements, and is a symbol of how from the differences and opposites can arise something amazing. The rainbow is a means of communication between heaven and earth, symbolizing the meeting of different worlds.

Total value

In the Nine of Cups, a person enjoys their happiness alone, and it is only in the Ten of Cups that they are willing to share that happiness with loved ones, bringing them joy and happiness, creating connections and planning for the future. This is an important transition from individual well-being to interaction and shared joy.

The rainbow is also often considered an omen of happy events. The Ten of Cups card reflects true, deep love, union with the beloved person, complete satisfaction in personal life. Here may be the moment of marriage by true love, successful family relationships, support and understanding in the family. This is a state when life is filled with bright moments, children are happy, and relationships with a partner bring only joy.

The Ten of Cups represents the culmination of positive emotions and harmony of feelings. Here a person experiences the fullness of happiness and harmony, and they appreciate how fortunate their life is at the moment. This is complete happiness and fulfillment of all desires.

However, a moment of choice may arise in the Ten of Cups. A person can relax, satisfied with the results achieved, but there is a risk of falling into a state of passivity, which can lead to a loss of inspiration and forward movement. Instead, the person may set new, more ambitious goals that previously seemed unattainable.

Relationship

This card symbolizes complete idyll in a relationship where absolute harmony reigns. In this couple there is a deep mutual understanding, and people agree in all aspects: physical, sexual, domestic, mental and spiritual. They share common goals and a vision for the future. These two people are closely connected, as if they were created for each other, their union is strong and blessed from above.

The card shows a notional hammock in the shape of a rainbow where the couple sits. The hammock descends from above, as if from heaven, which symbolizes the special purpose of this union. They have their backs turned to each other, which indicates that they trust each other completely and feel completely safe in this union.

This card also represents the protection of the family circle. The person clings to their family and loved ones and is not ready to move far away from them, as they feel incomplete without this support. Even if they are not officially married yet, they have already started to build a future together, looking ahead and considering long-term plans. This couple can quickly move on to official marriage and build their family dreams.

Work and finance

About rainbows in this context. Legends say that where rainbows touch the earth, incredible treasures can be found or places with rich harvests can be discovered. In popular European beliefs, the rainbow is often seen as an omen of wealth and prosperity, a prophetic sign indicating the location of hidden riches or a message of future abundance.

In the context of the card, this symbolism of the rainbow hints at the fact that the person leads a truly luxurious lifestyle, with the ability to live large, not denying himself in pleasures and the opportunity to pamper loved ones. He has excellent intuition in financial matters, knows exactly where finances can be "hidden", and how these funds can be earned easily and happily. Work brings this person real pleasure, and the team at work is so good that he feels them as a second family and in the working environment he finds comfort, as if he is in his home, feeling full satisfaction with his professional environment.

A person truly enjoys his work, and in such a way that it brings him not only material well-being, but also emotional satisfaction. Finances flow, providing not only stability for him and his family, but also a surplus of funds for the realization of all his desires and dreams. Work for him is not just a duty, but a source of vital energy, love and emotional well-being.

Occupation

Creative profession, psychologist, nanny, weather forecaster, child trainer, family psychologist, maternity worker, family psychologist, registry office worker, decorator, photographer, artist, a person who creates something beautiful, as well as a musician seven colors of the rainbow as seven notes.

PLACES AND FACILITIES

Bright, beautiful places, home, where there are holidays, festivals, daycare and places where there are children holidays, resorts, exhibitions, galleries, concerts.

Tip

To deal with family issues, to bring up children, to be a mediator between earthly affairs and the Higher Powers, just as the rainbow serves as a link between heaven and earth. The moment has come to establish relations with relatives, to strengthen the foundations of family life, to open our hearts to those we love, to keep loyalty to the hearth. It is important to plan competently for the future, to think seriously about what tomorrow will bring.

Warning

The card can also signal possible overprotection of family members by the questioner. There is a risk of losing personal boundaries, living solely in the interests of relatives, abandoning your own aspirations. It is important to exercise Temperance in trusting others and not to open up to them too quickly and completely. This is not the right time to strive for intimacy in relationships.

Page of Cups

S ymbolism

1. A person may be inclined to think of his own genius and feel elevated above others, even if his ideas seem ridiculous (pig with wings), he may believe that they are insights sent to him by higher powers. In the same way, a person may unreasonably romanticize and praise personalities who, in fact, turn out to be purely earthly and not always capable of insightful foresight (pig with wings).

2. When the Paj of Cups occurs in a chart, it can mean that a person's emotions override reason, like a singing bowl rising above their head.

3. Visually the card is overflowing with energy. One can see the outline of a second hand stretching from the character's hand, making a romantic gesture, symbolizing a connection to a love image, a dream cloud. This is not an illustration of a real partnership, but only the fruit of a person's fantasies. Such an image reminds of online correspondence, where hands touch each other through invisible streams of energy, and their gesture becomes similar to the emoji love sign, which is confirmed by real experience.

4. The heart of the character is like a source from which the light of high and awe-inspiring emotions bursts out in a stormy stream. The person depicted on the card may be overly emotional, unable to keep his feelings under control. Emotions overwhelm the mind, and from love he may lose his mind, with the feeling as if the earth is leaving under his feet. Here lurks the risk of becoming completely lost in his feelings, which in extreme cases can lead to tragic thoughts or actions, evoking associations with the image of

the Hangman.

Total value

The Page of Cups, representing the conjunction of water and earth, symbolizes the beginning of the formation of feelings. At this stage, emotions (represented by water) take over the entire human body (which represents earth). Through this influence, the Page of Cups becomes involved in the world of emotional experiences.

Here hormones cannot be restrained, and feelings are almost impossible to hide. The face of the Paje of Cups always reflects his inner world. A person corresponding to this card makes sometimes distant and unfulfilled plans, going into the world of his dreams and creating in them ideal realities.

He prefers to dive into his dreams and fantasies to escape from the pressures of reality. His view of the world may be overly romanticized and different from that of others.

The Pajas usually bring some kind of news or chance. In the case of the Wige of Cups, this news is associated with the opportunity to fall in love, find inspiration, or delve into new and exciting feelings. It can also be associated with news of a pregnancy.

The Page of Cups represents a young man or woman, a child, a younger brother or sister. This is a card of a person who is very responsive and empathic. He can become deeply involved in the problems of others, even more than they are themselves, and constantly worry about them. He can propose various ideas and solutions, sometimes absurd and unfeasible, because he is detached from reality.

Helping with practical matters is difficult for him, as he is not very adapted to everyday life. He may believe that the world should help everyone and show resentment if it does not. These people often behave like hysterical children, lacking wisdom, rationality and maturity.

The Pudge of Cups lacks inner stability and finds it difficult to stand up for his views and decisions. He tends to be malleable and too soft. Despite his age, he feels like an inexperienced child. Therefore, he often trusts others more than himself and puts himself second to others. His dreams of happiness for all and a world with butterflies may lead him into an unrealistic fantasy world, leaving little room for action in real life.

Relationship

From this card comes an air of romance and frivolity, of airy infatuations and superficial crushes. The relationship it represents lacks the maturity necessary to form a long-term and stable union. More often than not, one of the partners is immature, perceiving the relationship through the prism of obsessive idealizations.

Such an individual lacks maturity and the necessary inner strength to cope with the onslaught of emotions. They can overwhelm him like a tsunami, carrying him into the unknown.

The card depicts an unusually naive personality who can be exploited by a more cunning partner. His admiring gaze is directed toward his partner, as if he is looking upward at him. The dependence can be both emotional and material. This person may be so blinded by his feelings that he is willing to make excuses for his partner for any, even unfavorable behavior. The Page of Cups refuses to see the shortcomings of his companion, lives in a world of fantasies and illusions. He is capable of plunging headlong into a relationship without bothering to learn the true nature of the partner.

Also, this person is susceptible to influence from the partner and can go about his desires, even if they push to questionable actions.

Work and finance

The person is able to create large-scale projects and fantasize, however, he is often indecisive in matters of their realization and increasing financial income. Nevertheless, the Tarot indicates his tendency to emotional spending and making purchases subordinate to desires. Also, the card predicts the appearance of unexpected cash receipts, which can cause surprise and joy in a person. Money literally "falls from the sky" into his life, whether it is a lottery win, an inheritance or a gift, but not as a result of hard work. Financial success comes easily, and a person is able to attract them with his inner mood.

In this context, the pig symbolizes abundance and fertility, predicting monetary gains. However, given that the pig is depicted with wings and soaring upwards, there is a risk of spending the money received quickly and without thinking.

The Page of Cups is characterized by a good understanding of clients and customers, the ability to feel their needs. He often shows exceptional loyalty and puts his emotions and soul into his work, projects and products. However, this card can also indicate naivety in financial matters and excessive gullibility. The person may be inclined to spend money immediately because of fear of the responsibility of managing large sums of money. He finds it difficult to save for any significant purpose, as he does not know how to restrain himself and often allows himself petty distractions. His ability to manage his finances may be limited and he may easily become indebted and have difficulty in repaying loans.

Occupation

All creative professions, a person chases inspiration, artist, illusionist, musician, illustrator, hairdresser, poet, writer, designer, a person with an unconventional approach to work. The Page of Cups is engaged in all occupations where fantasy and aesthetic approach are required. He can be an excellent florist, designer, musician, stylist.

PLACES AND FACILITIES

The sea, bodies of water, exhibitions, gatherings of creative people, bohemian places, virtual places (communication on the Internet, this is hinted at by the heart-shaped smiley face), discos, concerts, musical instruments and speakers (the white lines coming from the page resemble the sounds of music).

Tip

To seek lightness, to get away from grayness, pragmatism and hard-headedness. To bring creativity into the world, to inspire and uplift others, to create unusual things. To open your feelings, fulfill your cherished desires and trust your intuition.

Warning

A person may lose self-respect, distrust himself and others without objective grounds. He may be deluded and live in illusions. But one should not be too distant from reality and live only in dreams and illusions, because in practice events may develop quite differently.

Knight of Cups

Symbolism

1. The lover is not just walking, he seems to be soaring, hovering on the wings of deep passion (and in fact, his sneakers even have wings painted on them).
2. Abundant bouquet of scarlet roses as if shouts about the storm of passionate emotions.
3. The fact that a person removes their hat shows that they have genuine respect for their significant other.
4. The scarlet plaid spread out in the background is a reminder of sensual pleasures, a strong indication of deep sexual attraction.
5. The emphasized presence of the letter envelope emphasizes the importance of correspondence and communication.
6. Since our protagonist chose the chair over the bedspread, the conclusion is self-evident: it matters to him to create an aesthetic environment, a culture of relationships, and a way of presenting himself.
7. He has a heart tattooed on his left wrist that looms among the other patterns, which emphasizes his responsiveness, caring nature, ability to empathize and be emotionally open.
8. Perhaps it hints at conception (grapes, like wine, are a symbol of rich vitality and fertility).
9. A snow-white horse is an emblem of a man who is faithful, not prone to jealousy, who values freedom. In this context, attempts to control or restrict his freedom will be useless - he will simply ride away on his horse, slip away, not allowing himself to be held. Bans on communication with friends, excessive jealousy or, let's not say, surveillance - all this will only repel him. Also, the white horse

symbolizes the highest and purest aspirations of man.

Total value

The Knight of Cups represents the harmony of the elements of water and air. Unlike the Dog of Cups, who was just beginning to understand his feelings, experiencing uncertainty in their manifestation, the Knight of Cups is already capable of open and confident expression of his emotions, thanks to the presence of the element of air, associated with communication.

In this regard, the words of the Knight of Cups can be seductively dangerous, as he has a talent for charming others with his compliments and verbal charm, which allows him to win the hearts of the ladies. It is extremely significant for him to not just experience feelings and emotions, but to share them, and to seek understanding and empathy from those around him.

The Knight of Cups card is associated with messages and tempting offers. Through it come exciting dates, various events, pleasant encounters and new acquaintances. It is a period full of emotional impressions, which promises a rich and exciting pastime, putting a pleasant imprint on everyday life. When life seems monotonous and routine, the appearance of the Knight of Cups promises a wave of activity and variety in everyday life.

It also symbolizes creative uplift, inspiration and deep love, a state in which you can put your affairs in order, successfully engage in creativity and solve many problems. The Knight of Cups is a reliable friend and a devoted lover with exceptional charm, mystery and attraction.

However, the Knight of Cups tends to experience stress, taking all events to heart. If he faces even mild criticism, he can show his emotional nature in two ways: either to burst out and make a scene, or to hold a grudge, for a long time maintaining dissatisfaction and interrupting communication.

Knights of Cups are not known for cynicism and cruelty, but they are capable of skillful deceptions, like all members of the Cups. They can create an illusory fog around themselves, drawing others into their world of tricks and mirages. They tend to live in illusions, attributing fictitious images to people, looking at them through the prism of their fantasies, and do not always want to recognize the true face of reality.

Relationship

The Knight of Cups has the ability to convey his feelings to the other person with hints and subtleties, inspiring romanticization of his object of attraction. His tenderness and romanticism require a delicate and gentle approach. Roughness and harshness can discourage him and dampen his passions. He is cautious in relationships and does not tolerate excessive insistence and rudeness. For example, if a girl persistently pursues him in search of attention, it is likely to only frighten him. The Knight of Cups is characterized by poems, letters, displays of sensitivity and admiration, as well as frank declarations of love and expressions of feelings.

Under the Knight of Cups there is often a period when people exchange sweets and bouquets, passionately tell each other about themselves and listen attentively to every word of their partner. During this period people are fascinated by each other, but behave more confidently and freely than when communicating with the Knight of Cups.

Here there is love, attraction, desire to be near each other and openly express their feelings. The Knight of Cups does not impose itself and does not seek to conquer the partner, as the Knight of Wands. At the beginning of a relationship, this arcana may use hot-cold tactics, sometimes responding with delayed messages or replying with cryptic answers to attract attention.

However, in a negative sense, the Knight of Cups can symbolize fraud or parasitism. Such a person may be dependent on his partner and use him to fulfill his needs, not wanting to achieve anything on his own. He may be more comfortable living on someone else's dime than laboring on his own. He may pay more attention to his own appearance and his own interests without caring for his partner, looking for a partner with material resources to use for his own benefit.

Work and finance

Grapes are a symbol of abundance, indicating that one will be better off financially in the near future. The horse, as a symbol of new opportunities, opens up his prospects, including the possibility of changing jobs to a better paying one. And since it is a cup, it could be associated with a more satisfying and inspiring job.

The chair a person sits on indicates a person's attachment to a place or a possible career advancement. It could be a sought after position that the person is striving for. He or she really enjoys what he or she does and it brings him or her not only pleasure but also financial reward. This person is active and creative.

The atmosphere in the work environment is filled with friendliness. A person easily makes deals and finds common ground in cooperation. The Knight of Cups shows diplomacy and willingness to compromise in negotiations. He does not give up before difficulties, but if work does not bring joy, his enthusiasm may gradually fade and he may stop striving for success.

Occupation

Tattoo artist, driver, rider, bartender, hairdresser, stylist, artist, event organizer, horse person, writer, poet, musician, remote profession. This workers in the beauty industry, bloggers, psychologists, actors, musicians, fine arts teachers, travel and pilgrimage specialists, meeting and dating organizers.

PLACES AND FACILITIES

The sea, bodies of water, exhibitions, gatherings of creative people, bohemian places, virtual places (communication on the Internet, this is hinted at by the heart-shaped smiley face), discos, concerts, musical instruments and speakers (the white lines coming from the page resemble the sounds of music).

Tip

Searching for lightness, avoiding grayness and pragmatism, rejecting stubbornness. Bringing creativity into everyday life, inspiring and supporting others, creating unusual objects. Opening your senses, fulfillment of cherished desires and trust in intuition.

Warning

A person may lose self-respect, distrust their own abilities and trust others without sufficient reason. Self-deception and immersion in a world of illusion is possible. It is important not to stray too far from reality and not to live exclusively in fantasy worlds, as events in real life may turn out differently.

Queen of Cups

1. Her pose conveys a sense of trust in the world. Her hands are up, expressing honesty and openness as we see her full palms. It is as if she is speaking to the universe, connecting with it through her open subconscious, which allows her to feel and perceive signs and signals from the world around her.

2. Her eyes are closed, focused on inner sensations and intuitive communication with the world around her. She has a good understanding of other people, using her emotions (like water) as a means to connect and relate to them.

3. Her feet are in the water, which makes her movements fluid and slow, and gives her a sexual nuance. The Queen of Cups gives herself completely to the creative flow and does not limit it to rationality or monotonous duties.

4. The circle of water surrounding the Queen of Cups symbolizes her ability to create her own space and hold others in it. She can charm a person like a siren, and this circle also serves as her energetic protection. She considers everything that enters her space to be her own, and therefore can be jealous.

5. The decoration on her forehead is a triangle downwards (symbol of water) and is located above her third eye, emphasizing her excellent intuition.

6. The crown hovers above her, indicating her ability to shift responsibility for her life to Higher Powers and her belief in the influence of the universe. This emphasizes that some forces are beyond the power of man, whether he be king or queen.

7. The cup the Queen holds in her hands serves as a tool for

187

meditation and divination. She attentively listens to the counsel of her heart and heals her kingdom.

8. The Queen of Cups embodies the muse, and her red hair blends into her dress, reflecting her emotional nature and emphasizing that her thoughts are driven by impulses, feelings and passions.

9. Her red dress reflects her passion, while the greenish color symbolizes her ability to genuinely experience emotions. Underwater, her dress changes color, reflecting her empathy, which affects the coloring of her aura and moods. She is deeply empathic and sensitive to the feelings of those around her.

Total value

After achieving mastery in expressing her emotions through the Knight of Cups, comes the Queen of Cups. Water plus water is her element, deep and mysterious waters. The Queen of Cups is completely immersed in exploring her emotions. She strives to feel every subtle vibration of her soul and to hear every word of it. She is fascinated by this process and it seems that there is nothing better in the world for her than to explore the vast and bottomless oceans of her inner world.

The Queen of Cups is sensual, artistic, creative and gentle. She is ready to come to the aid of those in need and can give wise counsel. The Queen of Cups has good intuition, clairvoyance and empathy. She can be overly worried about others, even strangers, be overly imaginative and sometimes wind herself up with all sorts of negative thoughts and scenarios. She may drown in her own illusions about events and people. She is ready to sacrifice herself for others, but most often sacrifices for feelings and relationships, sometimes even sacrificing communication with friends and career.

Relationship

In relationships such a person shows honesty, sincerity, openness, sometimes even naivety and gullibility. The Queen of Cups takes a passive position, passing the initiative to her partner. She is faithful to her partner and does not hide anything from him (revealing palms). A red dress symbolizes high libido and passion in a relationship.

Such a person is very caring and devoted to his partner. Sometimes he may show excessive care from the very beginning of the relationship. He is ready to come to the rescue, overcoming distances and even lending money, and some may abuse this kindness of his. The Queen of Cups should be very careful in choosing close people she trusts.

A couple where the Queen of Cups is present is characterized by tender and reverent relationships. It symbolizes endless love and unconditional acceptance of your partner with all his problems and shortcomings. This card represents attention and care for each other, as well as sensuality, trust, mercy and compassion. The Queen of Cups is ideal as a wife, mother and friend.

Such a person may also exhibit manipulative behavior, play the role of a victim, arrange scandals and tantrums. He or she may cry dramatically and playfully, accuse the partner of indifference and lack of attention. For reasons known to him, he may take offense and distance himself from his partner. At the same time, he may remain silent, making the partner feel guilty and panic over misunderstandings.

The Queen of Cups can also organize provocations and tests to find out the information she needs. For example, she can tell her partner that her friend saw him walking with some girl, although it really did not happen. If the partner does not hide anything, he will not fall into the trap, but if he does, the Queen of Cups will find out the truth with the help of these cunning tricks.

Sometimes she can seem windy and unreliable. She is not always very demanding in choosing her partners and can give in to sudden emotions. She is willing to open her heart to those who need warmth and love, without always considering whether the person is worthy of it. She feels compassion for those who are less fortunate in life and is ready to provide support in various forms.

Work and finance

The main obstacles to the promotion and development of personal business are the lack of well-honed sales skills, uncertainty in plans and unclear structure of actions. There are difficulties in accurate accounting of finances and their effective investment.

The Queen of Cups finds it difficult to protect her interests, promote herself in front of competitors and engage in power struggles. Her strengths are manifested in the role of mediator: she is able to charm and convince customers, business partners and investors. Possesses a fine intuition and the ability to find the right approach to people, feeling how best to influence them. Guided by her inner feelings, she achieves her goals and attracts favorable circumstances.

However, the Queen of Cups heralds the receipt of a significant amount of money and a life of abundance, as she is associated with the eighth house in astrology, the house of major finances. The image of a fish on her medallion, as well as the fish next to her, symbolize cash flow, profit, abundance and fertility. And this is confirmed in practice. If you get the Queen of Cups in answer to a question about financial prospects in the current month, you can expect prosperity in money matters.

In addition, the fish-shaped medallion with which the Queen of Cups is adorned can serve as advice in career planning, especially regarding financial investments. It symbolizes the need to invest in appearance, self-improvement, perhaps buying a valuable gift for yourself. This approach will positively affect the emotional state and will give additional motivation to attract new significant funds.

Occupation

This is a creative person who constantly needs inspiration. Feels people well, so it is possible to work as a psychologist, psychotherapist, psychic, esotericist. This is a person who subtly feels the world. The person does not work hard and clearly not "hands", it is intellectual, creative labor. The Queen of Cups engages her hands in the creation of the beautiful: paintings, sculptures, playing musical instruments, massages. It can also be work in the field of recreation and entertainment. It can be a job that helps people find peace and restore physical and mental balance - psychology, social assistance, healing, meditation, spa, as well as all sorts of creative circles, hobby classes, mainly related to creativity or esotericism.

PLACES AND FACILITIES

Places near bodies of water, places with light walls, places filled with light from the sun or artificial light, aquarium, esoteric stores, temples, places of power and rituals.

Tip

To relax in nature, near picturesque bodies of water, it is important to take time for yourself, immersing yourself in a world of peace with the help of relaxing procedures. Such a vacation will be a catalyst for restoring emotional balance, will help to get rid of excessive stress. Allocate time for yourself to avoid unnecessary fuss, be in a state of calm and spend time peacefully. Engage in self-development, working to strengthen your intuition and flexibility, cultivate confidence, empathy and compassion for others. This is the perfect time to open yourself fully to love, to immerse yourself in a world of sensuality and creativity, to be real in your feelings and to trust not only yourself but also your partner and the world around you.

Warning

It is worthwhile to remain down-to-earth, more functional and practical in your approaches, to consider the situation without unnecessary emotions. It is necessary to be careful not to give yourself away completely and not to show excessive trust. Remember that your openness and honesty may not be perceived and even rejected, they may remain unappreciated.

King of Cups

S ymbolism

1. The red color of his clothing symbolized consciousness and the element of Fire. Kings represent fire, and the King of Cups is the personification of fire combined with water. He controls emotions, both his own and those around him, and this is his realm. He knows how to manipulate the psyche and feelings of others, just as he moves his hand over a singing bowl, creating resonance with the world around him and filling the space with peace.

2. Its influence is immense. Water reacts to the vibrations of the cup and transmits the waves of this energy to the surrounding beings. Thus, the King of Cups has a significant impact on the emotional, sensitive and mental background of people. He easily reads the state of other people, which makes the job of attuning to people and influencing their state ideal for him. He can be a hypnotist, psychologist, esotericist or a brilliant creative person who with his notes or strokes on canvas penetrates into the deepest corners of human souls. He masterfully manipulates people, just as he leads his hand over the bowl, creating a certain sound that spreads in the surrounding space, and its vibrations are amplified by the structure of the water. He manipulates human emotions.

3. Sky merges with water, which means that a person gets knowledge and answers to their questions from their subconscious mind. Sky represents the air element responsible for information, while water symbolizes the subconscious mind.

4. A boat rising into the sky symbolizes a person's aspiration to know his inner world, as well as the world of emotions and feelings.

It also represents freedom and travel, indicating the possibility of moving, changing direction in life and opening new opportunities.

5. Like the Queen of Cups, the King of Cups wears a crown, which emphasizes the importance of personal responsibility for one's life. It reminds us that we shape our own destiny and are responsible for our own decisions. The King's eyes are closed, indicating that his attention is directed inward, toward personal feelings and intuitive communication with the world around him.

6. Starfish are able to regenerate lost limbs or cast them off when in danger. It symbolizes the ability to recover quickly from injury, illness or life's difficulties, both physically and mentally. The card is also associated with protection, indicating that there are means of preservation and defense, similar to the protection that starfish provide with their needles and claws.

7. The card shows an open heart radiating light, which symbolizes spiritual awakening and purity of intentions. This person is pure before himself and others and has a clear spirit.

8. The bracelets on the right hand and the rosary beads seem to add a layer of symbolism to the image of the King of Cups, emphasizing his outer influences and inner practices. Bracelets, as an extension of necklaces, may symbolize the connection between personal spirituality and impact on the world around him. The use of meditation beads indicates the King of Cups' ability to take a meditative approach to actions, which can signify their awareness and intentionality.

9. White bracelets and threads perhaps reflect purity of intention and a desire for sincerity and honesty in one's actions and influences on the outside world.

10. The ring on the middle finger of the right hand, which is associated with Saturn, the planet associated with power and discipline, can symbolize control over emotions and the ability to manage them competently, both your own and the emotions of others.

11. Silver hair, despite its outward youthfulness, emphasizes the King

of Cups' wisdom and ability to manage emotional flows, to soothe anger and stress through peacefulness and meditative practices. This indicates his depth of understanding and ability to balance emotionally.

Total value

After the Queen of Cups fully explored her soul, psyche, feelings and emotions, she discovered how to manage it all. The King of Cups, for his part, proved to be a gentle and intuitive leader.

The King of Cups is a kind friend, a loving husband, a caring father and a generous philanthropist. He is usually very polite, gallant and devoid of callousness. He has an outstanding sense of humor and is always ready to come to the rescue if he sees someone in decline. He does not pretend that nothing is going on, but on the contrary, he is able to support and inspire those around him. His gentleness and warmth make others trust him.

Relationship

In emotional relationships, the King of Cups shows itself as a person deeply in love and interested in his partner, characterized by subtlety of feelings and romanticism. When conflicts arise in a relationship, the King of Cups can avoid risk and not rush to go to reconciliation, preferring to wait for the right moment when circumstances themselves will unite partners, or when the initiative comes from the other half. Nevertheless, in certain situations, he may show impulsiveness, losing control over his emotions, and may sacrifice everything, just to return the favor of a loved one.

A boat, appearing in the context of a relationship, represents the possibility of frequent meetings, communication by phone, trips to visit the object of your feelings. This symbol can also hint at a long-distance relationship, foreshadowing a close encounter with a partner who lives far away. In a characteristic way, this image can reflect the situation when the spouse is a sailor on a voyage, and his faithful wife is waiting for him at home.

The King of Cups has the ability to lavish his beloved with the most exquisite gifts, flattering compliments, and if his feelings reach a peak, he may resort to writing poems, dedicating songs or creating portraits of the beloved, depending on what field of art he shows himself in. He tends to idealize his partner, to see him as a muse and a divine being. But if the lover begins to make demands on him, to show excessive practicality and materialism, the King of Cups may perceive it as an insult to his feelings and himself personally, which may lead to the fact that he will withdraw, spend time with friends over a glass of wine or comfort in the arms of other women, as his mental vulnerability and sensitivity to such things is very high.

Work and finance

This person has an excellent creative vision in his activities, but it is hard for him to promote and realize his products. Financially, he is doing very well, thanks to the cards Pisces and Star, which predict prosperity and well-being, as well as good luck in money matters and abundant profits.

The Star of the Sea in tarot is a symbol of intuition and the ability to overcome difficulties on the way to success, it gives these qualities to the person for whom fortune-telling, endowing him with a flair and the ability to overcome barriers on the way to achieving financial ambitions. Such a person instinctively feels where to go, with whom to do business, where to invest to increase income, in short, he has a special gift for recognizing financial opportunities. Pisces is a sign of abundance and fertility. A pendant in the shape of a fish symbolizes abundance and prosperity.

If such a person has to perform monotonous, uninspiring work, which causes him irritation, he will not hide his dissatisfaction. He may show himself irascible, nervous, and all the time express the idea that somewhere he will be better, and one day will decide to leave the usual place of work in search of something new and more suitable.

In general, as a colleague or business partner, this person is a valuable asset, treats with attention and is ready to support in a difficult moment. However, sometimes this person can let things run their course, relax and live by the principle "let anything happen". But he does not aspire to big risky financial ventures, because he values his mental comfort and is afraid of losing it.

This person shows excessive kindness to those who are sympathetic to him, ready to help in career advancement or some other important endeavor. He should be cautious to avoid exploitation of his benevolence.

195

His generosity may attract those who wish to take advantage, and he should be wary of such people to avoid being manipulated.

Occupation

Artist, musician, any kind of creativity. This is a creative genius, a talent from nature, a subtle flair for art. A good psychologist, esotericist. Sailor, a person working on a ship; a person working in water parks, swimming pools, oceanariums; diving, surfing; professions related to bodies of water.

PLACES AND FACILITIES

By the reservoirs, boats, ships, beaches, aquariums, travel stores.

Tip

Follow the path of your creative inspiration. Take responsibility for managing your feelings while remaining open and receptive to the world around you, however, without letting your emotions dominate your mind. It is important to remain empathetic and understanding towards those around you. Allow the other person to take the initiative, while you keep a close eye on developments.

Warning

Do not ignore obvious facts, do not comfort yourself with sweet illusions about other people or events. Do not resort to passive waiting and refusing to take an active role. Inaction and hoping that someone else will do all the work can ultimately lead to disappointment.

WANDS

Ace of Wands

Symbolism

1. In the Seer's deck, the Ace of Wands, as intended by the creator, represents the beads and Nets of Indra. These are mirror beads with knowledge of other beads, emphasizing the interconnectedness of all ideas and thoughts. Indra's Net in Hindu mythology is a vast network that permeates the entire universe, symbolizing time and space. At the nodes of this network are diamond beads reflecting each other, which speaks of the interconnectedness of all things in the universe and the fact that each thing contains elements of the other.

Total value

The Ace of Wands brings many ideas to achieve goals. A person pays attention to the ideas and ambitions of other people and gets inspiration from them. This contributes to broadening his horizons. As a result, the person has insights and more beacons for inspiration.

We observe a situation where thoughts move freely, people adopt them and turn them into concrete goals and ideas. This is how ingenuity and flexibility of mind are manifested. A person is able to look at a situation from different angles and change the usual view of the world. His thinking becomes flexible and agile, which allows him to see many different perspectives to achieve his goals.

The Ace of Wands also symbolizes the treasures hidden within the mind. This is a period of active mental activity accompanied by vivid and colorful dreams. Revelations come during meditations and dreams. An important feature of this card is the ability to synthesize ideas. A person can draw inspiration from various sources and transform them through himself, creating his own brilliant ideas.

The Ace of Wands also symbolizes a conscious personality. The person develops and cares about his personal growth. He has many interests, talents and hobbies. He is creative and artistic, strives for self-expression. The personality is self-sufficient and capable of generating ideas. It is constantly creating new neural connections, mastering new disciplines and accomplishing something new.

Relationship

A person is in the process of self-identification, looking for himself, trying to combine all his skills and abilities into a coherent system that will reflect his entire life experience. He shows a desire for active self-development and continuous learning. Has a fast thinking speed, developed intuition and excellent memory. Ace of Wands symbolizes impulse, spark, dynamics and movement. It is a card of enthusiasm and the opportunity to radically change something in your life.

In the Seer's deck, the Ace of Wands, as intended by the creator, represents the beads and Nets of Indra. These are mirror beads with knowledge of other beads, emphasizing the interconnectedness of all ideas and thoughts. Indra's Net in Hindu mythology is a vast network that permeates the entire universe, symbolizing time and space. At the nodes of this network are diamond beads reflecting each other, which speaks of the interconnectedness of all things in the universe and the fact that each thing contains elements of the other.

This chain of associations can be developed endlessly. For example, you have a backpack with a lock, you have a similar lock on your sweater, the sweater is made of velour, which is also used to make your curtain. The curtain is colored yellow, the same color as the pencil on your desk. The sketches made with this pencil are in a favorite notebook that an old friend gave you. Remembering your friend, you decide to call him or her and arrange to meet. This chain of associations can lead to action. The same way the process of creating ideas, projects, the birth of brilliant thoughts and plans works.

Work and finance

Launching new projects, generating ideas to develop existing business and founding your own enterprise. Burning passion for the chosen business, developing various projects and establishing branches to expand the business. Getting satisfaction from running your own business. Creative approach. Career growth, advancement and promotion. Business brings inspiration and energizes. Generating income through personal ideas and efforts.

Active search for ideas to generate additional income. Developing concepts for new products in the chosen niche. Realization of creative projects and collaborations. Partnering with other professionals. Knowledge of ways to make money. Ability to see perspectives, desire to learn and expand your horizons.

There may be a situation when the abundance of ideas can be confusing. In such a case, it is important for a person to gather all ideas into one meaningful and promising concept, not to waste his efforts on trivialities and focus on the main thing, but at the same time to draw inspiration from many sources.

Occupation

Inventor. A person who constantly engages his imagination, it can be a scriptwriter, artist, musician, can be a businessman, programmer. Professions related to passion and sex.

PLACES AND FACILITIES

Dry LOCATIONS AND OBJECTS, sands, deserts, cliffs, southern countries, dry climate, heat. A place with beautiful decorations, decorated with lanterns, candles, garlands.

Tip

Use the potential of your imagination to achieve the best results. Trust your intuition and pay attention to the signs that the universe gives you. Catch the moments of inspiration and learn to utilize the available opportunities.

Warning

Avoid spending long periods of time waiting for inspiration and insight, it is important to act quickly and with determination. Make decisions without hesitation. However, make sure you don't miss something important.

Two of Wands

S ymbolism

1. The personality reflected in the Two of Wands is at a crossroads between the familiar and the new. The Wand in the corner of the room symbolizes attachment to old habits and established order, craving for security and stability.

2. White sneakers on a character can reflect inexperience and apprehension before new endeavors. They symbolize doubt: whether it is worth risking cleanliness and comfort for the sake of uncertain paths that may or may not turn out to be successful.

3. The wand directed to the window represents the desire for freedom and development, the desire to break out of the closed circle and routine. It indicates an inner conflict between the desire for change and fear of change.

4. A surf and globe with a water image can symbolize plans for a trip or move involving water, sea or ocean and a desire for outdoor activities. However, there are doubts and worries about whether everything has been taken into account and planned correctly.

5. A protruding ear from underneath the hair can indicate insecurity and a tendency to consider other people's opinions, which can lead to hesitation and fear of making a mistake.

6. A bob hairstyle with clean lines emphasizes the need for order and structure, which can indicate a conservative mindset, a reluctance to step outside the box and a fear of new experiences.

7. In general, this card reflects the inner state of a person who stands on the threshold of change, but is not yet ready to make a decisive step forward, oscillating between the familiar past and the unknown future.

Total value

The person represented by the Two of Wands has the ideas and plans engendered by the Ace of Wands, but has not yet found the strength to realize them. She is busy planning, perhaps even planning to travel. A long wait is felt. This person spends a lot of time at home, in her comfort zone, and finds secondary advantages in the current situation that keep her from taking decisive action forward.

This person prefers coziness and comfortable conditions. He does not have full confidence and willingness to take risks and step out of his comfort zone. He is inclined to theorize, but does not resort to active actions. His thoughts are full of dreams and plans, but without concrete steps forward. He is not in a hurry to abruptly change his passive state to an active one - he prefers reflection before taking the first step. He has hope and anticipation of change.

A person wants to introduce the new into the old and get rid of outdated beliefs. He tries to find a solution to free himself from limitations and is in search of an answer. His personality is prone to procrastination and indecision. He procrastinates before changing himself and his way of thinking. He is concerned about losing a part of himself and being deprived of what he already has.

The person appreciates stability and a familiar picture of the world, but wishes to put his knowledge into practice. He has a fear of the future, but he also feels a strong desire for change. He remains in the swamp, holding himself back and making excuses for not moving forward.

A person is afraid of changes and alterations, thinks for a long time before taking the first step. Life passes, and he does not dare to plunge into its flow, remains a humble observer. He has old habits that hold him back from moving forward, and he lacks inner support. There remains hesitation within about his choices. The person enjoys reading adventure novels or watching such programs and dreams of the same kind of pastime.

Relationship

In a classic relationship, the person has a clear vision of what the relationship should be like. Common interests bring people together. It can be a mutual passion for traveling or active sports. However, such relationships can sometimes create a stuffy atmosphere in which a person feels constricted and longs for freedom.

We can talk about distant relationships. People often get acquainted online and limit themselves to communication through correspondence and phone calls. Sometimes a meeting is impossible because of certain circumstances. This is a time of waiting for a new stage in the relationship, when the barriers between the partners will fall, and they will become closer to each other. Anticipation of a meeting. According to this card, it is also possible that one person is secretly in love with another, does not admit his feelings, only gives subtle signs of attention.

It can also be uncertainty, when there is a choice to be made between two partners, between circumstances and relationships. There is a desire to meet, but external obstacles stand in the way. Communication takes place via the Internet. A person may live with one partner, but mentally be with another. A sense of obligation keeps him or her in place. One partner may restrict the freedom of the other, forbidding communication with friends and demanding to stay at home all the time.

A person may feel depressed because of the current circumstances, there is a desire to start over, differently, which symbolizes white sneakers. In relationships there is a search for new ideas that would help to find the best solution to get out of a stale situation.

There is an active search for ways to move the situation forward. Partners feel a longing for mutual communication. At the same time, a return to previous conditions can lead to depression, which is symbolized by the black corner.

Work and finance

Reporting, project planning and creating lists of objectives are key tasks. Detailed project management, schedule development and effective time management are also part of this process. Actively seeking employment, including overseas and in various fields such as travel, management, sports, tourism, education and geography is an important task. Developing strategies for business development, innovating, expanding the project and finding additional sources of income are also relevant.

Work fatigue, need for rest, desire to take a vacation or change the sphere of activity. The desire to leave the familiar place and get rid of the work routine, for example, to move from the office to the field of sports. The desire to find a new job that would bring inspiration, something fresh and unexplored. Radical change of professional direction, search for optimal solutions in career. Doubts about leaving your current job for fear of losing stability.

Expectation of better conditions at work, search for better career prospects. Acquisition of new knowledge, professional training. Striving to expand one's competencies and powers, as well as to increase salary. The possibility of remote work and cooperation with foreign partners. Availability of stable income and fixed salary. Expectation of return on investment.

The financial situation remains unchanged. It follows from the map that neither career growth nor a significant increase in business income is foreseen in the near future. However, the financial situation is not expected to deteriorate either. The situation will remain stable.

Occupation

Teacher, store worker with sports and travel equipment, travel agency worker, window maker, decorator, hairdresser, stylist, fashion designer, office clerk, accountant.

PLACES AND FACILITIES

Enclosed spaces, house, rooms with large windows, museums, travel and tourism stores, geographer's office, library, car, motorhome.

Tip

Stop waiting and start living in the present day, not waiting for the right moment, but creating it yourself. To take action, to overcome the barrier that prevents you from interacting with the world or a certain person.

Warning

There is a risk of being stuck in one's habitual zone for a long time, and this can last for years if one remains in a passive state, feeling sorry for oneself and only sighing. The situation requires immediate resolution and a way out of it. However, sometimes it is also possible to be moderately patient and stay in your comfort and safety zone.

Three of Wands

S ymbolism

1. The feeling of freedom is emphasized by the loose hair that curls in the wind. This indicates liberation from restrictions, the absence of stereotypical thinking and rigid frameworks, the character's gaze is directed beyond the horizon.

Total value

In the Triple of Wands we observe that unlike the Two of Wands, here the wands are set vertically and they are blazing, radiating strength and confidence. In the image, the girl is waiting for the wave to approach. This symbolizes the expectation of an auspicious moment and the first step towards success.

This is a card of getting out of your comfort zone, starting new endeavors, learning new sports including surfing and other extreme sports, activities and entertainment, especially water related.

If on the Two of Wands the character only dreamed of surfing, on the Triple he is already ready for action. Usually such a person observes others, learns, can be in the role of an objective observer, looking from the outside and not inclined to get involved in events. This is a loner, an individualist who knows what he wants, has will and determination, is talented and full of vitality, has many ambitions, inner support and fire.

Such a person realizes exactly what he needs to realize his desires. Since the character on the card is turned back, it may mean that he acts guided by his feelings and ambitions, not listening to other people's advice and instructions.

Can have many different hobbies and pastimes, interested in everything that is far and unattainable, as well as mysticism, religion, esotericism, spiritual knowledge, distant countries and their cultures.

Such a person is able to rely solely on himself, not to be attached to the place of residence, often change the place of residence, quickly tire of monotony and prepare for a trip or move to a new LOCATION AND OBJECTS.

Relationship

The person waits too long for circumstances to change by themselves, for the partner to act differently, to fulfill promises and so on. He takes a waiting position, hoping that others will make decisions, take action, invite him, and thus remains in a passive and waiting state, waiting for the partner to make the first step or offer.

A person can put off the bright moments of life for later, postponing the realization of his desires with his partner, instead of decorating and improving the relationship here and now. He repeats the same mistakes, gives his partner too many chances, does not show determination for radical changes, cannot give a clear ultimatum and defend his interests, demonstrating willpower and inner confidence.

Relationships can be distant. There is a desire to break out of loneliness, to leave one's refuge, to throw oneself into the whirlpool of life and make new acquaintances. The partner may keep at a distance, be selfish and not compromise, listen only to themselves, constantly expect perfection, being with one person but eyeing others. It can also signify joint plans, travel, the couple's long term prospects and a shared future.

There is a strong attraction to the partner, a desire to change something in the relationship, waiting for the right moment to make changes and diversity in the life of the couple. Sexual attraction is strong, a person is attracted to the partner, there is passion in the relationship. There are common plans and distant dreams, the desire to build the future together.

Work and finance

A person is ready to move to a new stage of his development, to expand his horizons and apply his accumulated knowledge and experience in practical activities. He or she has invested funds and efforts in a project and now expects a return on his or her investment. There is a desire to change work, a desire to leave the usual place and start something new.

Self-employment is preferable for this person, as working for hire may make them uncomfortable and they are unlikely to be willing to follow management's instructions. In terms of career growth and return on investment in projects, one should be patient and wait for the right time. The card also indicates the possibility of working remotely, finding new employment, new ideas and concepts for one's own business or project.

Occupation

Profession is related to travel, water, sports, art, fitness coach, surfing. Body art, tattoo artist, hairdresser, astrologer, astronomer.

PLACES AND FACILITIES

Beach, sea, river, ocean, lake, places near water bodies in general. Gyms, places where sports games and competitions are held, extreme resorts, abroad.

Tip

A person, as already being at a high enough level, realizes the importance of stabilizing his position. It is now necessary to maintain this level and ensure stability. This involves careful planning of the next step and a willingness to act as soon as the right moment appears. Expanding one's capabilities is also part of the plans.

Warning

However, it is important not to miss the important moment, and you should not make a decision if you do not see the whole picture or if the situation seems dangerous. All in good time, and the timing is important. It is better to wait until conditions are more favorable and then take action.

Four of Wands

Symbolism

1. Against a clear sky, the tambourine symbolizes true joy, purity and creative impulse. The seven circles on the tambourine reflect the alignment of a person's seven chakras, indicating harmony in all aspects of life. The tambourine also represents trance immersion, when a person can experience such bliss that he or she is completely disconnected from the outside world.

2. The character on the left is accompanied by energy emanating from his right hand, which is a giving hand. This suggests that he is sharing his joy with others, spreading positive vibrations.

3. Flags on a marquee symbolize togetherness and diplomacy. Two identical garlands of flags indicate that over time people tend to adopt each other's habits, becoming closer and finding common ground. The colors of the flags carry the following meanings:

- Red: luxury, passionate relationship between partners living under the same roof,
- Lavender: adventure, love and creativity in the home,
- Blue: tranquility and harmony, diplomacy in conflict resolution,
- Green: prosperity, balance and security. The placement of flags at the entrance can symbolize the hospitality of the hosts and their openness to others, willingness to share news about life in the house and personal relationships.

1. The tent is a symbol of comfort and protection, offering shelter from weather, heat and rain. It is also associated with comfort and security, emphasized by the four Wands forming a protective

square around it. A tent can allude to a nomadic lifestyle, traveling, living abroad or in another city, away from a familiar home. It also symbolizes the starry sky and the protection of higher powers.

2. The burgundy background color speaks of high self-esteem, confidence, courage and the ability to bring joy and positivity to any environment. The burgundy color of the earth symbolizes prosperity in the house and respect for its owner. Such a person prefers stability and comfort, avoiding unnecessary stress and nervousness, striving for an organized and comfortable life.

3. The ring on the index finger of the character's right hand on the left indicates a strong-willed character, a love of luxury, leadership qualities and the ability to be an organizer and mentor.

4. Red bracelet on the left hand serves as a talisman, protecting from the negative impact of others, the evil eye and spoilage.

5. The yellow bracelet on the arm of the character on the left attracts good luck, symbolizing a person being lucky or having an amulet to attract prosperity.

6. The dance symbolizes the release of energy, the discovery of feminine power. It expresses liberation, lightness, ease, ease, creative self-expression and openness to the world.

7. Bracelets worn on the couple's hands symbolize a harmonious exchange of energies: the woman's left hand receives, while the man's right hand gives. This indicates that the partners complement each other perfectly. A red bracelet promises happiness in personal life and portends a prosperous marriage.

8. Dance reflects people's openness in expressing their feelings for each other, encourages them to express themselves and creates an atmosphere of unity and harmony in the home. Through the movements of the arms, head, back and hips, the dance conveys the following messages:

- The back symbolizes the sincerity of the relationship between people,
- Hands reflect the ability to find common ground and come to

compromises,

- Hips are associated with sexual satisfaction in a couple,
- The head indicates the ability to disconnect from everyday life and relax in each other's company.

Total value

Under the majestic starry night sky, the Three of Wands symbolizes a man who seeks to expand his horizons and possibilities. However, shrouded in darkness, he is limited in his actions. But comes the Four of Wands, symbolizing the dawn, the thin boundary between the passing night and the approaching morning, when the first rays of sunlight touch the earth. The Four of Wands is a true celebration of life.

The Four of Wands depicts a person who radiates cheerfulness and a festive mood. This is the image of a person who looks at the world with unchanging optimism, is characterized by friendliness and willingness to help others. He loves his family and friends, is altruistic in spirit, always ready to come to the aid not only with good advice, but also with active actions to help people cope with their life difficulties. Such a person has kindness, honesty, openness and peacefulness, although his excessive gullibility can sometimes play against him. He is sociable and emotional, which makes him the soul of the company.

Relationship

The burgundy color of the earth on the map symbolizes stability and reliability, as well as conservative views on relationships and marriage.

The card also shows that one of the girls moves to the right and the other to the left, which symbolizes the combination of masculine and feminine. The right side is associated with qualities such as determination, purposefulness and activity, while the left side symbolizes flexibility, softness and intuition. This perfectly illustrates how the masculine complements the feminine and vice versa, creating harmony in the couple. The man is able to protect his woman and display noble qualities, while the woman understands and supports her man.

Work and finance

The burgundy earth color in the context of work symbolizes a person's entrepreneurial spirit, outstanding organizational skills and abilities. It is the color of stability, denoting regular and reliable income, material stability, prosperity and abundance. It is associated with good profits and successful completion of transactions, which leads to a secure and solid position in business and work, as well as possible promotions. The burgundy color also portends successful investments and material support.

In the career aspect, this color indicates success, effective teamwork, fruitful cooperation and profitable partnerships. It portends a pleasant working atmosphere, customer satisfaction and gratitude. In addition, burgundy can symbolize corporate celebrations or celebrations in honor of successfully completed projects.

Occupation

Professions related to design, interior design, hairdressing services. Musician, artist, dancer, circus performer, a person who works in the field of organizing events, celebrations, concerts. Jeweler, a person who creates jewelry, decorations.

PLACES AND FACILITIES

House, marquee, house in nature, venue, discos, clubs, parties, concert, circus.

Tip

It is necessary to revitalize, to get rid of the excessive seriousness that has enveloped everyday life. It is important to allow yourself a period of rest and complete relaxation, to organize for yourself a pleasant pastime, whether it is a holiday, weekend or vacation. It is time to pay attention to strengthening ties with loved ones, work on stabilizing relationships, joint receipt of joyful emotions and impressions, which can later serve as a reliable protection against potential conflicts.

Warning

It is important to firmly protect your personal boundaries and focus on serious tasks. It is time to get to work and stop chasing fleeting pleasures that do not bring long-term benefits. You shouldn't be overly relaxed or too open with others to conserve your energy for important matters.

Five of Wands

S ymbolism

1. The white top of the characters' clothing symbolizes the desire for social cohesion, the desire to purify oneself and reach a new level of consciousness, as well as to improve one's position in society. The color white represents initiation into a new life and the desire to connect with the divine light to which all aspire. It is a symbol of fair and open competition.

2. The red pants symbolize the will to win and the desire for mental clarity, which is achieved through physical effort, sport and work. The card emphasizes that it is necessary to work together to achieve the goal, as each character with his individual rod contributes to the creation of a common ladder to success.

3. Black shoes indicate persistence of character. The identical shoes of all the characters suggest equality of power, and no one can crush the other, as all have equal capabilities. The distant mountains and unworn shoes hint that the characters have not chosen the traditional path to the top, refusing to follow other people's scripts, they seek to build their own system, indicating their ambition and relatively little life experience.

4. In ancient times, mountains were considered the abode of the gods, such as Olympus, the realm of the gods among the ancient Greeks, a place where the gods dwelt at unreachable heights. On the map, people strive to reach the light and fire of Empyrea, the highest part of the heavens, filled with pure fire and light, which is higher than the mountains and even higher than Olympus itself.

Total value

In the Five of Wands, a person leaves the stability of the Four of Wands and enters into active competition to achieve their goals. This is a card of competition and tension, where social networks and human interaction play a key role. It symbolizes the protection of personal interests, rivalry, hustle and bustle and the desire to win in a kind of Olympics of life. The card reflects the need to make significant efforts to achieve a certain goal, the search for the light of knowledge, the dispute over an idea and the struggle for one's place under the sun.

The Five of Wands card reflects the desire of people to achieve high goals, sometimes even beyond their capabilities, which symbolizes the desire to "jump above their heads". Characters on the card are willing to act at the limit of their strength, showing persistence and will to transform reality in accordance with their desires. This indicates their desire for power and their ability to persevere.

People depicted on the card are active and confident in their beliefs, able to lead others and inspire them to stand up to opponents. They are radicalized, can be initiators of revolutionary changes and protests. They are characterized by sharpness, unpredictability, and a tendency to be talkative. The competitive environment is a stimulus to development and a source of energy for them. They are purposeful, venturesome and cannot sit still for long.

However, such people may lack internal stability and integrity, their inner world may be unstable. They are prone to irascibility, aggression and excessive emotionality. Despite this, they are courageous, energetic and passionate, dynamic and risk-taking, have good reactions and endurance, extroverts. These people are confident and determined, love the feeling of adrenaline and have a strong will to win. They are hard to stop, they strive to be the first and conquer new territories without thinking about possible consequences.

Relationship

The Five of Wands card in the context of relationships can symbolize the process of "lapping" partners to each other, where provocations and the desire to add fuel to the fire are used as a way to ignite greater interest and passion. It can be a desire to experience vivid emotions, where feelings erupt like a bubbling volcano. In such a relationship, the game is played on equal footing and partners strive together to achieve common goals, finding growth through crisis and tense moments.

The relationship described by this card is characterized by equality, where each partner tries to assert their authority. Shared activities such as sports, hiking or adventures may be part of their interaction. However, frequent disagreements, quarrels and conflicts are also possible, as both partners can be irascible and prone to emotional outbursts.

Jealousy provocations, such as one partner flirting in front of the other, can be used as a way to "tickle nerves" or test a partner's feelings. Partners may seek to dominate or get the other to follow, with one believing himself or herself to be more nimble and agile, encouraging the other to be active and involved in the turbulent flow of life.

Communication via the internet and phone calls can also be part of the relationship dynamics of this card. Partners may seek to impress each other through a variety of ways to get each other's attention, from demonstrative gestures to unconventional actions. This can include behaviors such as performing impulsive acts on emotion, such as getting tattoos of each other's names, which is an attempt to strengthen bonding and affection during times of turbulent passions.

Work and finance

The person is caught up in a multitude of small worries, strives to have time to do a huge number of things, works without respite, putting a huge amount of energy and effort into his work. He is determined to complete the project as soon as possible, is constantly in a whirlwind of activity to make a breakthrough in the field of finance, but his labor can resemble a fruitless effort, like a stormy activity. A person runs back and forth, tries to do everything at once, but does not achieve meaningful results. This is a constant rush and the desire to do many things at once, when a person is simply overwhelmed with a mountain of tasks. He is always in constant motion and his thoughts are occupied with his own affairs.

This card also reflects a situation where a person is trying not to drown in a sea of business or personal problems. He is looking for ways to regain stability, hiring marketers, working on improving the design of his website, looking for new products to expand his product range and seeking advice from other competent professionals.

This card also perfectly characterizes hardworking and enterprising people who do not miss any chance to earn money. Take, for example, a person who rents out his house, receiving income from it, then goes to a neighboring region to buy goods that can be sold more expensive than the house. He also grows vegetables on his plot and successfully sells them, as well as rents out various equipment. As a result, this person knows how to extract income from everything around him, using all his abilities and opportunities, and he does it all at the same time. This is the case when a person strives to earn all the money in the world.

In addition, this card is associated with career advancement. It symbolizes a person who works hard and tirelessly to achieve the desired level of well-being and career growth. Here it is appropriate to recall the myth of Prometheus, who stole fire from Olympus and gave it to people, which symbolizes the desire of the person described by this card to achieve more, to believe in his right to have everything he wants.

Occupation

Coach, rope walker, mountaineering (mountain and industrial), waiter, marketer, manager, firefighter, call center worker, stuntman, online store worker, weaving, embroidery, knitting, caving, work related to extreme, sports travel, survival in the wild, hiking.

PLACES AND FACILITIES

Gym, sports, mountains, rocks, caves, social media, internet.

Tip

It is necessary to act immediately, to pool all your resources and efforts, not allowing yourself to relax until the goal is achieved. Use every available opportunity and resource in order to realize your plans and ultimately be at the peak of success.

Warning

In pursuit of your dreams, it is important to properly distribute your efforts, so as not to run out halfway and not to be without strength. It is necessary to remain attentive to your surroundings, not to focus solely on one goal, so as not to miss significant opportunities.

Six of Wands

S ymbolism

1. The laurel wreath or laurel branch has long been associated with a symbol of glory, victory or peace. This symbol, which dates back to antiquity, represents greatness and success. The goddess of victory Nika, according to ancient legends, often depicted with a laurel wreath in her hands, symbolizing a crown of glory for the victorious heroes. The victorious warriors, as well as the winners of sports competitions were honored with a laurel wreath, and even statues of deities were decorated with this sign of triumph. Laurel wreath is a sign of victory, perfection, and also symbolizes the complete triumph over inner weaknesses and opponents. It represents the ideal of achievement and supreme recognition.

2. The mini-skirt on the card character symbolizes liberation and freedom, as it gives freedom to the legs and does not restrict movement, which in turn emphasizes independence and courage.

3. The girl on the harness does not notice people's faces, she only sees their hands that praise her. These hands, seemingly transparent and insignificant against her background, may symbolize her perception of those around her as something secondary. Her own hands, raised upwards, are associated with celebration and the joy of success.

4. High-heeled shoes depicted on the card symbolize stability of social status, and a thick heel reflects willpower and self-confidence. This person is the chosen one of fate, the favorite of Fortune.

Total value

A person has gained the upper hand in a competition symbolized by the Five of Wands. This card means a favorable and triumphant period in the life of a person, this is the era when he reached the top, overcoming all the obstacles associated with the Five of Wands. And now he is celebrating his victory, while the crowd around him welcomes him with applause, support and admiration.

A person has the opportunity to demonstrate his achievements for universal praise, loudly declare his triumph, the difficult path that has been traveled to reach the current position. He skillfully draws attention to his person and influences public opinion. This person is a real leader, he enjoys popularity and knows how to manage the attention of the public. This card can also signal some bright and significant event.

As for the spotlights illuminating the stage, a competent and professional approach is required, which includes not only adequate placement of lighting devices, but also selection of appropriate equipment such as spotlights, spotlights and soffits and so on. This indicates a detailed and professional preparation for some significant event. It can be preparation for an exam, for a celebration, for the start of a new project.

Stage lighting is key to creating a visual image of an event or person. This image should highlight and emphasize everything that is happening on stage in the best possible light. It follows that the representation of a person or event may not be entirely true, but rather artificially constructed and presented in the best possible light. The right light creates the right mood and atmosphere in the audience. Also, the light is set up in such a way that it hides shadows, which hints that some negative aspects may be hidden. This is especially true if the card falls in a negative position.

The card reflects arrogant self-esteem, the image of a conqueror, a person who seeks popularity and wants to stand out among others. It shows a person who cannot exist without support and communication with others.

The card also symbolizes an energetic rise and connection with the Higher Powers, which is emphasized by the light coming from above and illuminating the hero. The laurel wreath is associated not only with healing properties, but also with cleansing from mental illnesses. Laurel leaves were used for ritual purification, such as Apollo, who purified himself with them after killing Python. This symbolizes purification from negativity and purity of human energy.

It was believed that the rustling of laurel trees could carry divine messages or predictions of the future. Laurel became a symbol not only of special magical power, but also of clairvoyance and prophecy. Laurel branches and garlands were used in rituals, for example, they were thrown into the fire during sacrifices, which gave the action a special solemnity. This may mean that a person has developed psychic abilities and magical potential. The card may also indicate the need to sacrifice to the gods or the person's connection with such deities as Apollo, Daphne, the goddess Nika, Victoria or Fortuna.

Relationship

The partner or couple shows a love of attention and a desire to be at the epicenter of things. People in this relationship prefer to play a key role, they enjoy compliments and praise. Their external perception is extremely important to them, as well as their partner's appearance. They strive to make their couple visible and gain approval from others, they like to show off their successes. In such relationships, one partner often elevates the other, increasing their self-esteem through the attention and approval of their other half.

A laurel wreath in the context of a relationship can tell us a lot, as it is related to the myth of Apollo and Daphne. In Greek myth, Apollo, the god of light and male beauty, mocked Eros, the god of love, and his arrows. In response, Eros decided to take revenge by wounding Apollo with a love-inducing arrow and Daphne with a disgust-inducing arrow. This may symbolize a situation where one partner has deep feelings for the other, while the other may not feel reciprocated, even disgusted.

According to the myths of ancient Greece, to protect the nymph Daphne, who had taken a vow of virginity, from Apollo's persecution, the gods turned her into a laurel tree. This tree became sacred to Apollo, and he began to wear a wreath of its leaves. This could mean that in a relationship, one partner idealizes the other, perhaps even to the point of obsession, keeping things associated with the partner as precious heirlooms.

The transformation of Daphne into a laurel tree and its inclusion in the symbolism of Apollo, losing its independence and becoming an attribute of the god, may indicate that in a relationship one person may use the other to advance his career or to increase his status. Such a person may perceive his partner as an accessory that emphasizes his importance, without truly valuing him, but at the same time expecting admiration and worship from him.

A laurel wreath associated with Apollo can also indicate that a person has many love affairs and is prone to frequent romantic adventures.

Mini-skirt on the card can symbolize the partner's unwillingness to submit to control, emphasizing his desire for freedom and independence. No one can tell such a person who to be with or how to spend their time. The stage lights illuminating the couple can mean that all aspects of their relationship become a subject of discussion among other people, which can lead to the couple's private life becoming public.

Work and finance

This person achieves a successful career, recognition from clients and colleagues. He manages to make profitable deals and successfully invest funds. He is a person with ambition, who leads in his field of activity. His financial situation can be extremely stable and he is able to earn significant amounts of money. Nevertheless, he should be careful not to spread about his income, as many people may try to take advantage of his success.

The possibility of inspections at work can be associated with the Six of Wands card, which symbolizes success and recognition, but can also warn of the need to be prepared for scrutiny or evaluation. Spotlights and lighting making everything visible may indicate that a person's actions will be under scrutiny, and they should prepare themselves to present themselves and their work in the best possible light.

The Six of Wands conjunction with the sixth house in astrology, which relates to work and service, emphasizes that a person is likely to be a valued and respected employee whose work does not go unnoticed. He or she can expect positive feedback, rewards, and perhaps even promotions due to his or her accomplishments and diligence. Pleasant bonuses and recognition from superiors are signs of his professionalism and contribution to the common cause.

This card also indicates a person's ability to work in large teams and take prominent positions in them. His ideas and efforts are supported by others and he is fully committed to his work. This indicates that the person is heading in the right direction and his work will be rewarded with success and recognition. His self-esteem is strengthened and his successes inspire him to create even more ambitious plans in his career.

It is important for a person to have his work recognized and appreciated by others. Therefore, he attaches great importance to the quality of his work, and inattention to detail or illiteracy is not for him. He strives to do his work thoroughly and perfectly. If you have a question about whether it is worth ordering services from this person, the answer will be unequivocally positive. He not only wants to perform his work at the highest level, but also expects rave reviews and grateful words from clients.

Occupation

Artist, actor, musician, singer, clothing designer, perfumer, aromatherapist (as laurel leaves contain a huge amount of essential oils), work with stage light can speak about the profession of a light artist, producer, marketer, media worker, journalist, producer of a personal brand. It is also musicians, poets and dancers whose patron was Apollo and who were awarded laurel wreaths.

PLACES AND FACILITIES

Stage, concert, theater, disco, club, catwalk, clothing store, fitting room, dressing room, podium, model school, places for photo shoots.

Tip

Do not stop at what you have started, do not refuse support from the outside. You are worthy of success and accept it with pride in yourself and the path you have traveled. Proudly display your talents and accomplishments. Enlist the support of those around you.

Warning

Take a sober look at your capabilities. First achieve a good level in your business and then demonstrate it, so as not to be ridiculed. Look at the person's work, not just the wrapper. There can be a bubble effect here, a person may have an inflated ego, but in reality they may be nothing.

Seven of Wands

S ymbolism

1. The card shows that the girl's head is turned to the left, which symbolizes the presence of a negative experience in the past. This experience made the person become more cautious, limit his frankness and more detailed disclosure of events in his life. He now takes a more reserved approach and will not reveal his success in front of everyone. He has realized that excessive pride and boasting can lead to undesirable external obstacles.

2. The yellow, soft cushion on the card symbolizes a person who appreciates comfort and coziness. This symbol indicates that the person prefers to be in comfortable conditions, as if sitting on a soft cushion.

3. The yellow color on the card is associated with Manipura, a chakra that is located at the level of the solar plexus and is responsible for willpower, perseverance and the ability to achieve goals. The yellow cushion indicates that a person feels safe and comfortable when he or she is in a stable social position and can freely express his or her opinion and respect his or her boundaries.

4. The energy center Manipura stands out brightly on the map, which indicates the strong-willed and self-sufficient character of the person. He knows his price and is self-confident.

5. Also on the map can be seen rune Alghiz - a symbol of powerful protection. Rune emphasizes the importance of trusting your own intuition, as well as its use to establish a connection with the higher powers and get reliable protection from negative influences and stress.

6. On the card, the girl has her arms crossed in a gesture of prayer,

which indicates her faith in her own protection and trust in the universe. She has high hopes in the higher powers and feels herself under their protection.

7. The white upper garment on the card symbolizes connection with the higher powers, and the red lower garment represents connection with the earth, strength, vitality and good health. This card describes an independent person with a strong will, able to clearly set boundaries and defend his opinion. He is selective in choosing his social circle and does not allow his boundaries to be violated.

Total value

After achieving the recognition and triumph symbolized by the Six of Wands, the person decides to reduce his social circle and take time to rest. He also establishes himself in his positions, becoming stronger after the victory represented by the Six of Wands. The Seven of Wands emphasizes the importance of holding on to the results achieved. It is necessary to guard one's achievements from competitors, envious glances and other obstacles in the way.

This person is confident in his strengths and aspirations. He is persistent and strives to achieve his goals, has clearly defined values and rejects external opinions and influences. He is able to express his desires, feelings and emotions, to be firm and responsible for his life. This person strives for self-realization and creation, has organizational skills and knows how to deal with his emotions.

Relationship

One of the partners has adopted a stance of unapproachability, withdrawing from his companion. There is tension and resentment in the relationship. There is a lack of mutual understanding in the couple, which may indicate a period of conflict or time after the conflict, when both partners have not yet forgiven each other and retain resentment. Communication is reluctant and only by necessity. The relationship has cooled down and the partners have stopped taking each other's interests into account.

This can also indicate that one of the partners has a stronger will and begins to dominate the other. In some cases, the partners may complement each other: one makes decisions for both, and the other agrees.

The card may symbolize protection of the relationship from interference of outsiders. The partners distance themselves from those who might disturb their harmony, and do not allow outsiders into their relationship, limiting the circle of communication and spending time exclusively together. This may indicate jealous and possessive behavior in the couple.

One of the partners may restrict the other's freedom, control his social contacts, hold back development, not support ideas and projects, and even show jealousy towards them. Instead of direct criticism, he or she may completely ignore the partner's talents and skills, showing by his or her behavior that they don't matter. This behavior can be caused by various reasons, but often it is due to feelings of inferiority and jealousy of the partner's successes and hobbies.

Such a person may be excessively resentful, arranging long periods of silence to punish the partner, who may not even understand the reason for the offense and does not receive explanations during such periods. The card may also reflect competition for the partner's attention, where someone is trying to invade the relationship and one partner is trying to protect it from outside interference. According to this card, a person may hide their partner from others, not telling friends and family about them. The card may also symbolize pregnancy as strengthening the bond. One partner may be too intrusive, leaving no personal space for the other. The other partner gets tired of the constant attention and interference, causing a desire for privacy and detachment.

Work and finance

According to this card, the person may reject job offers, preferring to relax or focus on his own project, seeking to work independently. He may avoid collaborating with others, wanting the entire project and all its results, including financial gain and recognition, to belong to him alone. The card may also symbolize defending one's project or thesis, and protecting one's reputation from external attacks.

This card may indicate that a person has taken a break from work, gone on vacation or simply decided to rest. If a person works in a team, the card may predict his refusal to fulfill his duties, which may lead to conflicts with colleagues.

The card can also reflect the achievement of a certain social status or occupation of a high position, which indicates reaching a new level in the career. It may represent a successful person who is diligent about his success and financial well-being, actively protecting his savings. The person clearly understands his desires and strives to realize them, while knowing how to find time to rest and enjoy the fruits of his labor. This is a person of action and achievement, a leader, striving for a high position in society, career growth and financial prosperity, usually desiring power and satisfaction of his needs.

Often this card can mean that a person is immersed in work, has isolated himself from others, turned off his phone and disappeared from sight so that nothing will disturb him until the task is completed. The card can also advise to create a financial "safety cushion" for the future.

Occupation

A yoga teacher, a security guard, could point to the military.

PLACES AND FACILITIES

Yoga centers, retreat locations, customs, places where they check identities, luggage, confined spaces.

Tip

Focus on one significant project, limiting your contacts and removing unnecessary tasks from your sight. Don't let distractions get in your way and get serious about strengthening your position in your chosen status or direction. Overcome the temptations that may arise on your path to your goal.

Warning

It's time to overcome the barriers that prevent you from being close to an important person or a cause dear to your heart. This is not the time to take offense and create barriers to mutual understanding. It's also important not to get bogged down in a task that doesn't bring results. It may be worth distracting yourself and switching to something else to look at the situation from a new angle and regain your strength.

Eight of Wands

S ymbolism

1. All wands on the card point to one point, indicating that all desires and opportunities are concentrated on one goal. Sometimes this card can indicate the presence of obstacles or problems that may make it difficult to achieve the goal.

Total value

After strengthening its position in the Seven of Wands, the individual begins to enter more actively into the rhythm of life and seeks to achieve its ambitions. This card draws the image of a restless person who is constantly rushing somewhere and is characterized by hustle and bustle. He can simultaneously participate in several projects, perform many tasks and take on various obligations.

The individual is characterized by an extremely busy daily routine, which can be planned in detail literally by the minute. He lives in an accelerated time mode, performing all tasks twice as fast as usual. It is like an endless stream of events, which he himself initiates, and then tries to manage this kaleidoscope-like whirlwind, trying not to miss a single detail.

Such a person may be thirsty for new impressions, seeking to fill his life with a variety of activities in a rich and energetic way. He is interested in trying everything in a row, experiencing the maximum of possibilities. However, in this desire, he may not go deep into the essence of things, remaining on the surface, quickly jumping from one thing to another and not internalizing the essence of what is happening.

This person may be excessively talkative and have a sharp manner in his movements, sometimes showing a temper comparable to the instantaneous flashing of a match. He may burst into anger or enthusiasm in an instant and plunge headlong into a new endeavor. However, his anger is as quick to pass as it is to arise. He doesn't tend to harbor resentments or feelings, preferring to express his emotions openly. He is direct and open, which can sometimes seem to others too assertive and abrupt in communication.

Such a person is really hard to keep up with. He shows incredible initiative and enthusiasm. Wherever he is invited, he will find time to inform all acquaintances and come in advance. He does not like to wait, and during the wait will certainly find an additional occupation, as he is constantly looking for something to do. He is characterized by hyperactivity and strong purposefulness, shows great interest and curiosity, having a wide range of hobbies.

It can also reflect a person focused solely on one goal, not paying attention to the surrounding. Interpretation may vary depending on the neighboring cards in the layout.

The Eight of Wands warns of situations that require immediate intervention and quick reaction. There is not much time to solve the problem, just a day or two, otherwise serious consequences will follow. The card also indicates that in the near future will happen something unexpected and abrupt, which a person should think about and take action, relying on other cards in the layout or aspects of events. It can be an event like a thunderbolt from a clear sky, something unexpected, abrupt and uncontrollable, which is already inherent in the fate of man and carried to him.

However, as far as traveling and moving is concerned, this card portends a quick, easy and prosperous resolution of the situation. It symbolizes lightness, speed and impetuosity in these aspects of life.

Relationship

If it is the beginning of a relationship, such a person may tempt his partner to make very quick decisions. For example, he may ask questions like "Are you going to be with me or not? Decide quickly, I expect an answer tomorrow" or "Are you ready to go to another country with me? "I'll have an answer in an hour." And this can happen after only a week of acquaintance. Also, such a person can quickly offer to move to a more serious relationship, even on the second day after acquaintance to offer the partner to go to the registry office. As for sex, here you should not expect a long wait.

In such a relationship there is usually passion, intense emotions and the fire of passion. Partners are constantly on the move, often traveling, participating in parties and events. This card indicates deep and passionate feelings for the partner, the fact that the person is focused exclusively on his partner and does not notice others. He is always striving for him.

This card symbolizes constant communication and connection between partners. If you want to know if a certain person will write to you, the probability is very high. However, it can also indicate that a person can have many partners, a lot of communication with other people. Lots of calls, meetings, correspondence. This card can mean that the person is windy and wants to try different options. He can go from one partner to another without getting too attached. However, even here it is important to take into account the other cards in the layout for a more accurate interpretation.

Work and finance

This person may have many ideas and projects, and his workday is packed with a variety of tasks. He has a busy schedule and is highly reactive at work, which makes him highly explosive. It is best not to distract him from the tasks he is focusing on, because if he is interrupted, he may react too violently, like a powerful machine that has lost control.

This card reflects a rush at work, where many projects are concentrated at one time. It can also indicate high turnover in a workplace where employees change frequently. This type of work requires the ability to multitask and react to events. The card may also advise narrow specialization in work.

It speaks of urgency and the need to react quickly in a situation. It also emphasizes quick work results and instant rewards. Sometimes she advises focusing on a single project and narrow specialization.

This period is characterized by rapid dynamics, activity and quick action. There may be sudden advancement. It may also indicate synchronized action or a joint effort that produces excellent results in a short period of time.

In the financial sphere the card promises success, new sources of income, inflow of investments and successful interaction with banks. It can also be associated with obtaining a favorable loan or cash bonus.

Occupation

Business related to innovation, work in trains, planes, any means of transportation, as well as a person can invest in cryptocurrencies and constantly monitor the market.

PLACES AND FACILITIES

Railroad stations, airplanes, airports, cars, computers, telephones.

Tip

Quickly activate yourself, wake up and don't waste energy on idleness. Switch to something new, avoiding monotony, go on vacation. The desired results will be achieved only through prompt and decisive action. Another tip - be alert and receptive, turn to external influences. Unexpectedly appeared important information can be decisive, do not miss it.

Warning

Avoid excessive forward acceleration. Do not rush, as this can lead to mistakes. Take into account different possible developments, do not freeze on one strategy.

Nine of Wands

S ymbolism

1. The fence symbolizes that the person has accumulated enough life experience to be more discerning in his contacts. Now he is not in a hurry to let new people into his life, preferring first to thoroughly investigate their intentions before allowing them to cross the threshold of his personal space.

Total value

This arcana describes the moments when unexpected difficulties appear on the way. Take, for example, a situation when a person is planning a trip abroad, but encounters problems with documentary checks, and as a result he is denied boarding the flight. Or let's imagine that a person has an online store on a social networking platform and their account is suddenly blocked, thus interrupting access to business management. This card is a symbol of the need to prepare carefully for possible obstacles, to avoid situations where you find yourself powerless and unable to act.

The card also warns of the need for restraint and prudence in business, relationships or any other aspect of life. It warns that there comes a time when it is important to protect your own, not to open up to everyone you meet, to be cautious and carefully observe what is going on around you. During these periods you should behave with the utmost caution and be wary.

The Nine of Wands can symbolize a person prone to mistrust and suspiciousness, who does not trust others, sometimes even loved ones. Such a person may demonstrate arrogance and arrogance, treating others with disdain.

This card may reflect a person who has reached a new level in life, who is trying hard not to return to his former state, despising those who remind him of the past without compassion, with open condemnation. It can also represent someone who has completely renounced his past life and acquaintances, consciously seeking change.

A person with these characteristics sets clear personal boundaries. He will not be overly courteous to those who, in his opinion, violate his personal space. Nevertheless, he may be inclined to interfere in other people's affairs, shining his light all around, but he will not allow anyone to invade his territory.

Relationship

The Nine of Wands in the context of a relationship can illustrate a protective and distrustful state of one or both partners. This can manifest itself in the creation of an emotional barrier, with people building a wall between themselves, not allowing each other to get too close. There can be alienation and an unwillingness to share personal space in such relationships, whether it be a home, social circle, or personal thoughts and feelings.

Under the influence of this arcana, one of the partners may show contempt, be secretive and conduct various checks in an effort to retain control of the relationship. This can manifest itself in jealousy, an urge to check personal messages, calls, social media accounts and so on. As a result of this behavior, the relationship becomes stuffy and restrictive, with partners isolating themselves from the world around them and limiting each other's freedom.

Manipulative behavior can also be characteristic of a relationship under the sign of the Nine of Wands, where one partner tries to humiliate the other or make them feel insignificant and dependent. This may be part of an attempt to keep the partner in control and prevent them from leaving.

At the same time, the Nine of Wands may reflect a fear of repeating past mistakes. This can manifest itself in the fact that a person isolates himself, refuses new acquaintances and relationships, because he is afraid of experiencing pain and disappointment again. If a person has returned to a partner after a breakup, this card may represent his fear and uncertainty about the reliability and sincerity of the renewed relationship.

In any case, the Nine of Wands in the context of relationships points to the need to pay attention to how we set boundaries, to our attitude toward issues of trust and interaction, and to our ability to be open and honest with partners while maintaining our own space and individuality.

Work and finance

Work and projects may need to be checked, mistakes may occur, and the card recommends revising one's labors. In general, it indicates the need for inspections, such as tax and health inspections, as well as evaluating the quality of your work social media account. This card also hints at the need for re-training, exams, various certifications and professional development.

The card emphasizes that a person should be vigilant about his position at work. For example, if a serious competitor appears in his field, one should actively gather information about him, identify his weaknesses. The same applies to the arrival of a new employee who may cause dissatisfaction. In this case, you can ignore him, behave defiantly and even complain to your superiors.

As far as finances are concerned, the card recommends restraint in spending and spending with caution. It is important at this time to save the budget and avoid excessive spending. The card advises to save money, create a financial reserve fund, as is done in the Seven of Wands card.

You should be careful about your financial resources. Also, one should keep income matters confidential to others and not grant loans in the near future. One may have internal barriers about earning money, such as the belief that "there is no suitable job" or "I am above such a job". This can lead to inactivity and aversion to work for a long time.

The card also indicates an internal barrier related to attitudes towards money. Some may believe that money is dishonest and dirty, and they are not willing to chase after it. As a result, they may remain poor but proud. Another barrier may be the fear of losing money, investing in the wrong projects or being lured out by scammers or relatives. They may have negative experiences of losing large sums of money in the past, making them cautious in financial transactions.

Occupation

Security guard, security, inspections, sanitary stations, customs officers and people working in government offices, where they usually look down on the person, tax and so on.

PLACES AND FACILITIES

Borders, customs, x-ray rooms, doors, fences.

Tip

Maintaining your own positions and principles in the face of obstacles is of paramount importance. It is advisable to repeatedly double-check your work and make sure there are no mistakes to prevent possible failure in the future. It is important to be vigilant and not allow those who could cause harm to approach. It is necessary to show determination and courage in defense of one's own views and personal boundaries.

Warning

On the other hand, you should not isolate yourself from the outside world and potential opportunities. You should not shy away from new perspectives, hold yourself and others back because of your own prejudices and perceptions of the world. There is a risk of getting stuck in one place due to fear of failure and distrust of others.

Ten of Wands

Symbolism

1. For animals, the bell serves as a signal to keep them from getting lost. It is a bridge to the idea that one should pay attention to the advice and guidance of experienced persons so as not to get lost in a world of endless obligations. The bell here represents calls and messages, and it applies to many different areas, not just work. In the work realm, it can also suggest that making noise around you helps you stay in the spotlight so that as many people as possible become aware of you and your work.

2. The white skirt fluttering in the wind symbolizes the human desire for freedom and ease. It blows in the same direction as the person, emphasizing that freedom awaits ahead, but achieving it requires effort, will, and fulfillment of responsibilities.

3. Three burning wands, acting as signposts of the path, indicate that a person is moving in the right direction and is not going to lose his way. The flame of the wands speaks of his energy and passion, sufficient to achieve the goal.

Total value

The individual has left the comfort zone indicated by the Nine of Wands and set out on a long journey, taking with him accumulated knowledge, extensive experience and a sense of duty. The card image shows a girl dragging heavy valises and bags behind her, having already walked a considerable distance, and contemplating the possibility of leaving them behind, as physical exhaustion has reached its limit and painful sensations have engulfed her entire body.

At a crucial moment, a marvelous yak appears on the scene to take the weight of her baggage and remind her of the importance of asking for support when it is needed. This turn of events symbolizes in essence the cards that one should not be overwhelmed by all the difficulties alone, but rather share the load and ask for help.

This card usually reflects a period in one's life when there is work to be done that consumes a tremendous amount of energy. The person on whom the card falls lacks the energy to complete what has been started, and if there is no intrinsic motivation, it is probably the tasks imposed by obligations or a sense of position, but in any case there is a huge amount of work to be done in a limited time frame. These are times of total exhaustion, when things to do and obligations exceed all possible limits.

The map shows a girl facing the last obstacle - the mountain she has to overcome, and she is so weary that she is ready to give up the weight of her burdens. But it is in the most difficult hour that a yak appears, willing to support her without compensation. In general, this card often predicts tedious moves and trips, when, for example, you intend to take with you a lot of suitcases, trying to show ingenuity to transport them, your plane is delayed, then you are late for the bus, and the next one has to wait for an incredibly long time, then you have to make a change, and in the final of this route you fall from fatigue.

Also the card often implies that a person decides to realize all his ideas and endeavors at once, but it would be better for him to stop and carefully consider which actions to take first, and which can wait, because he is overloaded and there is no guarantee that performing several tasks at once will lead to a high-quality result.

The card can signal professional burnout, when a person is so overloaded with work that he loses the meaning of his efforts and more often catches himself thinking about giving up everything.

The card describes a person who is used to taking on a lot of responsibilities and work, and is always willing to do things for others. She may stay after hours to help someone or do work for others. This is a hyper-responsible person who can take on the entire family load in one fell swoop and provide support to all family members. This person finds it difficult to say no and say no, believing that it is her duty and purpose to be a hard worker and help those in need, regardless of gender.

However, this card can also indicate a personality who is not eager to carry the whole load by herself and is always looking for connections and contacts, people who could help. She actively works herself, may even lead the process, but gladly accepts help from others and never refuses it.

Relationship

We are going through a difficult phase in the relationship, when its weight is felt more and more every day, and it becomes more and more unbearable to stay in it. This is a test for both partners, which can either strengthen their union or lead to its ultimate destruction. There are relationships where one partner is allowed to dominate, exploiting the other in any way possible, while the other enthusiastically provides help, deep down hoping for genuine feelings of his companion. But this partner is only interested in material benefits: money, gifts, contacts or other support he or she can get.

This card symbolizes a person who can be relied on in difficult times, who will not leave you when you find yourself in a difficult situation. It promises to help your partner get out of difficulties and represents a time when both have to make excessive efforts to achieve a common goal. This may involve having to make a joint move, purchase a home, pay off a mortgage, or start your own business - situations that require a significant investment of effort from both parties.

The card can also reflect a difficult, debilitating relationship, an imminent breakup or departure that leaves behind deep wounds of the soul. It depicts moments when partners are forced to part with a heavy heart, keeping love for each other, but circumstances do not allow them to stay together, leading to an inevitable separation.

Finally, this card shows a relationship that resembles the situation with a suitcase without a handle - it is hard to carry, but it is a pity to throw away. One of the partners continues to pull the relationship with the partner, who has long been uninspiring and does not cause the former feelings, but he can not afford to leave, feeling pity for the partner and not wanting to leave him.

Work and finance

This card symbolizes a period when a person or company has a high influx of clients, an abundance of work and a variety of orders. His daily schedule is densely packed with meetings and deadlines, so that there is little time for respite, and there is a risk of forgetting something or missing something important because of the huge number of obligations. Although things are moving up the ladder of success, a lot of effort is needed and the path to the top seems particularly difficult and draining. In such a situation, a person should consider hiring an assistant to relieve themselves by delegating some of the tasks to someone else's shoulders.

In the context of this card, a person may experience a distinct lack of time for rest, or he may be deprived of the opportunity to relax and recuperate at all. He has an acute imbalance between work and rest, which leads to complete exhaustion. An excessive burden is placed on his shoulders. The card also reflects a scenario where a person sets an ambitious financial goal for the year and starts a marathon of tireless work, in which he immerses himself day and night, never stopping until he achieves the desired result.

A person may refuse weekends, regularly work overtime, and not take vacations for many years. Such a lifestyle is indicative of true workaholism, when a person literally falls off his feet from fatigue, but still continues to work tirelessly without ceasing his activities.

The card can also signal the need to analyze whether a person has not become a victim of someone else's irresponsibility, whether colleagues do not shift their responsibilities to him, whether he does not do the work for others without any reason. After all, it happens that in the team some employees regularly ask for help, resorting even to manipulation on feelings, and as a result a person, in order to help, agrees to take on an additional load.

Occupation

Can show movers, construction workers, people who work hard physically, travelers, pilgrims, a person who just works hard, has a responsible position, carries a lot of projects.

PLACES AND FACILITIES

Mountainous terrain, train stations, airports, farms, construction sites.

Tip

In order to develop stamina and endurance and to successfully complete tasks, it is important to prioritize your priorities. You should not rush ahead and take on too many responsibilities. It is best to unload yourself and decide how you can make your life more comfortable and efficient by realizing what you can delegate to others. You should not feel shy about asking for help and accepting support from others.

Warning

It is important to realize that asking for and accepting help does not mean shifting your responsibility to others. On the contrary, it is a healthy way to manage your resources and effectively achieve your goals. Striving to always carry the entire load can lead to exhaustion and an inability to complete important tasks. Unchecked priorities can also pose a risk of burnout. In addition, it pays to be cautious when traveling to avoid unforeseen difficulties.

Page of Wands

Symbolism

1. The Pagus of Wands has many salamanders on his pants, symbolizing his lack of restlessness and constant movement. This card also contains a lot of yellow color, which reflects his vigor, energy, joy and desire for success. The color yellow represents hope for the best and mobility.

2. The red laces and sleeves on Paj's sneakers emphasize his activity and willingness to move spontaneously. He is always ready to step forward and start something new, which is reflected in his lightness and mobility. The red sleeves indicate his energetic activity and lively work.

Total value

The Page of Wands usually symbolizes a person with burning ambitions, who may not yet have the experience to realize them. After experiencing the hardships of the Tens of Wands, he feels light and playful, dancing on the wave of life and enjoying the moment.

The Page of Wands combines two elements - fire (represented by wands) and earth (wands). It is the beginning, sprouting from the earth through the active and persistent actions of the Page of Wands. It is youth and spark, it is chance and exciting news that motivate to action.

The Page of Wands is attentive to what is happening and actively participates in the process. This is a situation that inspires movement and creativity. For example, before a holiday concert where a stage needs to be decorated, this card reflects anticipation and fascination with the action of improving and beautifying.

It is a kind of turmoil where uncomplicated tasks are performed, but with great enthusiasm. The Page of Wands is quickly ignited by ideas and is ready to try something new. For example, he may start practicing some section, but after seeing an interesting style of dance, he will instantly become infatuated with it. He can either stay in the old section or throw it away, but in any case, he is fully immersed in his new hobby, exploring it from all sides and improving his skills.

The Page of Wands is driven by pure and sincere urges to grow and mature. For example, he may begin taking guitar lessons and practicing diligently, more passionate about the process than the outcome. This is a time when experience is gained and new skills are acquired.

The Page of Wands craves attention, compliments and admiring glances. He is able to work for the public and do everything possible to attract attention, whether it is a one-actor theater or a demonstration of his abilities. His egotism and self-love can sometimes become very expressive traits of his character.

The Page of Wands represents an agile, young, energetic and athletic person. He can sometimes be obsessive, seeking to draw attention to himself, and even meddle in the affairs of others in order to stand out. He is constantly imaginative and inspired, but he often lacks the practicality and perseverance to bring his ideas to life.

Relationship

The Page of Wands indicates a superficial and frivolous relationship. Such relationships lack seriousness and maturity. Since the Wand symbolizes the fire of the earth, namely the fire of passion combined with the earth of the body, it can mean that this relationship is based solely on physical attraction and sex.

Such relationships are characterized by a quick ignition of passion and a quick fading. A person tends to change partners frequently to try something new. There is no question of permanence, but rather infatuation, flirtation and sex, which can arise and disappear as quickly as a candle flame. There is no desire for interaction and exchange coming from both parties in this relationship. The Page of Wands tosses the wand, makes a circle and comes back to himself, demonstrating that all of his actions are aimed at satisfying his own desires rather than creating a relationship.

Such a person may need a partner only in a moment of good mood. He may not be ready to support and share the worries and problems of his partner, and he can treat it all with lightness and humor. The Staff of Wands is a person who lives in the moment, today he is in love with one, tomorrow with another. He may also be infatuated with a famous person in some circle and is ready to compete for her attention, just to emphasize his victory. The Page of Wands is impulsive and fiery, he rarely thinks about the consequences of his actions.

In this deck, the circle represented by the Page of Wands card plays an important role. It often indicates that a relationship can end and start again, like a rotation in a circle. The card can also mean that the couple decides to reconcile and rebuild the relationship to rekindle the romance and give it another chance.

Work and finance

The Page of Wands usually heralds new prospects in the workplace, the opportunity to climb a new rung on the career ladder and overcome financial limitations. This card can symbolize the beginning of an exciting project, successful deals, profitable investments and money movement. A time when it is important to develop your skills, you may need training, professional development or an apprenticeship.

The Page of Wands may also indicate the beginning of career development, where a person still lacks experience, but has great ambitions to grow professionally. This card advises you to look at your own work from a new, more objective point of view. It symbolizes new and fresh ideas, as well as excellent prospects in the working sphere. The Page of Wands may predict the arrival of some important career-related news or the possibility of additional income.

The person depicted in the Page of Wands card seeks to express himself and show his abilities through work. This card does not promise great wealth; rather, it indicates that the money earned can be quickly spent. The many shades of yellow in the card indicate the importance of communicating with others and learning from others' experiences.

In addition, a circle on a map is often associated with finalizing deals, settlements, and a return to previous responsibilities and projects. It can also mean a return to a standardized work schedule and familiar working methods, as well as a repetition of similar work tasks.

Occupation

Fitness trainer, athletic trainer, dancer, gymnast, fire show person, juggler, entertainer, assistant, manager.

PLACES AND FACILITIES

Club, disco, festival, performance venue, exercise room, massage room, sauna, sandy LOCATIONS AND OBJECTS.

Tip

Show curiosity, actively engage in the question. Hone a skill. Take things easier and look at the world more positively. Invest time, energy and money in yourself. To try to repeat something, give something a chance and give it a chance. Close debts and tails.

Warning

One should not take the situation too lightly. You should also avoid being overly naive in this matter. Evaluate where you are going in circles, start acting differently and look for an alternative path. Otherwise, the situation may suck you in and you will feel like a squirrel in a wheel. You need to change your tactics, because doing the same things will not get you different results.

Knight of Wands

Symbolism

1. In addition, this card can indicate a relationship where one partner sets the pace and rhythm of the relationship (drum), puts forward new ideas and proposals, plays a leading role, and the other partner is ready to follow his leadership and adjust to it, as if dancing to the music of the first.

2. It can also symbolize a relationship where one partner is more risk-taking and impulsive (corresponding to the Knight of Wands) and the other more reasonable and rational (corresponding to the Black Horse). They may come together with common goals and interests to move forward together.

Total value

After a constant process of inspiration and training in the Page of Wands, the Knight of Wands flies in at the speed of light to meet his goal. The Knight of Wands carries two elements: fire and air. Air is constantly fanning the fire, spraying it in different directions, which emphasizes the swiftness of the Knight of Wands.

This card shows events that burst sharply into life like a fiery hurricane. This is a period that requires quick and urgent action to avoid missing opportunities. It is the drive needed to avoid stagnation and dead center. Perhaps it is a relocation, a decision to change one's residence, when one decides to leave, packing one's suitcases and leaving early in the morning without giving warning to anyone.

This card shows a person who is completely absorbed in the process of achieving it, seeking to accelerate his path to success. He can set a lot of ambitious goals and loudly declare them. Sometimes he may have a negative opinion of people who do not follow his example. The Knight of Wands can quickly switch between different areas of life, removing himself from social media and severing ties with others to start a new chapter. This person is always moving forward, full of enthusiasm, energy and competition, able to give movement even to situations that seem stalled.

He is ready to invest a lot of resources, including strength and money, for the sake of achieving his goal, which for him is above all. Knight of Wands believes in the permanence of his goal and always goes forward. In many of his lives he is just a wanderer, a bright spark, a comet that left a trace and moved on.

He is impulsive and always in search of adventure, capable of causing adrenaline and looking for new experiences. Usually such a person prefers a motorcycle or a bicycle and does extreme stunts on them. Adrenaline and new impressions are an important part of his life. He actively participates in creative projects, has good creative abilities and musical talent. He feels the rhythm of music and time, which helps him to always have time everywhere. He can also go out in public, show off and stand out with a colorful personality.

According to the idea of the author of the deck, this Knight was heading on his horse towards his goal, but on the way he saw a beach party and decided to join it. He engaged in this unexpected adventure with fiery energy and started playing a tune on his djembe. However, he then realized that he was distracted and this made it difficult for him to reach his goal. So he got on his horse and continued toward his goal.

Relationship

The Knight of Wands symbolizes a passionate and vibrant relationship where two fires meet. This union is filled with relentless dynamics, reminiscent of an explosive cocktail. Partners show sincere temperament, their passion seems restless. They can arrange passionate meetings in unexpected places and make quarrels over trifles.

This couple is always in a hurry to get somewhere, often going on trips. However, this union is often not long-term and may end when one of the partners gets infatuated with someone else and abruptly ends the relationship. In general, this is a relationship filled with passion, strong attraction and sharp emotional displays. But they are not always deep and intimate like the relationships of the Cups suit; they are often fleeting likes and attractions, similar to Mexican passions.

This card can also indicate a person who is passionate about his or her pursuits and does not pay enough attention to his or her partner. It may describe a passionate person who is proud of his victories in love feats and always sets new goals for himself, including conquering different people. Such a person may pursue the object of his passions with persistence and determination, even in spite of rivals. Marriage may seem like slavery to him, and he is in no hurry to put on the "shackles" of this institution.

Work and finance

According to this card, money is earned with passion and pleasure, bringing the joy of labor and anticipation of joyful results. A person can immerse himself in work in order to have time to fulfill everything in time. He is very active in the workplace, working at high speed and fully dedicated to the task, striving to complete it as quickly as possible. He is full of motivation, rushing towards the desired result and not paying attention to everything else going on around him. This high pace of work can lead to the risk of burnout.

In a team, the card symbolizes a warm and dynamic atmosphere, where there is always something going on, and there is no monotony. There are always new ideas and work activity. However, it can also indicate that a person is motivated by the desire to get ahead of his colleagues or competitors in business, and this competitive motivation becomes for him an additional source of energy for work.

The Knight of Wands often feels tempted to do everything at once. He is impulsive and fervent, starting many things at once but not always completing them. His goals must be achieved quickly, because if he does something for a long time, it can cause him to burn out.

Occupation

Musician, entertainer, worker with horses, person who works with means of transportation.

PLACES AND FACILITIES

A stage, a means of transportation, places for concerts and rehearsals, parties, a beach, a stable.

Tip

Music and art can be a way to find harmony, enhance mood and morale. It is important to feel the rhythm of the world around you, to get into the flow of time and to allocate your resources effectively in this flow.

Warning

It should be remembered that there is no need to rush, it is better to do something slowly but qualitatively. There is no need to avoid difficult situations and run away to new opportunities. Do not rush to change partners, jobs or locations, but instead allow time for passions to subside and consider the situation calmly and rationally.

Queen of Wands

1. The Queen of Wands portends that inspiration will be revealed to the individual in the near future. This discovery can occur in different areas of life, such as a long-awaited moment of insight, when previously hidden aspects become clear.

2. This card also symbolizes the light of knowledge, when a bright light breaks through the darkness of ignorance, bringing new insights. This aspect is illustrated by the abundance of candles and light in the palm of the Queen of Wands. Her open right hand symbolizes a willingness to share, help and inspire others.

3. This card speaks about the generosity of a person, readiness to share and give a helping hand to those who need it. Short haircut indicates businesslike, active and determined person. Her earrings in the form of triangles pointing upwards symbolize the element of fire. She is surrounded by light and fire, which conveys her inner power, energy and strength.

4. The Queen of Wands sits on a soft chair-shaped cushion that shines and glows like a candle. This suggests that the person represented by this card feels comfortable in a bright, dynamic and colorful environment.

5. The black cat at her feet symbolizes predatory instincts. In addition, the cat as a lunar symbol and the black color of its fur are associated with the night and its mysteries. In the context of the bright lighting on the card and the light in the hand of the Queen of Wands, the cat represents enlightenment and the uncovering of secrets, as well as the possibility of gaining knowledge and unraveling previously hidden aspects.

Total value

After the hot nature of the Knight of Wands, comes the moment of wisdom, represented by the Queen of Wands. The Queen of Wands combines the two elements of fire and water, where water symbolizes wisdom, calmness, understanding and caring. This card indicates situations that require leadership qualities, the expression of ambition to the fullest and the application of creativity to problem solving.

This card represents active and mobile people, emphasizing the importance of mobility, flexibility and openness to new opportunities. The person represented by this card can be a support and protector for the more vulnerable. The Queen of Wands can be enthusiastic about giving advice and guiding people through problems, whether or not her advice is followed. In her outlook, she is always right and seeks the best for others, even if this translates into pushy recommendations. She feels important and wishes to influence those around her, which brings her satisfaction. The person represented by this card appreciates the gratitude and compliments given to her for her advice and help.

The Queen of Wands can sometimes act under the influence of emotion and make decisions quickly. Her statements can be harsh and hurtful. She is prone to selfishness and always thinks first of her comfort. This queen has high self-esteem and is narcissistic. She usually remains optimistic in all circumstances and has a hot temper. The Queen of Wands is determined and impatient, does not tolerate long waits and prefers active action. Her creative mind is bursting with ideas, which is reflected in the many candles on the card.

This queen always strives for leadership and tends to stand out bright and dressy. However, behind all this ambitious fervor can hide an empty sound, as she sometimes overestimates her achievements and abilities. She may burn with a desire to earn someone else's fame and even appropriate someone else's merits. In negative aspects of this card, the person displays arrogance and pride.

The person represented by this card is ambitious and strives for social realization. He usually has many useful contacts and can successfully accomplish tasks thanks to his connections. The Queen of Wands is ambitious for self-reliance and independence, and she has confidence and charisma. Her energy and positive attitude can inspire others, and she is often a source of optimism for those around her. She is an artistic person who seeks to be the center of attention and draw attention to herself.

Relationship

This queen does not know how to hide her emotions; she openly demonstrates her feelings for her lover, seeking to surround him with an aura of romance and passion, so that he can immerse himself in this well-being. It is important for her to share her love, and she looks for all ways to make her emotions understood and felt by her partner.

In the same way, when she is seized with the feeling of falling in love, she makes it known to everyone around her. She never tires of talking about the man who has won her interest, shares her experiences with her friends, and publicly flaunts her liking. She may show his pictures on social media, introduce him to her circle of friends. At the same time, she may also listen to her friends' opinions about the new acquaintance to get their approval or opinion about him, to find out what they think about his looks, ways of socializing, personal qualities, and so on.

For her, falling in love is always an inspiring impulse that gives wings and breaks the monotony of everyday life. This is the state when thoughts of a partner fill every minute, it is a fire that encourages positive changes in life and motivates to move forward.

The Queen of Wands strives to cause admiration and genuine surprise in her chosen one. She is not accustomed to leave something to chance, and in any circumstances seeks to show herself only from the best side, to mesmerize and inspire. In addition, she will not stand idly by, waiting for the manifestation of initiative from the partner. On the contrary, she herself will be the first to write, call and schedule meetings to demonstrate her interest and participation.

This is the queen who can build a relationship solely on physical attraction, she follows her instincts more than others. And her partner, even if he is not a person from social circles, will demonstrate the behavior of a star of the screen or modeling business - such is his self-confidence and self-esteem.

If she is in love and believes in her chosen one, she can provide support both financially and give valuable advice. However, there is a certain trap in her worldview: she believes that any person is capable of sparking an idea, discarding laziness, pessimism, apathy and childish behavior. Even the most hopeless partner she is willing to give a chance, but if he does not respond to her suggestions and does not try to improve his situation in work, housing or other aspects of life within a certain time, she will end the relationship and walk away, determined to seek new adventures, love or just spend time having fun with friends. This is not a person who will put up with dashed hopes and homesickness. Through her actions, she will come out of a state of sorrow and sadness.

Work and finance

The Queen of Wands always strives to take a leadership position, to be the center of attention, and to become the head of something. However, sometimes she prefers not to take on all the responsibilities, but to have a person around her who can take care of household and routine tasks.

She's not afraid to take on responsibility and tackle big business challenges. No matter what she does, she always finds a way to get the right people to help her move forward and build her own brand. Connections are important to her and community plays an important role in the development of her projects. She enjoys being in the community, loves being the face of the company and building her own brand.

She is creative in her work, tries to express her individuality and make her contribution. She is active and open professionally, ready to offer her ideas and adjustments. She always has her own vision and opinion and believes she can do better than anyone else.

She is always full of ideas and opportunities on how to make money, and yet she values money and is not shy about spending it, mostly on herself, to look bright and stylish, and on her entertainment.

Occupation

Creative professions, esotericism, public personality, entrepreneur, speaker, seminar presenter, leadership position, motivational coach, space decoration, designer, decorator.

PLACES AND FACILITIES

South, hot places, parties, concerts, fire shows, circus, clubs, ritual sites, women's circles.

Tip

Take advantage of your charisma, actively use all your acquaintances and business connections to achieve your goal. It is necessary to brightly and visibly demonstrate to others all your talents and professional skills. It is important to show courage and do not hesitate to make bold decisions in the current issue. The situation is under your control, and it is your initiative that determines the outcome of events.

Warning

One should remain moderate and realistic about one's own abilities and skills. It is important to avoid being pushy in offering your services or advice, especially when they may not be needed. It is important to be clear about your strengths and not overestimate them. Be careful how you express your thoughts and feelings; not everything should be the subject of other people's attention.

King of Wands

S ymbolism

1. The image of the Lion behind the king symbolizes not only the importance of connections and contacts, which can be a reliable support, but also reflects the pride, generosity, and indomitable willpower of man. Lion emphasizes situations where it is necessary to show courage and heroism, to act honorably and with dignity. This symbol also calls to reveal personal charisma and erudition, pay attention to improving self-esteem. He personifies not only generosity and power, but also indicates that, being behind the back of the king, the Lion gives dominion over himself, saying that a person is not afraid to confront even a powerful predator. In general, it is a symbol of trust, first of all in oneself, trust in one's own strength and unbreakable self-confidence.

2. The King of Wands represents a man who is full of excitement, loves the extreme and is capable of causing shivers in the knees of himself and others. The crown on top of his staff indicates a preference to lead through others, managing events with a steady and steady hand. This character tends to place himself a notch above those around him.

3. The salamander on the King of Wands symbolizes the spirit of the element of fire. It reflects bravery, courage and the ability to stand in the face of adversity and resist temptation, as the salamander is known for its coldness and ability to withstand the flame, sometimes even extinguishing it. The red color of the king's clothing emphasizes his explosive, courageous and passionate character.

4. The medallion in the shape of the fire element symbol worn

around the King's neck confirms his power over the fire element - over temper, anger, passion and other fiery attributes. These qualities can bubble up in him, but unlike the Knight of Wands, the King is able to control them.

Total value

After the wisdom of the Queen, comes the moment of power over yourself and the world around you, in the person of the King of Wands. This King represents the double fire - the endless desire for power and the expansion of his horizons. It is important to realize that the King of Wands is confident in himself, in his desires, and in the correctness of his decisions and actions.

His ability to convince others that he is right is astounding. His desires always translate into active action. The King of Wands is an individual who is clearly defined in his goals and full of confidence. He usually has many ambitions and works enthusiastically to achieve them. The King of Wands is socially active and accomplished, he is enterprising and businesslike. His reputation is secure and he himself has put a lot of effort into making it so.

He is respected in society, and his word is always weighty. Even if he is engaged in a business that seems unimportant, he is able to describe it in such a way that others are left in no doubt: this person deserves respect, and so does his business. He strongly believes that he is better and more important than others, regardless of his field of endeavor or status. His ego is large, and he prefers to display pathos and theatricality.

It is not difficult for him to step out of his comfort zone, but he usually does not get into such situations. The card indicates the establishment of strong social ties, favorable positions in society and business opportunities. It also implies that in order to successfully achieve your goals, you will have to work hard, make important decisions, take risks and act without delay.

This card heralds a period of intense activity, when you will have to make a lot of effort. A time when life is filled with impressions because of constant movement.

The King of Wands is characterized by directness and determination. He will not be silent and patient, preferring to speak directly, even if it may lead to conflict. This is the type of person who fears nothing, protecting his interests and those of his loved ones by any means necessary. Social or physical fights do not scare him. Such a person will always be a defender and fighter, ready to help and solve the problems of those he cares about. And importantly, he doesn't shun responsibility. He may be rude and too direct with loved ones, which can cause resentment due to his hot-tempered and emotional nature.

The King of Wands card may portend events related to a man who is ready to make a commitment and give his patronage. The outcome of the situation will largely depend on this man, whose image coincided with the King of Wands. Usually such a person has the power and means to solve important issues.

Relationship

In the context of feelings and relationships, the King of Wands represents ardent passion, powerful attraction and sexual instinct. For this person, sex plays an important role in relationships, and he may view relationships through the prism of physical intimacy. He is able to enter into a relationship purely for pleasure, without developing a deep emotional connection with his partner, but rather to satisfy his own interest.

This person has outstanding charisma, and his personality is able to easily attract the attention of others. His peculiarity is manifested in his independence, high self-esteem and leadership qualities. He arouses interest with his persistence and ability to stand on his own.

If the King of Wands has shown interest in someone, he is not shy about showing his feelings and starts actively courting. He always expects attention and unconditional respect for himself, and he is known for his high ego. Selfishness is one of his characteristic traits. The King of Wands represents a proud man who values and respects himself, and will never grovel or show his weaknesses. He is generous, persistent and proactive, always takes the initiative in his own hands and tries to win the favor of a woman. He is a real player and hunter.

In relationships, the King of Wands is usually romantic and passionate. He likes to create grand gestures, stand out and be better than everyone else. Competition and rivalry are his element. The King of Wands card portends an exciting relationship based on a strong attraction to each other. In such a relationship there is always an emotional high and passion.

Regardless of the length of the relationship, this card indicates that the flame of passion between the partners will not die down and they will always be interested in each other. It can also mean that the partners in the relationship are both active and have common hobbies that they are passionate about. For example, it could be a sport such as cycling or diving that they are both passionate about and share with each other.

Partners will be on the same wavelength and constantly improving in their common passion, learning and sharing emotions. This relationship is characterized by temperament, yet it is mature and mature.

Work and finance

The King of Wands card in the business sphere predicts success and a favorable period. It indicates the need for hard work, activation of one's resources and constant forward movement. To achieve success, it is important to make decisions, work creatively and actively engage in professional activities. This card characterizes a person who constantly sets new career goals and actively develops his business contacts.

Financial success depends directly on a person's strength of character and punching power. This includes the ability to find common ground with the right people, negotiate and use one's skills to achieve goals. The King of Wands is able to manage such tasks with ease, and his card strongly recommends using these qualities to achieve success in the financial sphere.

The King of Wands does not shift responsibility to others and does not wait for help. He is a true leader who achieves his goals and strives to get better every day. He always strives to expand his business and influence. He knows how to manage work processes and delegate responsibilities competently to get results and move forward.

This King has great energy and organizes his workspace and schedule to maximize his productivity. He is passionate about his work and strives to stand out, be visible and earn respect and recognition in his field. He is always looking to become a leader and constantly evolve to reach new heights in his career.

Occupation

Self-employed, athlete, freelancer, politician, blogger, show business worker, producer, firefighter, motivational coach.

PLACES AND FACILITIES

Hot countries, south, zoo, wild places, safaris, gyms, director's office.

Tip

Develop a generous attitude towards the world and people. Recognize one's own value, build self-esteem and inner confidence, do not be afraid to take risks. Go after your goals and, if necessary, even defend them. Put yourself first and strive for success in your field. Strive to be the best in everything, surpass yourself every day and constantly evolve.

Warning

It is important to learn to wait for the moment with the manifestation of initiative, not to rush things and not to run ahead of time. First, strengthen your internal principles and improve your projects, do not rush to actively expand and take new positions, as otherwise you can fail and slide downhill.

SWORDS

Ace of Swords

Symbolism

1. The symbol of the spiral is deeply connected with cosmic algorithms and the universe. The spiral is a single code of the universe, indicating that the person who has this card, in the mind born in the whole worlds. Ace of Swords represents a very intelligent and creative individual who can easily generate ideas for global projects and develop existing ones. This person is always thinking long-term, exploring the depths of problems, revealing the truth, constantly learning and training his mind, having a mathematical mindset. He is able to be inspired by his thoughts and develop a variety of scenarios in his head.

2. The Tree of Sephiroth symbolizes life and represents the matrix of the entire universe. In the context of the Ace of Swords, this symbol indicates the ability to analyze the smallest details of the situation, to find connections between all elements and effectively process complex information. Star of Chaos, on the contrary, is the opposite of the order and structure of the Tree of Sefirot. In it we see the symbol of infinity, which denotes the ability of man to understand the various aspects of the universe. Therefore, according to the Ace of Swords, a person is able to transform chaotic thoughts into a clear structure and express them in words, even in the most difficult situations.

3. Mercury symbol and mathematical formula also serve as symbols of quick and instantaneous thinking. It indicates a mathematical mindset, logical thinking and high speed of information processing.

4. The symbol of sulfur, represented by the triangle up on the cross,

257

and the symbol of salt, represented by the crossed-out circle, symbolize the beginning and the original that make up matter. This emphasizes that thought is the beginning of everything, and it is through thought that we create reality and shape the world around us.

5. A prominent ear indicates a person's high sensitivity and vigilance. He is very curious and interested in everything that happens around him. This symbol also indicates that the person is an excellent communicator and is able not only to speak, but also to listen attentively.

6. The raven, as a symbol of wisdom and a messenger of the gods, gives the person on this card the characteristics of a wise decision. He pays attention to the voice of reason, is not in a hurry to act, but, on the contrary, shows deep thoughtfulness and foresight.

7. The symbol of the ray represents the act of creation and denotes enlightenment and penetration of the light of knowledge into the darkness of ignorance. In this case, the person depicted on the card, has the ability to penetrate through the information noise and separate truth from falsehood. He is always focused on the search for truth and true knowledge, has a clear focus on a particular idea, situation or person.

8. The long neck of the character on the card symbolizes the connection between body and mind, as well as the ability to express one's thoughts and ideas in the world. It indicates that such a person is always ready to express his opinion and share his thoughts.

9. The character's closed eyes indicate that the person is primarily paying attention to their inner mind and analyzing their thoughts before paying attention to external information.

10. The earring in the nose, as a highlighted facial element, symbolizes the person's ability to detect the right information and highlight the right thoughts from the vast information flow.

Total value

Ace of Swords represents a person who makes decisions based on logic and analysis. He has high energy, serious character and self-confidence. Such a person is able to remain cool-blooded in difficult situations and quickly find solutions. His straightforwardness and rigidity can sometimes manifest itself, but he is always principled and ready to fight for his beliefs.

The Ace of Swords symbolizes clarity and determination, representing the beginning of action, taking a firm and confident path. Sometimes it indicates conflicts and verbal disputes. This card represents strength of will and intelligence, requiring full understanding of the situation and transparency in thought without unnecessary embellishments.

The Ace of Swords also implies the need to show fortitude and fight against oneself, enemies or illusions. It calls for control over one's thoughts and emotions, as well as clear and decisive actions. This card teaches you to say "no" and clearly define your personal boundaries, not allowing them to be violated. The Ace of Swords represents the beginning of concrete actions and the triumph of one's own strength, whether it is the victory over bad habits or overcoming conflict.

The Ace of Swords emphasizes the importance of thoughts, from which all actions and results originate. It emphasizes that correct and competent thoughts shape our lives, and that changing thoughts can lead to a change of life. The spiral, as a symbol of development and change, indicates movement towards enlightenment and wisdom.

Relationship

The Ace of Swords symbolizes a heated and frank discussion of unresolved issues in the couple. This is a time of revealing grievances and bringing clarity and truth to the relationship. This is often accompanied by conflicts and sharp angles that make the relationship uncomfortable.

According to this card, one of the partners may carry out tests and provocations to test the other. Such a person is prone to overthinking and coming up with different scenarios. In a relationship, couples set strict boundaries and prohibitions, such as not seeing friends or communicating with someone on the Internet.

Fibonacci spirals indicate the desire for perfection. One of the partners may constantly pressure the other, demanding improvements in appearance or other qualities. There may be no room for emotion in such a couple, and people may be together because of ideal physical parameters or education. However, they are not necessarily attached to each other, and may break up if someone else "perfect" comes along."

By feelings the card indicates the lack of deep emotions and passion. The person may feel interest and desire to win the partner, but the relationship may be characterized by rigidity and lack of true feelings. It may also mean that forgiving a partner for mistakes or shortcomings is a problem, and the person constantly revisits these negative moments. The mention of abortion may be one of the aspects that the Ace of Swords card can imply, as can the other sword cards, but this does not always necessarily make sense.

Work and finance

The Ace of Swords in matters of work indicates the need to define a goal and focus on it. It implies excellent career prospects, possible career advancement or plans for advancement. The person is totally immersed in the idea of advancement in career and is willing to work hard, even day and night, to overcome financial barriers and advance in work. He can be tough and determined against those who try to distract him from his work. It is also a symbol of financial growth and financial empowerment.

The person depicted on the map does not stop at what has been achieved, but always strives for development and expansion, makes plans for greater achievements. For example, if he has a travel agency in one city, he can think about expanding the network to several cities, and then about entering the world market. This person is climbing the career ladder that he creates himself.

In addition, the Ace of Swords card recommends taking additional training, upgrading your skills and replenishing your knowledge for a successful career. It is important to build your work strategically, following a clear plan, and not just perform tasks on inspiration. This requires a clear and confident view of work, taking into account numbers, facts and deadlines.

Also the Ace of Swords implies working with information, such as online seminars, meetings and sharing information. It is a way of financial empowerment and also involves using creativity and developing mental skills to achieve greater results.

Occupation

Translator, diplomat, linguist, notary, casino worker, hypnotist.

PLACES AND FACILITIES

Fields, sandy places, deserts, roads, crossroads, places of influence of scales: courts, notary offices. Places where people's consciousness is stupefied: sects, slot machines, casinos.

Tip

Appreciate time, realize it as the most valuable resource that cannot be returned. Instead of delaying decisions and procrastinating, it is better to take small but regular steps. This way, time will be filled with lessons learned rather than passing in emptiness and indecision. Learn to make decisions, get rid of the toxic environment, choose your path and start moving forward with more confidence.

Warning

Do not stay still, do not postpone things and do not overthink. It is important to address situations with action and dare to take the first step. Avoid getting bogged down in your own thinking and start moving forward with small steps. Instead of trying to find a solution only in your mind, it is better to try and act, for experience and practice will always shed light on a situation. Trust your own intuition and do not always listen to the advice of others.

Two of Swords

1. In this card a person is facing uncertainty, his eyes are closed, which symbolizes the need to pay attention to his inner world, listen to the voice of the soul and achieve inner balance, as indicated by the sign of Libra on the hand of the girl. Only after achieving inner balance, you can make decisions calmly, without panic and fuss. On the hand of a man is also depicted the sign of Libra, which indicates his desire to maintain balance in two aspects of life, but the map shows that it is difficult for him, and he does not know how to do it correctly.

2. This card reflects the situation when a person has lost his way, does not know which path to choose, and is not oriented in the current situation. It also indicates that his plans have no reliable basis and may remain only empty fantasies. The person looks indecisive and uncertain. He will take a long time to think over his every move and discuss them with other people. This constant slow decision making leads to missed opportunities and time slipping through his fingers.

3. Two of Swords symbolizes the inability to make decisions and the fear of making a mistake. It is like a fork in the road to the goal, and it is important that this fork did not turn into a dead end and a person is not frozen in it, losing opportunities, as time inexorably slips away like sand, and a person feels his weakness before these circumstances. After all, sand is impermanent and symbolizes the time that passes away.

4. The girl stands at a fork and feels difficulty in choosing a direction, she appeals to the Universe for help. In response, two ravens arrive,

reminding her of Odin's two ravens. One of them pulls her toward the east, showing her memories, and the other pulls her toward the west, advising her to listen to logic. The girl realizes that her own choices lie only in her hands. The raven's claw serves as an amulet, reminding her that she has her own wisdom and foresight, and that she must trust her inner voice to make the right decision.

5. Gray hair symbolizes tension, anxiety and stress. It is also a sign of wisdom and the ability to make good decisions.

6. Black lipstick indicates that the girl holds back her opinions and may often copy other people's, as the color black absorbs individuality and she may present other people's ideas as her own. She also has a tendency to be pessimistic and see everything in black colors.

Total value

After the Ace of Swords thought occurs, there comes a moment when a person is faced with a choice: which of the thoughts to develop further, which perspective to build? To go to the right or to the left? Or to remain in the dark? To listen to one's own voice or to listen to others?

The person personified in this card often feels guilt and tends to see himself as a victim. This is reflected in the way the crows shout at him and he accepts this as the norm. He pays a lot of attention to authority figures and often listens to their opinions, as well as those he considers more competent than himself. He has difficulty making decisions and taking steps without the approval of others. The person seeks wise mentors, but because of his untrustworthiness, he may fall victim to unscrupulous people.

This card also indicates that the person may tend to shy away from problems and tasks that need solving and prefers to "hide his head in the sand". He avoids taking responsibility and is reluctant to make choices, wary of looking ahead. There is intense mental activity going on inside him, even if outwardly he appears inactive. He tends to be distrustful and suspicious of those around him.

For the person represented on this card, it is important to carefully think through his plans and be able to negotiate with himself. In dangerous situations, he should be able to take a wait-and-see and neutral position. Various fears and insecurities can hide here. It is important that a person does not let doubts and thoughts prevent him from listening to his intuition, and that he does not ignore it, remaining only reasonable.

Relationship

A person faces serious problems in his personal life and has difficulty making a decision. He has to choose between two partners, to decide whether to stay in the relationship or leave. The difficulty is that he may love one of the partners, but the relationship has become unbearable and he does not know what to do next or how to resolve this difficult situation.

There is also the possibility that one partner manipulates the person by imposing their point of view and claiming that they cannot walk a step without that partner. In a relationship, there can be a situation where a partner convinces a person that they have a problem with their head and they are unable to get along without that partner. The detrimental influence of the partner can be so strong that it prevents the person from thinking, planning and seeing the future. This is reflected in the dominant position of the crows on the chart.

The partner may also use the person as a puppet, closing the person's eyes to the truth and indoctrinating them into their world view, and may also lie to the person. Since crows are generally considered wise and long-lived, the person may prefer a partner older and smarter than himself. In such a relationship, he will depend on the partner to show him the way in life. The relationship may end up being fickle and unsatisfying, as indicated by the symbol of sand. Sand also indicates the destruction of relationships over time, making them fragile and unreliable.

A person may not notice the shortcomings of the partner or turn a blind eye to them, as well as not see his positive qualities, talents and merits. According to this card, people in a relationship may try to negotiate, make an agreement among themselves, find a compromise or reach an agreement. The person may also not fully realize their feelings for the other person and hide them from themselves.

Work and finance

The person stands still or seems to be rushing forward, but in fact he is not moving forward in his finances or career and does not know how to start moving. He feels difficulty in expanding and growing, and even taking one step in the right direction seems like an impossible task to him. Money moves out of his control like sand on a map that falls from a woman's hand. The man may make foolish and imprudent financial investments as the sand flies out of his right hand and his eyes are closed.

There is also a possibility that he may be used and advised to invest money in projects that are unprofitable for him, but profitable for those who give advice. There may be gossip spreading in his inner circle. His material condition is extremely unstable, as is the symbol of sand, which indicates instability and unsteadiness.

Double-bottom deals can be made here, where a person does not know the whole truth about the deal. There may also be deferred payments, delayed payments, and frozen accounts. There is a lack of vision of future prospects and one has doubts about the chosen path. There are difficulties in reaching consensus with partners, and people try to reach an agreement, but encounter difficulties and obstacles, which slows down the work process. The person may feel insecure about their abilities, experience imposter syndrome, and overlook their professional accomplishments. It may also indicate an impasse, where a person has left one job and does not know where to go next in their career.

Occupation

Translator, diplomat, linguist, notary, casino worker, hypnotist.

PLACES AND FACILITIES

Fields, sandy places, deserts, roads, crossroads, places of influence of scales: courts, notary offices. Places where people's consciousness is clouded: sects, slot machines, casinos.

Tip

Appreciate time, realizing that it is the most important resource that cannot be returned. Instead of wasting it on long deliberation and persuasion with yourself before making a decision, it is better to take small but regular steps. This way, time will be filled with accumulated experience rather than empty indecision. You need to learn how to make decisions, get rid of toxic environments, choose your path and start moving forward with confidence.

Warning

Do not stay put, do not allow procrastination and avoid overthinking. Situations should be dealt with by action, just take steps forward. Don't let the mind confuse you and start moving forward in small steps. Do not try to find a solution only in the mind, experience and practice will show all the answers. Trust your own intuition and do not listen to other people's opinions.

Three of Swords

S ymbolism

1. A dry tree on the map symbolizes death, while a withered tree reflects a barren and bleak period. These images represent changes that turn life upside down and bring suffering. The tree occupies an important place on the map, indicating something that has been lost, gone, or died, something that the person has forfeited. It could be something he did not value, and when he lost it, realized its value, causing a momentary feeling of despair. The loss has a great significance in his life, having become part of his being.

2. Gray color on the map symbolizes anger, frustration and depression. Suffering becomes routine and an integral part of human life. The Three of Swords indicates a crisis in life, in a certain area of life or a crisis of personality. This is a period when a person does not agree with what is happening, when his eyes are sharply opened to something.

3. In the distance on the map, crows can be seen flying away. Even their cries seem piercing. This indicates that excessive emotionality, impressionability and nervousness can push people away.

4. On the arm of the character are three swords that seem to be imprinted into the skin, like a tattoo that will stay with the person forever. This symbolizes deep stress and mental trauma, a serious event that may not let go for a long time.

5. The tree, as a symbol of memory, has dried up. Threads from the heart are pulled to it, suggesting that the memory of some moment of the person has faded. It draws the strength out of him, and he is slowly withering away, emotionally drained, just like this

tree.

6. His heart is bound up with the past tragedy, and it is unable to forget it. The person is continuously suffering, and it destroys him. A broken heart indicates love longing and emotional pain. The heart is sewn with threads and tied to a tree. The noose is caught on the tree and prevents the process of stitching the heart together from ending. This means that the person is constantly going back in time and rubbing his wound, not allowing it to heal. The red threads, like the red color of the heart, originated from the heartbreak and tied the person to a tragedy in the past. They cause him to drain energy through his longing emotions over the loss. In the context of this card, the thread symbolizes memory, vulnerability, doom and connection to the past.

7. There is a heart threaded on the thread, thanks to which it is still beating. There are knots visible on the thread, indicating that it is not whole and has been torn. It also indicates a disturbed stable state and the knots serve as barriers. It is a thread of pain and memory that is trailing behind the person.

8. A gray background expresses complete sadness, anxiety and absolute disappointment in a person. Also gray color means powerlessness, depression, complete indifference and coldness on the part of the person to whom the heart of the character on the card is attached.

Total value

This card, depicting boundless sorrow and pain, occurs after a person has made the mistake of taking the wrong path in the Two of Swords. It symbolizes deep disappointment, feelings of injustice, and devastation. During this period of life, a person may simply not want to live, because everything around seems gray and gloomy, and it seems that there is no end in sight.

It is a time of utter collapse and destruction, extremely intense and heavy. It is the moment when the truth hits a man hard and shatters his world. It is a painful life lesson, a blow that can shatter. It is the time when a person loses faith and hope, sinking into sadness and hopelessness.

This card represents a person who is in an extremely vulnerable state. He is so deeply affected by a certain situation that he is ready to vent his anger on the world, feeling powerless before his problem. This person's emotions are uncontrollable, and he may yell at someone one moment and cry the next, immersing himself in his own suffering. He seeks attention and sympathy from others, wanting his problem to be recognized. This card can indicate a person's real problems, but it can also indicate his tendency to manipulate his suffering, using it to elicit compassion and attention.

This person is emotionally unstable, lacks inner support and is prone to frequent tantrums, which creates discomfort in the environment. In addition, the card reflects a person who has experienced a heartbreak, after which his heart has closed to new emotional experiences. He has lost faith in people, in love and other emotional joys, believing that investing feelings in this is pointless, as it will always lead to disappointment and suffering. This person considers himself a realist, always criticizing the world and looking at it through the prism of gray shades, which makes his life dull. His fear is to get attached to anyone or anything because he fears that it will lead to pain and destruction of his illusions, so he avoids close relationships with other people.

Relationship

In relationships, this is a period filled with drama and tragedy. Cheating and a partner who behaves tyrannically can manifest themselves here. A person may love his partner very much, but is no longer able to be around him, as the partner constantly humiliates him and being around him becomes unbearable.

This is a time of constant tantrums, scandals, tears, resentment, sometimes even physical aggression. In this card a person reaches the peak of these sufferings and must make a decision: to stay with a partner, suffering emotional humiliation, or to leave, despite the pain of parting. This is also the moment of breakup, when the person has not yet recovered from the loss of his love, and his mind and heart are filled with only one person.

In terms of feelings, this card symbolizes unrequited love and a broken heart. The person may long to be close to the one he or she loves, but due to some circumstances cannot achieve this. There may also be third party interference here, where the partner's attention is divided between two people. This is also a period when a person faces harsh reality, illusions are shattered and he or she experiences total disappointment.

Work and finance

According to this card, losses, monetary losses, betrayals from partners, dismissals, bankruptcy and serious setbacks on the work front are forthcoming. The person feels that he is surrounded by difficulties and obstacles that prevent him from moving forward. This is a period when it feels as if sticks are being thrown from all sides.

It is also possible for a person's reputation to be seriously damaged and vilified. This is the moment when, for example, a person is forced to close his business due to unprofitability, or, for example, there is a fire in a warehouse with goods. In the case of this card, you need to be especially careful when entering into contracts, as there is a high risk of losing everything in the future.

The card describes a person who finds himself or herself "stripped bare", with nothing to spare, experiencing financial poverty and destitution, and suffering from a dire financial situation. This is a real crisis in financial affairs.

A dry tree on the map symbolizes the futility of labor efforts. The person has invested his efforts for many years, but the results are unsatisfactory, and he regrets the wasted effort and time. Also according to this card, the person has an agonizing feeling, as if he is at work as a penal servitude, and his work takes away all the energy and joy of life. Here there is a possibility of trouble in the workplace and in the team. These are also situations when a person is engaged in a business that he does not like, and which does not bring proper income. The card may indicate a debt pit and the need to divide property.

In addition, this card may indicate negative ancestral attitudes about money. This thread of fear and aversion to money stretches from deep roots, from parents, grandparents and so on, which indicates a connection with the family. A person may have the mentality of a poor person who believes that he or she will never make much money, and life will be filled with hard and low-paid labor. The thought of money causes him to panic as he associates it with agony and laboring for pennies. It is a tremendous fear of money and wealth associated with poverty and stress. The person may believe that money brings misfortune, that once rich he is bound to become a victim of theft, and that money will ruin his life. This may discourage them from starting their own business or starting a new endeavor because they are convinced in advance that failure is inevitable and do not want to face potential disappointments.

Occupation

Cardiologist, cardiovascular, surgeon, medical examiners. People who travel to the sites of various incidents, accident sites, dumps, ashes. Indicates military action, as well as a psychologist who works with difficult, crisis situations.

PLACES AND FACILITIES

Dumps, ashes, scorched fields, forests, houses, abandoned areas and towns, cemeteries, operating rooms, the creepiest and most unpleasant places.

Tip

Stop reveling in the suffering and stop torturing yourself with memories of the tragic past. Accept your feelings and emotions, however uncomfortable they may be, and allow yourself to live them. Work on the fear of disappointment and remove unnecessary expectations from the situation. To have no illusions about someone or something and to look at the situation as soberly as possible to avoid disappointments in the future.

Warning

Something can go completely wrong and ruin the plans both lengthwise and crosswise. Therefore, you should definitely take a different path and develop a new strategy so that the efforts are not in vain. Expectations may not be met and there is a high possibility of disappointment.

Four of Swords

Symbolism

1. On the Green background you can see the man's desire for peace. The card depicts a nest, which he built from dry branches, similar to the previous card. The nest symbolizes safety and protection. It is also associated with healing and the end of illness. However, the context must be taken into account to determine whether the nest is associated with illness or recovery.

2. On the arm of the character can be seen rune Inguz, which symbolizes growth and is on his left hand. This may indicate that the person is thinking about growth and development, but does not yet take concrete action. His focus is on inner growth and spiritual development. Perhaps he has hopes that things will improve on their own, without his active participation, and he does not seek initiative. The map also shows that the rune Inguz is on the left hand associated with the inner world, which emphasizes the person's focus on inner rebirth and strengthening. Rune Inguz also symbolizes the continuation of life and family.

3. On the card, the girl takes a pose reminiscent of the position of the embryo. This image is associated with rebirth and the second beginning. This rune may indicate pregnancy, the presence of a family nest and the possibility of restoring relationships after the conflict.

4. On the other hand, a tattoo in the form of flowers on the right side of the body of the girl expresses her desire to blossom and create a new life. She is ready to give love, but the flowers are drawn faded and dull, indicating that her intentions are not strong enough and she does not have enough strength for full realization. In her heart

she is ready for love and joy, although it is not yet fully manifested. The girl's skin symbolizes interaction with the outside world.

5. Next to the girl is an almost healed heart, resting and undergoing the healing process. The threads stitching the heart are protected by sharp spikes, indicating that it has become more cautious and protective. The person is not yet ready for a new relationship and continues on their journey of healing. The thread going down under the nest indicates that the past has not completely left the person, but he is in the process of healing. It is important to give him or her time to fully heal.

Total value

In the Four of Swords there comes a time of rest, recovery of strength and emotional state after the ordeal with the Three of Swords. This period takes time, and a person here is not in a hurry. He freezes, concentrates only on one thing: the past is left behind, and now it is possible to move forward in peace.

This is not an active stage in life, rather a break after a tumultuous period. The person has already moved away from active events, but has not yet fully recovered his strength. At this point, he needs to pay attention to rest and recovery. The worst has passed, and now you can relax and rest. This card symbolizes a halt, a temporary standstill of events, peace and tranquility. It is also a time for planning, reviewing goals and waiting for the right time to act.

The person shuts himself off from the world around him and seeks solitude to recover and gather his thoughts. He becomes passive and relaxed. Immersion in himself, a moment of reflection and meditation. The situation here is inert, everything moves slowly and the person remains unconcerned. This is a temporary depressed state, when there is no energy for active participation in social life. The person strives to resist and restore his balance. This is a period when everything goes on as it should and the status quo is maintained.

The Four of Swords represents passivity in a person. He may show laziness, be clumsy in his movements, and his emotions are hidden deep inside. In society, he prefers the solitude of home to noisy company. This person is not inclined to leave the comfort zone, and for him changes in life can happen only in case of extreme necessity, when his coziness is disturbed by external circumstances.

He cherishes his inner harmony and fears that external factors may disturb it. He avoids sudden movements and loud sounds. This person does not actively fight for his goals and often allows events to develop spontaneously, floating on the stream of life. He is not ready to take responsibility for his life and does not seek changes for the better, preferring to keep his cozy "swamp".

Relationship

The nest on the card symbolizes home, family, and a place of comfort and tranquility. It can also indicate a marriage bed and married life, which may not have too much emotion, but seems comfortable and familiar. In some cases, this card represents quiet and family harmony. However, in some contexts, the nest may indicate a tired relationship. Perhaps the person is submissive to his partner, giving in to everything, and does not have enough strength and will to resist. In such cases, the partner may excessively influence the person and deplete his energy. It can also indicate a pause in a relationship, when a person temporarily withdraws from love and relationships to allow their heart to heal and recover.

Often the Four of Swords signifies a period of loneliness and the absence of love or any active relationships. A person may be in the process of healing from past wounds and protecting their heart by suppressing feelings for another person or relationship altogether. This is a way of protecting oneself from possible disappointments in love and maintaining emotional balance.

Work and finance

The Four of Swords card indicates a slowdown in business and the need to rest and reboot. It indicates that the person is tiring of work and needs a pause. Things may move slowly and the person may feel tired of projects. He or she may find it difficult to maintain regular work activities and build a career. In certain cases, the card may indicate a person who is not inclined to be hardworking, tiring quickly of work and even unemployed. Such a person may feel lazy and unwilling to look for a new job or make changes in his life, and it is hard for him to get off the couch.

However, a nest can also symbolize working from home, in comfortable conditions where there is no need for physical exertion. It can be associated with intellectual labor, reflection and analysis. The card can also indicate the presence of passive income.

In the financial aspect, the nest signifies the protection of savings and their slow growth. Rune Ingwaz also indicates the potential for financial development, but in this case the slowing or stopping of growth can be associated with the postponement of projects and plans. This may be a period of burnout at work, when a person lacks motivation and strength for work affairs. He may be in temporary suspension from work.

The card may also indicate a person working in the same position for many years, even if it does not suit him according to various criteria. This person may have a stable income, but does not strive to develop and improve his financial situation. Perhaps he has unused resources and opportunities to increase his income, but due to apathy and inactivity he does not perceive them.

Occupation

Freelancer, tattoo artist, ritual worker, analyst, sanitarium or hospital worker, ultrasound technician, cardiologist.

PLACES AND FACILITIES

A bed, a cell, a ward, enclosed spaces.

Tip

Immerse yourself in peace, slow down the pace, take a pause in current affairs, move away from events at a decent distance and look at them objectively, abstract yourself and do not get emotionally involved in what is happening. It is important to spend time alone with yourself and thoroughly analyze the situation, avoiding unnecessary fuss and haste.

Warning

The need for rest and lack of activity should not be neglected. It is important to break down the barriers of calmness and break out of the comfort zone. Standing still and slowing down processes do not help to improve the situation. This is not the time for inactivity and prolonged thinking and planning. Now is the moment to leave the zone of habitualness immediately.

Five of Swords

Symbolism

1. The posture of the victor on the mountain is similar to that of the victor in the Six of Wands. However, in the Six of Wands it is a reflection of honest success, while in the Five of Swords it is a path through hardship and sometimes even darkness. A path where every step is accompanied by effort and struggle.

2. There are traces of blood on the snow, indicating that the man, despite the difficulties, was able to achieve his goal. He does not feel sorry for himself, does not succumb to weaknesses, and does not stop in the face of difficulties. He goes to his goal, no matter what, with perseverance and determination.

3. Brown is closely associated with the material world, its stability and animal laws of survival. This color symbolizes a life that can be less active, preferring physical rest and repose. This can sometimes be a trap, inciting laziness and inactivity, distracting you from achieving your goals. However, brown also represents permanence and stability.

4. A man lost his crows in a foul fight, but one of his favorite birds stayed with him. This bird, as if pushing a man out of his comfort zone, encourages him to take risks and change something in his life. It encourages not to be afraid of critical turns on the road to success, not to wipe your feet getting to the top of life. Those who prefer brown colors are not inclined to set themselves up for hardship and find it easiest to hide their head in the sand. Here we see similarities with the Four of Swords, where one avoids difficulties. However, in the Five of Swords, circumstances force him to face them, and this can cause obsessions and a depressive

state.

5. The man's left hand is holding his head, trying to relieve the stress and tension that may accompany his journey.

Total value

It is a departure from the familiar cocoon and relaxation of the Four of Swords, it is a breaking down of walls of comfort and an abrupt change of scenery in which one must be flexible, quick to react and adapt. After the stagnation and sleep of the Four of Swords, the Five of Swords is shock therapy.

This card indicates an unscrupulous and vindictive person who for the sake of his goal will go against everything and everyone, it can be his personal goal, for example, career, and a mean goal, for example, to take away the wife of a friend, as the Five of Swords carries a destructive imprint. This is meanness from the outside, loss of trust and illusions about the person. Intrigues, enmity and aggression, the card can indicate dishonest, mean deeds, such as a crowd attacked one, robbed, beaten and so on. This is a loss of honor, shameful and unpleasant situation. Also you need to look at what role the person on this card, the role of the victim or aggressor.

Also this card indicates that the person leaves the Four of Swords reflections, breaks the old worldview and vision of the situation, leaves himself old, with unnecessary mental attitudes and patterns in the past. He realizes that he spent a lot of time digging into unnecessary speculations and lived not at all the way he wants to live now, this person says goodbye to the old habits, average life, environment, despite the discomfort, he goes to growth and development through the crisis, internal or external, depending on the situation.

This card brings out secrets and other people's dirty laundry. Masks are thrown off, faces and true motives of people are exposed, this card forces a person to get out of the sweet veil of representation of others, this card of cold and critical thinking.

Relationship

A cold landscape symbolizes a feeling of coldness in a relationship, while a sparkling glow indicates a change in atmosphere, which may indicate unfavorable changes in a relationship. This card traces elements of deception and trickery, as well as disappointment in the partner and the relationship when expectations are not met.

In addition, one partner may sacrifice the other in search of better prospects and a more favorable position. This card can also indicate a short-term victory when one person uses the other sexually and then disappears, leaving the partner bewildered.

In a couple, one partner may be cruel and abusive to the other by humiliating, controlling, cheating, betraying, and deceiving. This partner may also try to crush the other's self-esteem, complain about him or her in front of others, discuss his or her shortcomings, and humiliate him or her in public. All of these are indicative of dishonest and cruel play on feelings.

Jealousy, ultimatums and restriction of the partner's freedom can also be inherent in relationships where one partner seeks to control the other, their finances, meetings and even personal correspondence. One partner may try to make the other feel helpless and unworthy, which triggers feelings of guilt and vengeful attitudes.

This card can also predict a breakup, which can be cold and painful. One partner leaves and the other stays behind, trying to figure out where they went wrong. This is a time when the other partner may feel regret for their behavior and reflect on what they have lost because of poor decisions in the relationship. The one on top of the mountain may leave the partner with a heavy heart, despite strong affection, but because of an unbearable situation.

Work and finance

The symbolism of the ascent up the mountain is related to life's tasks and challenges that fate sets before us. We see traces of blood on the ground, indicating the complexity and danger of this path. In this card, a person is ready to go to success, not stopping in front of opponents and ready to go through many difficulties.

The card also warns of the possibility of deception or betrayal, where someone may use dishonest methods to get ahead or cause damage. It can also indicate dishonest deals and unprofitable partnerships, as well as dishonest behavior by a boss at work who may use his subordinates for his own ends. Sometimes it can lead to disappointment and shattered expectations when plans don't come to fruition.

The card can also indicate difficulties in adjusting to a new schedule or work system, where the person may feel behind and unable to keep up with current trends. This can cause confusion and a search for ways to improve, such as better promotion and marketing methods.

The card also reflects disputes related to finances and competition for a job or promotion. This can create a tense atmosphere in the team and lead to competition between coworkers. Sometimes it can lead to one employee framing another due to jealousy or personal animosity, such as giving harmful advice to a newcomer to undermine his position.

This card also indicates envy, which can be destructive when one feels passion and anger when seeing the success of others. Investing in work that does not yield the expected results can cause feelings of frustration, resentment and anger. The card can also indicate a competitive victory or defeat at the hands of a competitor, depending on the person's role in the situation.

Also, this card often symbolizes victory over oneself and personal weaknesses. Achieving the goals of this card requires effort and self-discipline. A person is forced to mobilize their resources and limit themselves in some aspects of life, which resembles a difficult climb up the mountain. Rewards exist, but they are achieved through hard work and mental effort. This includes constantly developing new strategies and testing ideas to improve one's financial situation.

The person depicted on this card does not stop at a place and does not give himself a rest. He lives in constant tension, his mind is always busy striving for career growth and financial success. He constantly absorbs a huge amount of information for his own development, and his work on himself never stops. He lacks time even for rest, and he is ready to sacrifice moments of relaxation for the sake of achieving his goals. Regardless of all the difficulties, he does not stop.

This card also reflects the difficulties and obstacles on the way to success, as well as the high price one has to pay to achieve goals. It shows the base of the iceberg, what lies beneath the water, and reveals the difficulties and trials that a person has overcome to reach his or her goals. The card also indicates financial fluctuations, alternating periods of prosperity and recession. Therefore, for financial success here it is necessary to work hard, do not stop in front of temporary setbacks and keep moving forward.

Occupation

A forensic expert, also a person connected with crime, trade in illegal drugs, owner of slot machines and any organization where a person can be fooled and cheated out of money. Wrestling, boxing, martial arts coach, military man, mountaineer.

PLACES AND FACILITIES

Cold terrains, mountaintops, places amidst harsh, wilderness and places of battle.

Tip

To stand up for what is ours, regardless of circumstances, not to stop halfway and to overcome difficulties up to the end, despite their complexity. Let go of everything that hinders personal development and pulls us down, even if it is difficult, otherwise we risk stagnation and degradation. It is important not to be afraid to express one's own opinion, even if it contradicts others, and to boldly enter into disputes, defending one's beliefs and ideas. Sometimes it is necessary to give vent to negative emotions such as anger, jealousy, rigidity and harshness in order not to repress them within ourselves.

Warning

It is important to remain attentive to one's surroundings and not to go outwardly against one's own beliefs and principles, not to neglect conscience and kindness. You should not use other people for the sake of your own ego and do not turn a blind eye to the problems of your loved ones to avoid possible disasters in the future. It is also important to be alert to the world around you, to protect yourself and not to trust too easily, protecting important information and not allowing others to treat you with disrespect.

Six of Swords

S ymbolism

1. The card shows traveling, moving and leaving, as well as the arrival of guests. It also symbolizes parting with the past - people, place of work, city and habits. The boat on the map is a symbol of a person's life path and the transition from one state to another. This transition is accompanied by changes and alterations, often causing a variety of emotions, as the map depicts a lot of water. The person is in a boat, which means rebirth and the beginning of something new. The boat also symbolizes spiritual growth and connection to one's own root and lineage. It provides additional support from family and lineage. The card is also associated with the passage to another world and the journey of the soul along the river Styx.

2. The suitcase symbolizes hard-acquired but necessary mental and practical skills. The person carries with him from the past resentments, disappointments and memories. He values and respects having useful and practical skills, and his luggage of knowledge is extensive. The suitcase is a symbol of luggage and all that a person needs to take with him into the future.

3. The light ahead symbolizes hope for a new future. It suggests that a person will meet a new day and a new beginning of their life in the future, even though they may feel lost now and not know where to go.

4. The star acts as a reference point, showing a person the way. It is a star of hope for a bright future.

5. Ravens on the map help the girl to move forward, pulling the boat, which suggests that the person will not be alone in his work, and

other people will certainly come to his aid.

6. Also, the other crows are pointing towards the star, indicating that there will be people, pointers and signs on the person's path to help them get in the right direction.

Total value

The Six of Swords represents a transition from a difficult and conflicting situation that was depicted in the Five of Swords card. The person on this card seeks to break out of the problems and difficulties that haunted him on the previous card. The direction of his movement is not always clear, but the very fact of movement is important, because it is a movement to new opportunities and prospects.

The Six of Swords also indicates a person's inner changes. Water, depicted on the card, symbolizes the subconscious and inner world of a person. The person depicted on this card seeks to find answers to his questions and is engaged in self-development. He can turn to a psychologist or engage in spiritual practices, but in any case, his goal is to expand his consciousness, moving away from outdated beliefs and explore his inner world. The Six of Swords represents the expansion of horizons, flexibility of thinking and constant opening to new knowledge.

The Six of Swords man tends to change his surroundings often and does not stay in one place for long. He is constantly studying and learning something new, adding to his luggage of knowledge. This is a card of knowledge. This person is always ready for new discoveries and does not want to stay in places he does not like. He may not have confidence in the future, but he is always on the lookout for new opportunities.

Relationship

The Six of Swords symbolizes the arrival of balance and reconciliation in a relationship, which follows the storm depicted in the Five of Swords card. This card represents the couple's desire for consensus and finding a way out of conflicts. The relationship is at a new level of quality after going through difficult times together. The partners are moving towards new experiences together, focusing on the development of the relationship. Both parties reach agreement and fulfill their commitments, strengthening their bond and moving in the same direction.

Often this card indicates a long-distance relationship, as a transition from an old relationship to a new one, a move from an old shore to a new one. It can also signify one partner moving in with another, or a couple moving into a new apartment. It can also foretell both a breakup and the beginning of a new relationship.

A suitcase symbolizes a rich life experience, storing many experiences and memories. It can also symbolize a person's secrets, which he does not want to share with others. A closed suitcase indicates that a person seeks to keep his feelings, thoughts and desires in secret, not revealing them publicly.

The red shawl symbolizes freedom and courage, and its presence on a person's shoulders indicates that he has taken responsibility for his own freedom. The person has been able to free themselves from the role of victim or aggressor in a relationship, as in the Five of Swords card. The shawl also envelops the person, providing protection and care, indicating that he has taken care of himself and his well-being. Despite the fear and uncertainty of the future, he is moving forward, sailing towards new horizons while maintaining his freedom.

Work and finance

According to the Six of Swords card, a person may decide to change his job, field of activity or even completely change his profession, if the previous one did not bring satisfaction. He decides to start with a clean slate, but at the same time he has a rich life and work experience, which is reflected in the symbol of the suitcase, which is a treasure trove of experience. This experience may not necessarily be in a new field, but in general it develops important qualities such as discipline, responsibility, customer relations skills and advancement. The person carries this experience with them and will use it in building their new career.

The Six of Swords card can also indicate business trips, relocation of a work company to another city or abroad, and remote work. Its meaning can also cover dismissal.

This card is one of the cards of knowledge and indicates the need for constant learning, additional courses and advanced training. It reflects investment in education and knowledge, which is confirmed by the symbol "suitcase of money". A person realizes that investment in knowledge will bring him more income and help him to advance in career and in life in general.

Sometimes the card can indicate unplanned spending, an inability to manage finances, or spending money quickly. In such cases, it emphasizes the need for a more cautious approach to financial management.

It also indicates the importance of choosing the right direction for investment, managing finances well and being knowledge-oriented. In the area of learning, information and career development, it indicates a desire for professional development, learning new aspects of one's field of work and demonstrates an interest in work, as well as a desire to explore one's field of work.

Occupation

Sailor, trucker, bus or boat driver, person who travels frequently for work, freelancer, delivery person, education field, person who sells info-products, person who promotes others: marketer, tagger, producer.

PLACES AND FACILITIES

Means of transportation, car, boat, places near bodies of water, phones, computers, bags, suitcases, online chat rooms, online or offline study rooms.

Tip

Gaining knowledge and learning is a key factor for advancement in life and career. Learning helps you to manage life more wisely, control your emotions and make wise decisions in relationships. It is important to make choices that can open up new perspectives for you. Expanding your horizons and acquiring new knowledge play an important role. Finding yourself and doing things that bring you joy is also important. Changing your routine can be helpful.

Warning

It's not a good idea to give up what you've already accomplished now, or to quit your current job and leave an established relationship. Instead, it is better to stay where you are and strengthen your position. Making the wrong decisions can lead to dangerous consequences and the loss of everything gained. It is important to immerse yourself in your current situation and strengthen your existing position before thinking of expanding. You should not impose your point of view on others and consider yourself smarter than others, as stopping to gain new knowledge can lead to degradation.

Seven of Swords

Symbolism

1. The city, as a symbol of the center of civilization, remains off limits for this character, indicating his disregard for societal norms and living by his own rules.

2. Backpack in this context means traveling and wandering. It also carries important things for a person while concealing them from prying eyes. The backpack is worn on one shoulder so that it can be quickly removed and concealed if necessary. The brown color of this backpack is associated with the material world and survival, emphasizing the need to conceal certain information to maintain safety.

3. The hood symbolizes invisibility and going into the shadows. It covers the head, also symbolizing reflection and the spiritual aspect. The hood gives a sense of protection from the outside world and indicates a person's hidden thoughts and plans. The white color of the hood is associated with coldness, indifference and secret actions. It emphasizes the emotional alienation of the character from others and his ability to deceive and conduct a hidden game without remorse.

4. The knife, as a symbol of danger, indicates critical thinking and a sharp tongue capable of causing damage to those around you. The knife can be a tool of deception, use it for seduction and information manipulation.

5. Just as the moon reflects the light of the sun, the character is able to adjust to others and show himself in a way that benefits him. He is a master at reincarnation and manipulating others solely for his own benefit. The Moon distorts the truth and brings ambiguity

into relationships.

Total value

A Six of Swords person finds shelter in a new place, but the place is uncharted and the people are unfamiliar. In a new place one must be on guard, not relax and not trust the first person one meets. You need to watch your safety and the safety of your belongings.

Emanations, dastardly deeds, theft, various kinds of induced atmosphere require from a person not only caution, but also vigilance. According to this card, deceptions, dastardly deeds, theft, all sorts of tricks occur, and a person can not only be left without any things, but also become a victim of fraud. It can also be magical tricks, when something mystically falls into a person's possession, under the door and so on. This card is very reminiscent of pocket thieves who are active at train stations. For example, a Six of Swords person has arrived at a new place, got off the train at a train station, and a Seven of Swords thief or fraudster may appear here.

The Seven of Swords indicates the need to avoid direct conflicts and to approach problems covertly, using cunning and the ability to persuade the opponent. People associated with the Seven of Swords avoid open confrontations and prefer to act cunningly to avoid negative consequences. Their actions are determined by their own interests, and they do not always take into account the opinions and needs of others. Under the Seven of Swords you can get something for free, it is a kind of freebies. The famous expression "If you want to live, you have to know how to spin!" is applicable here. The Seven of Swords represents a creative way out of difficult situations, and under this card it is necessary to act quietly, carefully, quickly and skillfully.

The Seven of Swords symbolizes a person who avoids direct answers and serious decisions. He tends to avoid responsibility and shift it to others. Such a person avoids honest answers and serious commitments.

His cunning and resourcefulness help him hide his real intentions and actions. He is attentive and suspicious, able to read people, their gestures and facial expressions, and to sense lies. It is peculiar to him to influence the consciousness of other people, hypnosis and esotericism, as well as the ability to manipulate their thoughts and decisions in his favor.

Relationship

In a relationship, sincerity is out of the question. There are constant secrets, reticences, avoidance of responsibility, and there is no trust in the couple. Snow means that there is no mental closeness or warmth in the couple. This is a cold and unemotional relationship. The person is not afraid to deceive even a very clever partner (crows are clever). He walks on a knife blade and often does things behind his partner's back. He may give him tests and watch his partner's reaction.

Quite often a cuckoo lays one or two eggs in a crow's nest. Despite the fact that these eggs are significantly smaller than crow eggs, crows do not throw them out, but feed them. This means that a person can use his partner, tossing him his obligations: to give him a loan, to deal with some problem and so on. The partner, because of his trust, agrees and fulfills this person's requests. In a relationship, it is often playfulness in front of others and in front of each other. There are no feelings, people live together and everyone plays his role, a theater of lies and hypocrisy.

The card shows the hysterical nature of the partner. Can raise panic and throw tantrums for any reason. Scenes of jealousy and distrust. The person may go through the partner's phone and cling to every little thing. May spy on their partner. A person can drive his partner to the point where he starts doing many things secretly from him: going out with friends, doing some activities, planning, traveling somewhere. One partner may bring out the problems in the couple, complain about the partner, accuse him of all mortal sins. Pressing for pity, throwing mud. Like a crow screaming.

The bird's nest is the place where life is born, it is the family nest, matrimony. This card shows interference in someone else's life, family. The person interferes with the quiet conjugal life of others. It can be people from the outside, gossip, intrigues, sticks in the wheels, or someone has his eye on one of the partners. Also in this card, it is not uncommon for one of the partners to destroy the marital idyll with bad habits, such as alcohol or gambling addiction, and do it in secret from the partner. Then it comes out in the form of debts, loans and other problems, and then trust in the family and stability in the relationship is undermined.

Seven of Swords also shows a person who shows interest in another, but does not dare to directly express his feelings. Therefore, various pickup tricks and manipulations are used. Such a person can secretly learn information about the object of his interest through other people, the Internet and so on. He studies it from a distance, his habits and preferences, and based on this data knows how to act and where to set traps to get this person caught in his net. A person in the Seven of Swords, as in the Five of Swords, can use another person for a night, and in the morning disappear and do not pick up the phone. For him to bind himself in a serious relationship is like putting shackles on himself, he seeks freedom and irresponsibility in relationships.

Work and finance

This card is used for planning, developing new ideas and analyzing the work situation. It requires flexibility and the ability to adapt to external circumstances. Artists can draw inspiration from the ideas of others and creatively transform them. This process is commonplace and normal. Also copies, forgeries, plagiarism, and copyright infringements manifest on this card. Unsafe deals, dishonest agreements and cheating partners can be found here. Inaccuracies in documents can be exploited by dishonest partners. Work may be marred by intrigue, gossip and meanness in the team.

There is a folklore motif about collecting magic herb from the nests of certain birds that allows one to open locks. This symbolizes a person's desire to use other people's resources to achieve success, financial growth and career advancement. The character on the card dreams of rising above the ordinary, avoiding punishment and responsibility.

The card also reflects envy because the person sees injustice in the fact that birds can fly and he cannot. This can lead to spitefulness and attacks on others because the person believes he is entitled to more. He does not want to work hard to achieve goals but prefers to take them away from others.

The person in this card is responsible for his life, but he refuses to realize it. He often expresses resentment towards the world and perceives it as unfair. His behavior is childish, capricious and vindictive.

A person can resort to various tricks to achieve his goal. According to the card indicates that he really needs what he is trying to get, and he thinks over his actions in advance. He remains inconspicuous and cautious.

To improve your financial situation, this card recommends using unconventional methods and experimenting. You should create provocative content and use subtle psychology in sales. The Moon provides an opportunity to attract new clients and get people's attention.

Occupation

Lawyer, IT field, programmers, hackers, esotericists, marketers, managers, mediators, negotiators, diplomats, intelligence officers.

PLACES AND FACILITIES

Hidden places, locked gadgets, secret places, hidden rooms and rooms, places outside the city.

Tip

In this situation, you should avoid open conflicts and seek to resolve disputes. It is important to be creative and resourceful in finding solutions, while being willing to flexibly change your strategy to ultimately achieve your goals.

Warning

Vigilance must be maintained as there is a risk of deception, theft, set-up and betrayal. Some may deliberately distort information and create misinformation. It is important to be careful about divulging your secrets and not to confide them to any random interlocutor.

Eight of Swords

Symbolism

1. This is a projection of her own perception of herself. If in the Two of Swords there is an opportunity to fight and overcome opposing forces, in the Eight of Swords the battle is fought with internal obstacles. The eyes are called the mirror of the soul, and if in this mirror they are closed, it symbolizes a loss of faith and contact with the inner voice that would guide her soul.

2. The mirror has the property of amplifying any manifestation, so it multiplies the feeling of despair. It can not only reflect but also absorb energy, reflecting and magnifying fears that paralyze the girl, reinforcing her sense of helplessness. The mirror could distort her perception of reality. Associated with the element of water, the mirror serves as a reflection of her emotional world, emphasizing the unconscious aspects of being where one may be influenced by unfathomable forces. It suggests that the way out of a predicament is through a change in one's inner worldview, where one must rely on intuitive feelings as opposed to logic and rationality.

3. This card illustrates irrational fears and perceptions that someone is a negative influence or responsible for personal adversity. It reflects the image of the victim. The girl is depicted as if paralyzed, unable to take active action or influence circumstances. She sits passively in the mirror against a background of greenish sky and stars, and it seems that this state of affairs suits her. She does not want to change her usual position, where everything is stable and safe, where she feels protected from the outside world.

4. Her hands are not bound in reality, but in the mirror they are bound. The mirror reports her own feelings of having her hands

tied and her eyes closed. In reality her eyes are open and looking upward, she is looking outside herself for help because she does not feel able to help herself and is waiting for a savior to come. In her relationships, she feels herself as a victim.

5. She occupies a seat on a white rug, which symbolizes her desire for peace and tranquility. This indicates that she is comfortable in her current posture and location. She feels comfortable in this environment and finds it dangerous to leave it. She may have secrets under the rug that paralyze her with fear that someone may reveal those secrets. She sits motionless, afraid to get down from the rug and leave it unattended to avoid other people's gaze underneath and discovering dirt, some personal and unpleasant secrets that she does not want to share with others.

6. Wooden floor symbolizes stability and reliability of her current position. It reflects a person's worldview, his fixed habits and beliefs, which he is not going to change. Therefore, such a person very rarely changes himself in a relationship, and if a partner expects him to change his behavior, which could improve their relationship, he has little chance of seeing such changes.

Total value

In this state, the person seems to fall into a trap, when he loses the understanding of what steps to take next. In the Seven of Swords he finds that he has been tricked and betrayed, and the Eight of Swords plunges him into a deep slumber of despair caused by a sense of helplessness. He puts his own limitations on his ability to think clearly, constantly exacerbating this condition because the mirror effect serves not just as a reflection, but as an amplifier of his current state.

In this position, she seems completely immersed in her inability to act decisively and her will to compromise with circumstances, without actively seeking to change anything, allowing herself to float along indefinitely until external circumstances or other people interrupt this passive process. Her capacity for a balanced perception of reality she herself weakens, reinforcing this state again and again, as a mirror by its nature tends to double what is displayed. It is a reflection of her inner view of herself, she needs to find the strength to overcome. The person reflected by this card is frozen in place, he avoids mistakes and the acquisition of personal experience, afraid to live fully and try new ways of action.

The person associated with this card has many internal inhibitions and psychological barriers, he restrains his emotions and desires. His inherent dogmatism and lack of adaptability in thinking put walls of self-restraint in front of him. It seems better to him to suppress his needs and put up with inconveniences than to take bold steps to change the situation. This card symbolizes limitation and helplessness, in risky situations it serves as a warning of possible failure, and in situations involving the circumvention of rules, it warns of the risk of being caught.

Relationship

One partner may show a tendency to be compliant, having low standards and similar self-esteem. He is characterized by uncertainty in the correctness of his actions and limitations in self-expression. A lot of complexes prevent him from expressing himself, and he is afraid to make an extra step to avoid being judged by his partner. This person is afraid to express his desires and is almost incapable of open dialog, he constantly restrains himself.

Excessive shyness and indecisiveness prevent him from openly sharing his preferences and plans. He creates many fictitious fears and erroneous assumptions about his partner. This person is afraid that his partner will leave, leaving him in a difficult position, and believes in the most negative scenarios he has drawn up for himself, later transferring this to his partner and feeling hatred and jealousy because of his own internal conflicts.

Lack of willingness to open up to a partner leads to the accumulation of fears, resentments and emotional feelings within oneself. This person also reflects his inner states on his partner, causing a corresponding reaction in his behavior.

According to this card, partners may ignore each other, block each other on social media and be in a state of cold conflict. The warmth in the relationship disappears and unexpressed grievances and resentments accumulate, which only worsens the situation. There is a feeling of loneliness, even as a couple.

Work and finance

The threads held by the four crows symbolize the stable position of a person. He is surrounded by protection, keeping his boundaries from the outside world and remain in his fortress, unwilling to let outsiders in. It seems to him that his position is unshakable and unchanging. These threads also represent obligations and ties to others, such as debts, alimony, and loans. According to the card, money may appear "frozen" or restricted, and the person may feel limited in financial spending.

A person faces financial constraints and cannot afford excessive spending. However, it is important to realize that this is just a reflection of his beliefs and mental limitations. It is his own mindset preventing him from breaking free from financial blocks and distress thinking. This is when a person believes that he is not worthy of decent wealth, is self hindered and does not believe in his own strength. Nevertheless, this is not a hopeless situation, and a person can change his worldview, get rid of negative financial attitudes, develop his willpower, take responsibility, go beyond his comfort zone and not be afraid of mistakes.

The card can also indicate external restrictions such as blocked sites, social media, accounts that can affect a person's earnings. It could be a team atmosphere that creates tension and makes the person feel out of place. The card also indicates a job that consumes all of a person's time, depriving him or her of the opportunity to do other things.

Occupation

Psychiatrist, ophthalmologist, hospitals.

PLACES AND FACILITIES

Closed stuffy places, places by mirrors, prisons, hospitals, mental institutions, traffic jams.

Tip

It is important to look closely at where you are limiting yourself and why you are not allowing yourself to express yourself. Think about why you are restraining yourself and what benefits you get from such restrictions. In some cases, it may be helpful to try ascesis, temporarily restricting yourself from excesses, such as eating or drinking alcohol. It is important to try to find ways to get out of the vicious cycle and not deny yourself the opportunity to act. You should not shift reality and should try to see the situation as it is, introducing more realism into your life.

Warning

Perhaps now is not the right time for active actions and changes in the situation. Everything has its time, and perhaps it is not yet time to take decisive steps. It is important to wait until the situation becomes clearer. This card insists on the need for awareness and encourages you to wake up and leave the "prison" that you may have created yourself. It is important not to make up unnecessary problems or let paranoid thoughts and fears creep in. Be vigilant not to become ensnared by ideas or relationships that limit you, such as joining a cult or succumbing to the power of a dominant partner.

Nine of Swords

S ymbolism

1. The heroine of the card is faced with a shocking realization of reality, from which she turns away, hiding her face in the palms of her hands. Whereas in the preceding card her eyes were open, now, despite her open eyes, she chooses to remain blind to what is happening, to ignore the cruelty of her situation. The rain pouring down on her makes her situation even more tense and requiring immediate action. Rain symbolizes sadness because it hides the sun and darkens the light, which can represent long oppression or hypochondria. However, it is the rain that can help release the weight of sadness by washing away all that is superfluous and outdated.

2. In the picture, the card represents only the ghostly outline of a bed. The situation is full of anxiety and in some aspects is dangerous, as the person is unable to feel relief even for a moment - this causes enormous stress, not allowing to gain strength, especially when relaxation on the wet ground and under a wet pillow is impossible. A wet pillow is a symbol of lost emotional security. The pillow, which is usually associated with sleep, coziness and comfort, is now lying on the wet ground, emphasizing the deprivation of the girl's usual sense of comfort she had in the Eight of Swords. The ephemeral appearance of the bed alludes to the person's desire for relief and comfort, the desire for a vacation from stress so that the hard times are behind him and he can finally relax and alleviate the accumulated tension. Lack of quality rest and sleep adversely affects cognitive functions, weakens immunity, reduces libido, which indicates that the person

represented on the card is experiencing nervous overstrain and his mental faculties are clouded due to worries.

3. Hair, symbolically associated with our thoughts and spiritual connection with the Higher Powers, in the character of the Nine of Swords is in disorder, which reflects the confusion of her thoughts and confusion in the face of circumstances. Disorder in the hair also symbolizes the loss of connection with spirituality, the disappearance of a spark of faith and hope. Hair in a ponytail indicates that all the girl's thoughts are focused on her hopeless situation.

4. The black birds hovering over the heroine are like dark thoughts about the hopelessness of her situation, and only one white bird of hope stands out among them, soaring above them all in the distance. That is why it becomes unusually difficult to break through the darkness to this person ray of hope. The card hints at the presence of intrusive thoughts, up to thoughts of suicide, and this is a really difficult condition. The same experiences include panic attacks.

5. Dress, as women's clothing, becomes an expressive means of expressing human emotions. Women, by their nature, tend to be emotional, and through the dress they reveal their feelings to the world. In it, they can completely immerse themselves like a girl who wears a red dress. The red color adds expressiveness and drama to these emotions.

6. The familiar comfort is gone, instead the girl is sitting on green grass, which symbolizes a new stage in her life. The green grass represents life and the possibility of renewal after the rain. However, at this moment, the girl is too immersed in her emotions to think about it. Rain brings water, which is always associated with emotions. In this context, rain indicates that the person has entered an emotional phase of his life where it is important to manifest and purify his feelings in order to be ready for new opportunities. Rain symbolizes intense emotional cleansing and hints at sadness in the heart.

Total value

The character of the Nine of Swords card finds himself outside the bounds of comfort, deprived of shelter and a warm floor with a carpet, which was characteristic of the Eight of Swords. In the Nine of Swords, the character has to leave the usual confines of her comfort. Before her, circumstances arise when inaction and passivity are no longer possible.

Relationship

According to this card a person may feel guilt for his bad behavior towards his partner, which led to his leaving. At this point, the tumult and storm of emotions took him apart and he realized his foolish actions, realized the loss of an important person because of his foolishness. This sense of guilt and loss keeps him going.

The card can also mean that a person suffers because of their relationship, whether it is an unhappy love, a complicated relationship or a long loneliness. Very often, against the background of this card, a person feels lonely and sees no way out of this situation. He may not start a new relationship for years, but at the same time tormented by memories of past love. This is a state when a person is unable to eat and sleep, constantly thinking only about his lost love.

In the context of an existing relationship, this card indicates excessive jealousy, mistrust and constant worries about the partner. The person may suspect that the partner is communicating with someone else, cheating on him or thinking about it. This is constant suspicion and distrust of the partner. Also, the partner may intentionally drive the person to the edge, squeezing emotions out of them, emotionally pressuring them. Constant accusations, exaggerating a person's shortcomings, destroying his personality. The person is so dependent on the partner and has lost so much faith in himself that he does not know how to cope with this situation.

Sometimes this card reveals hard truths such as infidelity, betrayal and deceit, which shocks the person and causes deep sadness and suffering. It can lead to stalking the partner, desperately wanting to be with them and learn nothing else in life. It is endless tears, humiliation and suffering in the relationship.

In terms of feelings, it is self-injury, guilt, and painful memories of a favorite object. This object may appear in dreams, glimmer in the street, or seem in every face one encounters. It is tears and anguish over the loss.

Work and finance

This is suffering from financial difficulties, when a person finds himself in a difficult situation and does not know how to earn money. For example, he may be far from home, have no accommodation, and the bed marks on the map indicate his homelessness. Finding a job also proves difficult and the person is tormented by his hopelessness. In addition, he may have financial obligations such as loans that he is unable to repay, which is often accompanied by sleepless nights and anxious thoughts.

Lack of funds and a depleted financial cushion can only leave a person with a hard life, as shown on the map. It can also be a situation where a person is forced to step out of his comfort zone, for example, he has not been able to find a job for a long time and now he has to deal with this problem, but the idea of working makes him afraid. He is afraid to take responsibility and is under a lot of stress.

Often this card indicates an unloved job that brings a person a lot of suffering. He may feel that he is hitting a ceiling and missing out on his life by working in a hated position. Due to lack of alternatives, he stays in this job and sinks into deep depression. There is also envy of those who live a better life than he does, according to this card. It is envy of the financial position, status and success of others. The person believes that he does not succeed in anything and finds pleasure only in his failures.

This card can also mean deception in financial and business matters, disappointment in partners, deals and projects. It symbolizes failures and setbacks at work, and expectations about career growth are unfulfilled. A person may feel stressed before deadlines, when he fails to complete his work in time or fails to manage his work. He is disappointed in himself as a professional and in his profession as a whole.

The card also indicates fear of audits and reports, as well as of major career changes, whether it be a promotion or a move to a new level. The person may experience fear and doubt that he or she will not be able to cope with the new obligations, that he or she will make mistakes and fail. This can create a tense atmosphere at work, team problems and a discomforting work environment.

Occupation

Psychologist, neurologist, anesthesiologist, anesthesiologist, caregiver, people working with stressful and critical situations, bedding manufacturer or retailer.

PLACES AND FACILITIES

Hospitals, mental hospitals, a place that reminds a person of a trauma experience, movie theaters showing horror movies.

Tip

Concrete actions should be taken to overcome anxiety, as a lot of thinking can lead to panic attacks. It is important to shift your attention to other tasks and not to escape from reality, as well as to make decisions and take responsibility for your life.

Warning

It is necessary to change your attitude to the world and stop seeing the situation in a negative light. It is important not to create unnecessary problems for yourself, as anxiety can lead to the destruction of something that has no real grounds. Fears can paralyze a person, and giving up a familiar and comfortable position can be risky.

Ten of Swords

Symbolism

1. There is a vague shadow on the girl's back - it represents what she seeks to forget, to hide from the gaze of others and not to bring into the new life, into the light to which she is heading. Her face is illuminated by the light of a new day, her gaze is already forward, into the future, and there is a clear desire to end the past. The scars on her back are the sword marks of past trials, of the painful and treacherous path she has traveled. She dreams of healing and has no intention of going back to the way things were.

2. She lifted her right foot off the ground, preparing to take a step forward. The step has not yet been taken, but her intentions are clear - to cross the invisible boundary between the past and the new beginning of her life's journey. The raised foot is a symbol of departure; it no longer touches the ground, which is a metaphor for a secure foundation. This lack of contact with the ground suggests that the girl no longer sees a foothold in the past, in what surrounded her, and is looking for a new foothold, a new foundation. Her right foot, indicating the direction of movement, is her desire to go forward, to the new.

3. The bright orange color of her clothing symbolizes a thirst for change. Orange color is associated with vitality and the beginning of something new, probably because of the similarity with the morning dawn. It suggests that the girl is fully prepared for a new day that has already begun.

4. Sand is considered a symbol of purification in the East, as it is used for purification rituals instead of water. It suggests that one is going through a period of separation from the past, ending the old

life cycle and purifying oneself from it. The unsteadiness of sand also reflects the passage of time and can symbolize fear of death and concern for health, as it reminds one of the transience of life.

5. The prevailing sky on the map is a symbol of the soul, freedom and infinite space. By freeing oneself from the outdated, one becomes free and begins a new life cycle. This is a complex and painful process, a critical point of existence, marking the transition to a new phase of life.

6. A round bracelet on a girl's hand is a symbol of infinity and renewal, marking the end of the old and the beginning of the new. Its placement on the right hand emphasizes the renewed future, because the right side is traditionally associated with the future.

7. Ravens flying to the right emphasize the direction to the future, and no one on the map no longer looks back - all movements are directed only forward, to the dawn and renewal. Ravens can symbolize foresight, foreseeing the best way. They fly to where they foresee a favorable future, and the girl follows their example. During this period, new allies, advisors, friends or valuable insights may appear in a person's life - as if signs from above.

Total value

The individual makes the choice to end a long period of suffering, puts a decisive point, cutting the bonds of despondency, even at the cost of his own wounds. He realizes that the breakup will be painful, but staying in the state personified by the Nine of Swords is no longer bearable for him, and he decides to end it. He is determined to leave the circumstances behind, however painful they may be for him.

The Ten of Swords symbolizes deep pain, the end of an era, emptiness, complete disintegration, the need to say goodbye to the obsolete, whether it be relationships, profession or beliefs. This is the moment when old projects, expectations and tactics fail and a new direction must be sought. In the Ten of Swords a person has to face his fears; while in the Nine of Swords he could still be plagued by these fears, in the Ten of Swords they have already been realized in his life. For example, if in the Nine of Swords a person was afraid of parting with his partner, then in the Ten of Swords this parting has already taken place.

The Ten of Swords depicts a personality pierced by the swords of past failures, tragic moments, disappointments and personal tragedies. His heart resembles a sieve and it is difficult to heal. Such a person is depressed and extremely heavy, and his negative aura can pull those around him into an abyss of calamity. He may have a harmful component for the psyche, endure a lot of psychological traumas, which turns him into either a masochist or a sadist, depending on in what light the divination presents him. The self-esteem of such a person is destroyed, and his eyes are written with tears, he perceives his existence as a continuous series of troubles leading to an inevitable end. His life foundations may be shattered, he may exhibit cruelty and coldness. This person feels the weight of failures and encounters with harsh life circumstances. He may be overwhelmed by complexes and lack the will to resist difficulties.

Relationship

These are torturous relationships in which deceit, humiliation, and taking advantage of the partner may occur. They may indicate that people in this relationship do not value each other, constantly inflict emotional bruises on each other, and seek to hurt each other. There may also be ignoring in the couple, stopping communication, emotional blackmail, scandals, and fights.

This card can also indicate that one of the partners is suffering a lot from the relationship with the other, as he/she is not getting proper respect, feeling neglected by the partner. The person may not give enough time to their partner, constantly criticizing them, comparing them to others, destroying them emotionally, wearing them down and draining them of their energy, bringing pain and frustration. This card can make a person feel so depleted that they may begin to contemplate ending the relationship and sometimes even their own life.

This card also indicates the exhaustion of the relationship itself. When partners negatively affect each other over a long period of time and bring each other to the point of nervous exhaustion, the relationship can become a burden. It can also indicate a toxic partner who doesn't value their partner, making them unhappy and insecure, putting sticks in their wheels and ruining their lives.

This card predicts a breakup and the end of a relationship. It can also mean an abrupt end to a relationship, when one of the partners loses their footing and feels lost. These can be divorces and hard breakups, where one says goodbye to their partner as if saying goodbye to the meaning of their life. This period of a relationship can be very difficult and frustrating, both in terms of the partner and the very notion of a relationship. In this card, the person may no longer look back, although suffering greatly, but he is ready to move forward, opening a new page in his life. In addition, this card symbolizes a new beginning, the unknown and the anticipation of something new and pure after a difficult period.

Work and finance

A difficult financial situation forces a person to work without a break, without a day off. This is similar to physical illness and emotional exhaustion. The level of fatigue from finances and work is such that even walking seems like a burden. Nothing brings joy and work is seen as something that just has to be done, including paying off debts and loans. All the money earned goes immediately and there is no motivation to work. Additional expenses may include medical costs or unexpected problems, such as an accident at home that requires a significant financial outlay.

There may also be circumstances that drain a person for a long time. A person who has been working for many years may support relatives who depend on him and he is unable to refuse them, which causes a feeling of helplessness and lack of support. Moreover, a person may set overly ambitious goals, for example, setting himself a goal of completing 150 orders in 3 months, while he usually manages five, and he is forced to maximize his efforts to keep in step and reach his goal. This can lead to exhaustion as well as possible health problems once the goal is achieved.

It is excessive spending and financial losses, crisis in finances and professional activities. It is the disintegration of plans and hopes related to a business or project. It can also mean that a person is no longer able to generate new ideas and their mind is exhausted, requiring immediate rest and reboot. In some cases, it can mean a complete change in the field of work or niche, if a person has experienced failure in a previous job and has become exhausted, and now decides to close that chapter and look for a new job or field of endeavor.

Occupation

Massage therapist, acupuncturist, trauma therapist, critical care specialist, and ritual worker.

PLACES AND FACILITIES

Abandoned places, buildings, ruins, emergency rooms, construction sites, with iron bars sticking out, junkyards.

Tip

It's time to put a stop to a situation that has been going on for quite some time and has been draining your energy. If you feel unhappy about something and are suffering, you should not continue to tolerate it. The situation will not fix itself, and now is the time to put a decisive end to the past.

Warning

It is important not to rush into making decisions about ending and leaving. The card also warns against a possible abrupt and unpleasant end to a situation. It informs you not to enter into a relationship that is doomed to failure or to take on a job that will exhaust you. The card emphasizes that the consequences can be very severe.

Page of Swords

S ymbolism

1. The Page of Swords has the specialty of cleansing and healing the mind. The sword that used to bring misfortune has become a weapon that clears the way. It now leads us to the truth that keeps us above the abyss of the unknown, as we move from one state to another. The Jack leads out of difficult experiences, from the Ace to the Ten of Swords, onto the road that leads to truth.

2. The henchman goes barefoot, so it's easier for him to balance himself on the sword. But his shoes are nowhere to be seen - this apparently does not matter to him, as he does not yet have enough experience to realize how important proper footwear is. After all, it becomes very important when coming into contact with the difficult terrain on the path.

3. The Pazh's hair flutters in the wind, symbolizing freedom and flexibility of mind, readiness to absorb new knowledge. It also indicates his simplicity and sociability.

4. The four bulbs symbolize the ability to structure the knowledge gained. The henchman walks on his toes, which indicates his ability to balance and not be overloaded with excessive information. It also indicates good coordination in the learning system. Birds on the sides symbolize news and knowledge received from other people.

5. The henchman moves forward, but does not get distracted from reading the book. He assimilates knowledge carefully, and receiving information helps him move forward. The light bulbs that appear represent insights that arise after receiving information, which helps him maintain balance on the sword.

He has a balance between knowledge gained externally and that which is born in his own mind. He is able to analyze and ponder on his own. The book exudes a variety of colors, indicating that what he is focusing on is very fascinating to him and provides an escape from the gray of everyday life.

6. The bandana on Paj's head is bright red, expressing his enthusiasm for learning and gaining knowledge, as well as his passion for information saturation.

7. The crystal around his neck symbolizes concentration, clarity of mind, and indicates good memory and learning ability.

Total value

The Page of Swords is a guide to the world of swords and their influence. The henchman resolutely casts aside his sword and begins his journey through a land inhabited by swords and their arcana. This card often serves as a guiding star in difficult moments, leading one through storms and tumultuous times. This path is like a pilgrimage, where in the beginning point A and at the end point B, but the traveler is no longer who he was. On this path a person is completely purified and transformed.

The Page of Swords embodies impulsiveness, inquisitiveness, and mobility. It is a card of opportunity, news and information. The Page of Swords helps you find the best solution to difficult situations, even if it means accepting unpleasant news or having long discussions. His curiosity knows limits and he always wants to know everything that is going on, which can sometimes irritate others with his questions and excessive curiosity. His sharp mind allows him to analyze and understand those around him, investigating their actions and intentions.

This is an independent person who is willing to expose himself to risks and provocations for the sake of curiosity. The Page of Swords has critical thinking and is willing to take risks for the sake of experimentation to see what comes out of it. He is an explorer, studying the world around him. In his relationships with others, he can be straightforward and cold, without hiding his opinions or using unnecessary words. His cunning and shrewdness allow him to reveal the truth and does not stop in front of obstacles. The Page of Swords is characterized by good logic and a broad outlook, always acting in his own interests.

Relationship

Immature relationships, manifested by infantilization in the relationship and attempts to control the partner, often include reading correspondence and stalking, as well as pointless arguments. Criticizing one's partner, teasing about their shortcomings, and pointless recriminations are all common manifestations of such relationships. In certain cases, a person may issue ultimatums to his partner, forcing him to choose between himself and other aspects of his life, this is done in order to confirm his importance in his own eyes. Such a person often seeks to predict their partner's actions, as well as to understand where the relationship will lead and what benefits they can derive from it.

The card may indicate that someone is scrutinizing the couple, spreading gossip and harboring jealousy. It also represents an independent person who does not want to be suppressed. Such a person may use strange and inappropriate jokes and find it difficult to establish harmonious relationships. In such relationships, fears of breakup, endless quarrels and reconciliations are not uncommon.

Immature relationship, lacking deep soulful intimacy, special feelings and warmth. The partner may criticize and interfere in all areas of the other person's life, offer advice and ask a lot of questions. This can cause tense moments in the relationship when you have to talk to resolve conflicts or clarify situations. Unhealthy jealousy, suspicion, provocations, tests and intrigues related to the partner and his/her personal life may also be present in the relationship.

The Page of Swords can excessively interfere in the life of the partner, being interested in his past, former relationships and everything related to them. He may ask provocative questions and always suspect his partner of something. The Page of Swords is a rebel and he does not tolerate his freedom being restricted. If he sees rivals in his lover's heart, he may seek to black mark them, make up their faults and defame their reputation in his partner's eyes. He is adept at managing information and can manipulate it.

Work and finance

News related to finances. The Page of Swords emphasizes the importance of analyzing one's own income and expenses, keeping detailed records of expenses, prudent management of finances and thinking about possible investments for their effective multiplication. In general, you need to rationally assess your financial capabilities. This card also indicates an increase in customers, purchases and orders, especially through online platforms.

The general meaning of the map implies the need for additional control, careful analysis and revision. Work requires active thinking, and everyday tasks cannot be performed mechanically. It is important to actively participate in the process, plan strategically and experiment with new ways of working. For example, if the current advertising campaign is not delivering the expected results, you should look for reasons, modernize the approach and, based on the results, adjust the strategy.

This card can also indicate disorder in the workplace, situations when a person is simultaneously studying and working. Important aspects in this context are professional development, acquisition of new knowledge and skills. When performing tasks, there may be nervousness and a desire to cover everything at once. The card also indicates possible conflicts at work, gossip, intrigue and attempts to gather information about others. In general, it advises to actively make new contacts, interact with people, share information and use communication for career advancement.

The card emphasizes the importance of persuasive skills, the ability to present the advantages of your business or service to attract customers. The Page of Swords is skilled in the art of handling information, and in order to increase income one should emphasize this aspect by properly presenting and disseminating information. If the question is whether the client base will grow and the expected profit will come, this card gives an affirmative answer.

Occupation

Nurse, gun person, assistant, translator, negotiator, manager, marketer, writer, chess player, IT specialist, detective, teacher. Intellectual labor, info-products.

PLACES AND FACILITIES

Places in nature, bluffs, cliffs, mountains, hiking, pilgrimage sites, libraries, computers, books, phones, ceilings, lamps.

Tip

It is necessary to carefully double-check all documents, messages and available information. The card emphasizes the importance of additional training and learning new knowledge. It also emphasizes that despite the potential risks and volatility of the situation, it is important not to remain in a state of stagnation and despair, which could bring the previous cards, but to move forward, enriching your mind with new useful information. In relationships, one should adhere to the principle of "trust but verify" - not to immerse oneself in illusions, but to strive to understand the real picture.

Warning

It is advisable to avoid excessive curiosity and not to interfere with advice or unnecessary information where it is not very appropriate. You should also avoid allowing others to intrude into your personal affairs. Since the environment can be volatile, you need to remain alert and ready for unforeseen circumstances. To avoid serious mistakes and downfalls, it is important to pay close attention to detail and have reliable information to help you navigate the circumstances.

Knight of Swords

Symbolism

1. The motorcycle merges with the sky, indicating a human desire for boundless knowledge. And the motorcycle stands on the path, emphasizing that for this man only knowledge gained through his own experience is true.
2. The raven in the sky symbolizes speed, courage, high ambition and the desire for freedom.
3. A crossbow indicates a person's willingness to overcome difficulties. It also symbolizes the ability to wound with words, like arrows fired from a crossbow.
4. The white sweater and the hood speak of this person's indifference to others. His emotional aloofness and coldness are expressed in the fact that he puts on a hood, turns his back to others and does not take into account the opinion of others. He has his own opinions that are difficult to change. He is like ice, inaccessible and prickly.
5. We do not see his past (the path he has already traveled, the left foot). We see only the future, only goals and aspirations (the road ahead and the right foot), which means that a person can harbor his past experiences and mistakes without revealing them. This is not a person who will reflect on the past; he is consumed with the future and his path to his desired future. The red sole on the shoe symbolizes a bright change in life, an advancement achieved through his perseverance, dynamism and determination.

Total value

The Sword henchman, who is gingerly testing the ground beneath his feet, tries to find his balance by steadying himself on the sharp blade of his sword, while the Knight of Swords rushes forward at full speed. He will reach his motorcycle and increase his speed even more once he gets on it. The Knight of Swords symbolizes unexpected and dynamic circumstances involving mental tension and increased activity, during which a person is hyperactive and strives to achieve a goal or solve a problem with unwavering determination.

The Knight of Swords is extremely confident in his conclusions and statements, trusting in the rightness of his thought processes, and is ready to stand for his views stubbornly and categorically. It is incredibly difficult to change his mind about anything, as he is convinced of his ability to quickly and accurately analyze situations and believes that he is superior to others in this art. This Knight is a whirlwind of thoughts and words, pumping them up to inappropriate magnitude and seeks to fill them all available space, penetrating these thoughts of others.

His ability to speak and think becomes his main tool: he is often blunt and ruthless in his expressions, not caring about the possibility of offending someone with his harsh words. If the Queen of Swords with his honest words illuminates a person, seeking to prevent him from getting lost in illusions, the Knight of Swords does this because of deep dissatisfaction with the imperfections of others, seeking to confirm in every possible way his rightness and superiority.

For a certain period of time, the Knight of Swords is able to realize a lot of things, thanks to his vigor and focus on the goal. He is characterized by vividness of mind and speed of reasoning, is intelligent and quick-witted. Knight of Swords is a brave warrior who bravely rushes into battle with problems, resolutely eliminating them on their way. He is able to overcome any obstacles. He shows coldness of feelings and emotions, but if necessary, he can become an advocate for others, regardless of whether they are right or wrong. If their views are similar to his own, and he considers them his allies, he will persistently defend their interests. The Knight of Swords can display a fanatical drive and belief in the justice of his actions, no matter how harsh they may seem to those around him.

312

The Knight of Swords always seeks to destroy outdated concepts, throw off the shackles of stability and get rid of any restrictions. He is constantly looking for new goals and achieve the advancement of his ideas. He is not afraid to leave behind those who could previously be considered his close friends, if he is convinced that their views and goals are different. Without further explanation, he can simply cut ties and no longer include these people in his social circle. He is not attached to anything at all, and if someone is limiting him or preventing him from moving forward, he will quickly sever those ties and move far away.

This is a cynical and provocative person who easily makes enemies and happily engages in arguments and squabbles. He can also be fickle in his views and unstable in his interests, as he is like the air of air, often changing his life orientations and mental concepts. But he has a strong will and perseverance, and for him the end always justifies the means.

A person who corresponds to the image of the Knight of Swords, unlike the Doge of Swords, who seeks to accumulate knowledge and information, believes that he is well aware of everything around him and does not need additional information. He believes that he can come in and share all the knowledge and ideas he needs and impose his views and opinions. He is prone to temper, aggressiveness and sarcasm. Such a person appreciates speed and height, he has grandiose ambitions and broad goals. He is ready to explore the world and learn, extracting new knowledge from different sources.

Relationship

The couple are two extreme sports enthusiasts. They prefer traveling, outdoor activities, hiking and fast driving. There is often tension in their relationship and the partners sometimes compete with each other. This card can indicate two possible scenarios: either one partner is running away from the other or trying to win his attention. The Knight of Swords is characterized by spontaneity and a tendency to be prompt in relationships. He does not procrastinate and does not exaggerate in the preliminary stages. This person is ready to quickly start a relationship, and perhaps after a short time will offer his partner to live together or even marriage.

It is important for him to have something to talk about with his partner. It is important to him that his partner has life goals and plans, and that his partner strives to achieve them without staying put. Common goals for both are also important. The intellectual development of the partner is also important to the Knight of Swords. Although there are no manifestations of pure love in this card, there may be feelings of jealousy, coldness, anger, and even indifference.

This card can also indicate that the person is now focused on his or her own affairs and more important goals, and has no time or interest in his or her partner. It may indicate that the person is around their partner for some favorable reasons or plans of their own, and that there is no true love in their heart. In addition, the card may indicate possible conflicts in the relationship and cooling between partners. The Knight of Swords is considered to be a person who is reserved in expressing emotions and can sometimes seem rigid and unfeeling. Romance is not close to him.

The person represented on the Knight of Swords card can show pronounced toxicity in relationships. He is prone to constant criticism and reproaches to his partner, is able to stir up scandals and cause nervous tension. Jealousy of such a person can reach extreme manifestations, and he is ready to react aggressively to anyone he perceives as a competitor. In relationships, he shows intolerance, nervousness and selfishness, and can take revenge in cold blood if he believes that his dignity has been hurt.

The Knight of Swords can create a tense and conflictual atmosphere in a couple. Relationships with such a person can be accompanied by frequent quarrels, mutual accusations and conflicts. Partners literally live on the edge, often facing disagreements and dislike for each other. Their relationship may become so strained that they may even hate each other and constantly compete and argue. Dramatic scenes of jealousy and violence may occur in the relationship. Partners may take revenge on each other and hurt each other, even going so far as to destroy their partner's love life.

Such a person may interfere in the personal space and life of his partner, criticize him and impose his worldview. He may display tyrannical traits and ignore the feelings and condition of his partner, bringing him to extreme negative states. He constantly seeks to cause conflicts and is capable of suddenly losing his temper and blaming his partner for various situations. His behavior can be tactless and excessively harsh. Despite his jealousy, he is ready to protect his partner and fight for his interests. He prefers to discuss the relationship with his partner openly and honestly.

Work and finance

In this sphere, the Knight of Swords follows the beaten path, guided by his own logic, intuition and accumulated experience. He also relies on intuition and visual perception in his work. Thanks to his well-developed intellect and logical thinking, he is able to compose a chain of future events in his mind and determine how promising an opportunity is. This person is ambitious and strives for his career goals, quickly moves up the social ladder and develops his business.

He realizes that to achieve financial success it is necessary to be proactive, not to wait for a convenient moment, but to make decisions quickly and put them into practice. He is focused on long-term success and is ready to overcome obstacles on his way. The image of an eagle in the sky symbolizes his ability to cover large scales of work and effectively plan his actions. According to this card, you can expect a sharp increase in income.

The bracelet on his hand resembles the shape of a watch and indicates his high speed and the value of every second. He strives to stay ahead of the competition and maximize his productivity. According to this card, a person is often ambitious to surpass others and excel in his career, which motivates him to reach new heights.

He is determined to overcome financial barriers and is eager to advance his career and develop his business. He is intelligent and competent in his field, but has not yet achieved the mastery that the King of Swords represents. The Knight of Swords is on the way to his goal, and his movement towards it is intense and fast.

He can ignore the generally accepted rules at work and act on his own. He is not ready to delay processes and work slowly; his working style resembles that of a sprinter who strives to achieve goals quickly and efficiently, overcoming time and space constraints. By this card, one can expect a quick flow of money, but conflicts over finances are also possible. The person represented by this card tends to change jobs and avoid routine.

Occupation

Analyst, information technology specialist, litigator, investigator, blogger, stuntman, military, mathematician, lawyer.

PLACES AND FACILITIES

Fields, places for sporting events, biker and motorcycle rallies, stores for touring, bicycles, motorcycles and cars. A shooting range, a place in nature, mountains, as the eagle symbolizes height.

Tip

At this point, it is important to focus on mobilizing your own resources for an energetic breakthrough. Postponing things for later and looking for excuses for inaction will not bring success. The situation calls for swift and decisive intervention. It is important to show courage, responsiveness and boldness, it is necessary to be able to defend yourself and your activities, to be ready for quick and decisive action.

Warning

You should not rush without prudence and carry exorbitant responsibilities. In the current situation, it is important to pay attention to detailed planning and re-evaluation of many trifles. It is important to first thoughtfully consider each step, and then proceed to action. This card also warns that you should not be rude and rash to others, avoid groundless conflicts and scandals involving other people. Now is not the best time to demonstrate your uncompromising and strictness in your relations with people.

Queen of Swords

S ymbolism

1. The Queen, unlike the Page, wears shoes, which shows her concern for comfort in her daily movements. She has enough experience to realize that going barefoot is not the most comfortable way to get around.

2. By sitting on a sturdy and secure seat, the Queen demonstrates her self-sufficiency and confidence in her own life. It is also a symbol of her steady attitudes and inner stability. The high position from which she sits allows her to observe the world around her from all sides.

3. The flag she has hung clearly marks her territory and her concern for her own safety. For all queens, it is a symbol of water, which reflects their concern for their own space. The flag serves as a sign of belonging to a certain social status and self-identity. The blue color of the flag indicates the Queen's self-sufficiency, self-confidence and ability to control her life and limit access to outsiders. She has strong personal convictions and high intelligence. Her thoughts are systematic and she has high stress tolerance and equanimity. Next, from the Queen, are the brown and red flags, with brown above red, indicating her predominance of earthy and rational traits over impulsive and fiery ones.

4. The water element, representing emotion, in her case, is like being under lock and key. But there is always the possibility of accessing this emotional side of the Queen, her ability to understand and care for others. Her concern, however, is to help others see and understand the true nature of things, sometimes this can be abrupt, but always for the good of the individual.

5. Her hand holds the hilt of the sword, which symbolizes her willingness to react to scoundrels and unfair looks, she is ready to critically perceive many situations. The Queen of Swords tends to be distrustful of those around her. The point of the sword is pointed downward, indicating her reluctance to start conflicts, but any attempt to violate her personal space, she will raise her sword to protect her interests. The hand at her chin indicates her ability to analyze a situation and make important decisions.

6. She is planted high up in the mountains, which speaks to her resilience and determination through the hard road of life. The Queen possesses experience and sagacity. Snow symbolizes pause, peace, neutrality, and the aspects of life she holds in coldness and indifference. The frosty sky represents the wisdom and clarity of her mind.

7. The open knee speaks of her vitality and resilience in the face of any adversity. The raven in the sky indicates her ability to think on a wide gamut and independence in opinions. This symbol emphasizes her free thinking and ability for global analysis.

8. The rim on her head serves to keep her thoughts in order, giving them structure and organization. The leather material of the rim symbolizes the strength, flexibility and durability of her thinking. The ring on her ring finger expresses her desire for spiritual development and her belonging to a certain social status.

9. Mountains are a symbol of success and achievement, a symbol of career success. A difficult path to the top of the career is like climbing a mountain. Such a person can sacrifice relationships, feelings for the sake of achieving their goals. Queen of Swords shows purposeful, focused on a particular task of a person. Such a person clearly and competently prioritizes to achieve financial results.

10. The blue flag shows the symbol of the air element. This flag means the kingdom of the Queen of Swords. The flag is turned to the right side, like the Queen of Swords herself, which speaks of her foresight about the future, the ability to calculate steps, to see comprehensively (from the mountain), her desire for new

accomplishments, to new levels and achievements in life and career. This indicates good job prospects, but suggests that they can only be achieved through effort, firmness and character, as well as analytical ability.

Total value

The Queen actively seeks to expand her knowledge in various fields, while for the Queen of Swords is extremely important absolute transparency of everything that happens. She prefers the bitter truth to any seductive tall tales. Thanks to her vast life experience and pronounced shrewdness, her developed mind is able to accurately analyze the moves and actions of others, as well as to predict the development of events. In the image of the Queen of Swords crystallizes the enlightenment of the intellect, wakefulness of the mind and ruthless gust of wisdom, which penetrates everything in its path.

Queen of Swords has a well-developed ability to critically analyze information, and she is not afraid of conflicts and disputes arising because of this. She is characterized by emotional restraint and objectivity. This card symbolizes a person who has experienced many difficulties and disappointments that helped to form a realistic view of the world, devoid of illusions and naive expectations. The Queen of Swords knows that dishonesty can lurk everywhere, and her wisdom and experience are enough to not trust anyone unconditionally. She relies solely on her own judgment, accumulated experience and logic.

The card can signal that in the upcoming situation there may be an escalation of conflicts, the emergence of a tense and hostile atmosphere, all in the name of revealing the truth and restoring justice. The Queen of Swords is imbued with the elements of air and water, due to which she has the unique ability to penetrate deeply into the essence of various thoughts and concepts, like water that penetrates into the most secret corners. It also has the ability to accurately and thoroughly analyze, recalling in this aspect the properties of the element of air, which represents purity and precision of thought.

The Queen of Swords appears to us as a strong and independent personality, characterized by logical thinking and rational approach to life.

It is inherent independence in views and actions, it avoids excessive attachment to both cases and people. The Queen of Swords can afford to abandon personal relationships in favor of professional self-development, for example, immerse herself in academic research, devote her time to creating innovative ideas or a comprehensive search for truth.

Relationship

The Queen of Swords does not have high feelings and deep emotions. She is a perfectionist and wants a partner who will fully meet her requirements, but she is rarely satisfied with the result. The Queen of Swords may indicate a woman who is angry with men, completely disillusioned with them and with relationships in general. She may have experienced severe stress in the past due to the loss of a loved one or a breakup. May indicate a widow, a divorced woman or just a lonely woman who does not let men near her. It may indicate such individuals who do not know how to cry, who strictly forbid themselves to cry, suffer, and suppress these emotions, not giving them an outlet, and thus they develop into neurosis.

In relationships it is usually cooling, unwillingness to reconcile with the shortcomings of the partner, deep resentment, disappointment, unwillingness to communicate and reconcile with the partner. Unwillingness to show their feelings, a person turns away and closes himself off from his partner. This can be a quarrel, as well as a review of the relationship, when a person sits down and really evaluates the picture, how good the relationship is, how pleasant or unpleasant it is to spend time with the partner, whether it is worth spending time on him or her at all.

Behind the bars we see a bowl of water, as a symbol of the fact that the Queen of Swords does not allow her emotions to take over, in general she is little empathic and sometimes insensitive, hides his feelings and does not give them free will. Can suppress emotions. Guided by cold reason, not paying attention to emotions, neither on their own, nor on others. In general, to feel feelings for her may be forbidden, she is belligerent to others, cold and arrogant towards people. Queen of Swords has an even emotional background, makes decisions with a clear mind, rarely relying on the heart and feelings.

The Queen of Swords is very independent and will not allow her partner to limit herself in any way, so it is better for her to be alone than with someone who in any way claims her freedom. Queen of Swords relationships can be tense, the partner can criticize the person, sarcastic, point out his shortcomings, point out where he miscalculated. It can indicate that people in the couple are honest with each other, but at the same time are not very close, it is like the relationship of two scientists who are madly passionate about their intellectual work, and they have sex once a year. But they are interested in each other, they are asexual but very intellectual, and it is their high intelligence that attracts them to each other.

Work and finance

The card advises not to give up in the face of difficulties and do not get discouraged, not to go on the emotions, and with a cold and clear head to calculate your steps on the way to the top of the career. This map recommends to work methodically, to have a clear plan of work, so that everything was as in the palm of your hand, calculated and scheduled, how much earned, how much invested, how much sold, how much you need and what to buy, where and how much to invest, to get what is planned, here are important figures and facts. A clear vision of the situation and a sober assessment of your activities. In your work you should not give yourself a break, you need to be more demanding to yourself and your projects.

Financial situation depends on how much a person is able to negotiate with others and competently calculate his steps in financial matters. Also to improve the financial situation one needs diplomacy, increase one's competence, have a good understanding of work issues.

Occupation

A doctor, a teacher, a military officer, a servant of the law, a lawyer, a researcher, a tax officer. This is intellectual labor, work with technology, IT specialist, journalist, architect, customer service.

PLACES AND FACILITIES

Mountains, snowy places, skyscrapers, borders, also abroad, what the flags say, that is, it can mean another country. Libraries, a doctor's office, a lawyer's office, a teacher's or scientist's office, a programmer's workplace.

Tip

The situation requires more confidence in your abilities. You can only truly rely on yourself, but the ability to negotiate and resolve issues diplomatically can also be useful in this situation. It is important to be honest with yourself and fair in your decisions, as well as to rely on reason and logic. It is necessary to look at the situation from the outside, rise above it and evaluate it fully.

Warning

The card may serve as a warning of vengeful and envious enemies. However, it can also indicate that a person can become his own enemy by excessively restricting himself and depriving himself of the pleasures of life. For example, by forbidding oneself time with friends or the ability to relax to avoid distractions. This card also suggests that you should not be cynical and cold in your communication with others. It is important to take off the snow queen mask so as not to alienate people close to you.

King of Swords

S ymbolism

1. The King of Swords is towering in the mountains, surpassing the Queen of Swords. His boots are torn and the soles are abraded, a testament to a long and difficult journey tempered by experience and a wealth of knowledge.

2. The owl symbolizes wisdom and discernment, the ability to see around you at night without moving, reflecting shrewdness and attentiveness. It reveals a person capable of unraveling deception, without prejudice, with a great outlook and intelligence.

3. The raven represents justice and wisdom. On the card, the person wears shoulder pads made of raven feathers, embodying their qualities: constant striving for justice, wise decisions, excellent communication skills and the ability to learn.

4. The multitude of animals around the King of Swords indicates his excellent communication skills and ability to extract the right information. He is an intelligent and sociable intellectual with good logic.

5. The bat symbolizes vigilance and alertness, reflecting caution and continuous reflection, always ready for new challenges.

6. The dragonfly on the sword symbolizes lightness of thought, a bright mind and the ability to self-heal, which means keeping a clear mind and an active way of thinking.

7. Two swords and two feathers indicate that the King of Swords is always guided by logic when making decisions. He is capable of being both light and decisive, and has a strong defense and intuition.

8. The King of Swords sits on the peak of a mountain, representing

impregnability and wisdom, the path traveled and experience gained. His relaxation and confidence are seen in his readiness for action and defense.

9. The sword bears the symbol of air, which defines this person: where he thrusts his sword, that is his territory. Unlike the Queen of Swords, who has clearly marked out her territory, caring for safety, as water is her domain. The King of Swords, like all kings, possesses fire and is a conqueror, not confined to a specific space. This could mean that the person is still in search of the perfect match in life. If he likes someone, he will boldly express his feelings and may claim that person. Even if they are not yet in a relationship, he may still be jealous and push away the competition.

10. A person's shoulder pads are made of raven feathers. Usually shoulder pads symbolize responsibility, but since they are made of feathers, it means that the person does not feel the weight of responsibility for external circumstances, another person's feelings or any obligations. Feathers symbolize lightness and freedom, showing that the person is carefree and not attached to anything.

11. Gray hair is associated with wisdom and life experience, it shows an experienced and knowledgeable professional with deep knowledge and great authority in life. The peeled off sole of the shoe indicates a person who has seen a lot and managed to experience, overcome many difficulties. This person is probably a professional in his business, with a lot of training and practice under his belt. He is light on his feet, has the speed of thought, words, ideas, and the sharpness and suddenness of a sword-like response.

Total value

The King of Swords has within him the powers of air and fire. After the Queen of Swords has carefully opened her eyes and found the truth, the King of Swords becomes the guardian of the mind. He rigidly controls the mental processes, carefully regulating the flow of thoughts. No thought can escape his control or slip away unnoticed. He fully realizes the importance of keeping the mental plane clear and pure, avoiding outbursts of emotion.

The King of Swords realizes how powerful thought is and realizes that the art of controlling it opens the way to controlling one's destiny. He is serious and persistent in his search for truth and accurate information, displaying equanimity and judgment. His critical thinking prevents him from taking words on faith; he always verifies information, realizing its effect on the individual.

The King of Swords has outstanding intellectual abilities and is a true genius. He is passionate about researching nanotechnology and is capable of creating projects aimed at developing various technologies, including space programs and futuristic concepts. The King of Swords is characterized by fearlessness and determination. He has a strong inner backbone and is able to rely on himself in any circumstance, without fear of problems and prepared to solve them. He is irritated by the weakness and indecisiveness of others, and considers those who allow their emotions to interfere with important decisions to be weak.

Relationship

In relationships, he is not too romantic and prefers to provoke his partner to get information. However, more often than not, the King of Swords personifies a man who has lost interest in passion and may even be hostile to it. Unlike the Queen of Swords, he does not sit on a cushion, but on the ground, and for him comfort, security and stability in a relationship are not so important.

For the King of Swords, it is important that there is something to discuss and think about in a relationship. It is important to him that his partner is intelligent, and feelings and sex are not highly prioritized. He can easily hide his feelings and not show tenderness to win his partner over. He prefers to create intrigue and try to interest with his cognitive abilities. In a relationship, he keeps his partner at a distance and gives the impression of an impregnable rock.

Work and finance

The King of Swords card is surrounded by animals, indicating the possibility of generating good income through interaction with groups of people and collectives. The image of an owl on the card promotes rational spending of money and helps to ensure the advantage of income over expenses.

In the field of finances, it is necessary to calculate everything carefully and keep everything under control, or find a worthy specialist for this task. The King of Swords card speaks of skill and professionalism, as well as a serious approach to business. It requires an analytical approach to increasing capital, which implies clear and precise math, where every step, every investment and every interaction is calculated to the smallest detail.

It is important to remain objective and draw on your own experience. Money can come through interaction with others and communication. The King of Swords card speaks to the need to gain authority in one's field and describes a successful entrepreneur who is visionary, intelligent and able to carefully consider his or her steps to scale his or her business.

Occupation

Doctor, military, inventor, IT specialist, space explorer, creator and designer of new technologies, lawyer, judge, pilot, policeman, philosopher, critic, journalist, mountaineer, traveler.

PLACES AND FACILITIES

Mountain LOCATIONS AND OBJECTS, northern countries, cold places, doctor's office, military recruiting offices, observatories.

Tip

In this situation, it is important to show restraint and equanimity, as well as the ability to think without wearing rose-colored glasses. You can also seek the help of a professional with a rational and mathematical mind, who will help to take control of the situation thanks to his insight. It is also important to take a creative approach to problem solving, to act outside the box and to remain objective and impartial.

Warning

It is necessary to reconsider your attitude to the surrounding and close people. You should think about whether your relationship with them is not deprived of sharpness and coldness, whether you are not hiding behind the mask of a tough and cynical person? Also, it may indicate that other people may have a harsh and cold attitude, which can have a negative impact on relationships and other aspects of life.

PENTACLES

Ace of Pentacles

S ymbolism

1. Pentagram is a symbol representing a star with five ends bounded by a circle, and named Pentacle. Pentacle is associated with financial prosperity, stability and health of a person. The word "penta" stands for the number five, and each corner of the pentagram symbolizes separate elements: spirit, fire, water, earth and air. The pentagram is a symbol of good luck and protection. If the seven-pointed star symbolizes the entire universe, the five-pointed star represents man, his individual self in the world.

2. The presence of mandalas in a round shape indicates their integrity and completeness. In the center of the mandala is a pentagram, emphasizing that man is a key figure, harmoniously fitting into the system of the Universe and uniting all the elements. The Universe supports the human being, providing care and concern. Mandala made in yellow tones symbolizes effective interaction of a person with the world around him, his optimism, good luck and prosperity in health.

3. Sprouts symbolize the awakening of life, creative growth and improvement in the field of work. They signify the beginning of new projects and the creation of new sources of income. This card heralds the successful implementation of plans and emphasizes that the efforts invested will be rewarded. The sprouts indicate that plans can be turned into reality and what has been conceived can be realized. They also indicate that what was hidden may become visible, for example, a person may not expect success for his project, but suddenly a buyer or investor will appear.

4. Roots symbolize the connection to the earth and family. They

point to home, native places and ties to relatives. Therefore, there may be a family business or a craft that has been passed down from generation to generation and a person may learn it to earn a living. The expression "a person with roots" indicates that such a person is firmly rooted. Therefore, this card indicates a stable income and confidence in the future. It also emphasizes the importance of going to the heart of things, looking into the depths and analyzing the situation from within, rather than a superficial attitude to matters.

Total value

Each Ace symbolizes the beginning, provides a chance or a new perspective, and in the context of the Ace of Pentacles, this chance appears in a particularly clear form. He does not slip into the vague distances of the future, and offers a clear and tangible path associated with material benefits. The Ace of Pentacles promises material prosperity through financial bonuses, opportunities to increase income, valuable gifts, important acquisitions or decisions related to real estate.

This card provides an opportunity to lay a solid foundation for a relationship, career, significant acquisitions, or other endeavors that require stability and strength. It hints at the fact that building strong relationships requires an impeccable foundation, not undermined by grudges or claims, and strengthened by common pleasant experiences, care and understanding. In the field of earnings Ace of Pentacles implies the creation of a solid base for future growth and expansion of business through the attraction of knowledge, skills, contacts, investment in self-development, attracting valuable personnel and effective promotion. The Ace of Pentacles portends that the development and growth of anything requires a strong support. Thus, the Ace of Pentacles symbolizes well-being and prosperity in the area that is the focus of attention. It is a state of well-being, harmony and stability.

Yellow symbolizes the ability to see, perceive and understand. It represents the development of individuality and independence, and is considered the beginning of a new life and a time of joyful hope. Yellow is also associated with efficiency and physical endurance. The earth represents a fertile field where you can plant the seeds of any endeavor, knowing that in time they will grow and bear fruit.

The Ace of Pentacles describes a practical person who appreciates material possessions. He never denies the importance of money or carries negative beliefs about finances. He does not believe that money is evil and realizes that a lot of money can be earned through honest work. Such a person appreciates quality things, enjoys good food and knows how to relax. He is hardworking and ready to perform a variety of tasks. It is important for him to create a comfortable environment for himself and provide for his life with a financial safety cushion. He is also willing to give practical support, whether it be financial help or physical involvement, such as helping with repairs. The Ace of Pentacles is a trustworthy person with whom you can make plans and count on his reliability, he sticks to his decisions and promises.

Relationship

This card indicates a stable and harmonious relationship in which there are shared values. In this relationship, people place a significant emphasis on physical pleasure, including aspects such as sex, going to restaurants, sharing food and wine tastings, going for massages and spas, and shopping. They are hedonists who seek to enjoy life and their partnership, and therefore make efforts to enrich their relationship with a variety of pleasurable moments. This relationship has a strong foundation of mutual trust and care for each other, which provides stability and reassurance.

It is a feeling of happiness and comfort in a relationship where the partners are comfortable with each other. They know each other inside and out, understand each other's preferences and live in harmony. In such a relationship, it is important to show care in material and physical terms, such as cooking dinners, giving gifts and arranging meetings in favorite places. This card can also indicate the financial side of the relationship, where money and gifts play an important role. One partner can support the other by providing financial support and fulfilling various desires. The card can also symbolize the possibility of conception and birth of a child.

In a relationship described by this card, partners often participate together in household chores, decorate their home, and have romantic evenings. Their feelings are mature and grounded, and they show strong affection for each other. This relationship values a sense of comfort and security, as well as a desire to build a shared future and develop family bonds. Partners care for each other and stay close to each other for a long time, growing the seeds of love and supporting each other with tenderness and care.

Work and finance

This card is very favorable in financial aspects. It symbolizes the arrival of gifts, profitable deals, successful investments and investments, the possibility of inheritance, as well as any kind of material support. It also indicates quality purchases and investments in yourself and your home. The Ace of Pentacles card represents various types of financial bonuses, such as bonuses and other pleasant material benefits. It predicts a comfortable and stable work environment where employees can enjoy a variety of perks including free lunches, extra paychecks and other material bonuses. This card also indicates an excellent chance to prove yourself and be generously rewarded for your efforts.

The card also speaks of valuable opportunities that should be taken seriously and nurtured as if they were seeds that could grow into something beautiful. The Ace of Pentacles drawing of roots and sprouts emphasizes that the opportunities received should be carefully tended and not overlooked. Just as a gardener cares for a plant, it is important for the person in this card to patiently nurture their chances. Overall, this card portends support and good fortune as it depicts two hands holding the Pentacle. This is a symbol of blessing for success, wealth and prosperity in work and housing matters. The card also indicates successful investing, increased income and savings.

Occupation

Family business, artisan, sculptor, gardener, landscaper, numismatist, bank employee, realtor, construction business, midwife, nanny.

PLACES AND FACILITIES

A house, a plot of land, a dacha, places in nature, a garden, a vegetable garden, a place where one feels safe.

Tip

Do not be afraid of labor, do not be afraid to get your hands dirty with hard work. It is necessary to actively begin to fulfill tasks and work persistently. Do not miss the chances that fate provides, accept them with gratitude and develop them to obtain significant results. Competently invest your efforts, get on your feet and avoid laziness. It is important to be more practical and judicious in various situations.

Warning

You should review your investments in yourself and your business and determine if they are really producing the desired results. It is necessary to find a balance between pragmatism and passion. One may also encounter over-generosity, where one is willing to give much or even everything they have to help others. It is important to be wary of what you take or what you give away, given that resources that have been earned by one's own labor may be given or given to others.

Two of Pentacles

Symbolism

1. The girl has a pair of pentacles in her hands, one of which has quite a material form - it is a bag. This bag is a symbol of life experience, knowledge and skills accumulated during her journey. The pentagram, decorating her bag, emphasizes that the burden of life, consisting of experience and established habits, as if chaining her to a certain place, making movement on new paths more difficult. The closed nature of the bag hints that the accumulated knowledge and experience will be useful in the future, that she does not wish to lose or forget them, as they are of the greatest value to her. The physical presence of the bag also hints at earthly aspirations and gaining confidence in reality.

2. A foggy bag, like a reflection, indicates the desire for novelty, for exploring the unknown and the desire for adventure. It suggests that a person is ready for change and feels the need to go beyond the boundaries of the usual worldview. The pentagram on this ghostly bag is a symbol of protection, which suggests some carelessness in the girl's aspirations, that her dreams may be built on an unstable foundation, ignoring potential risks. This ghostly bag is a sign of dreams and the desire for change, reminiscent of the Moon.

3. The thread that holds the two pentacles together is limiting, but at the same time offers a solution that can help to get out of confusing circumstances. It symbolizes the opportunity to use the accumulated experience as a map that can point the way to new opportunities and horizons.

4. The girl's closed eyes express her thoughtfulness and unwillingness

to face the necessity to make a choice. It is as if she is trying to evade the upcoming decision, hiding from the immediate need to look at the situation openly.

5. The beads, along with the skirt, form a single thread of events and decisions, emphasizing that each action must be carefully weighed and considered. It is a reminder to consider the pros and cons and to create a complete picture of the consequences of a choice.

6. The bright orange skirt symbolizes the pursuit of pleasures and pleasures, making one ponder that there may be even more joys lurking in the unknown. And the beads on the skirt, facing the side of the misty bag, emphasize this longing.

7. The white void around creates an atmosphere of calm and concentration, providing a space for gathering thoughts and meditation, and is also a symbol of the desire to start over, with a clean slate.

Total value

In the Ace of Pentacles card, the person feels solid and full of confidence in the future, but when the Two of Pentacles appears, he begins to feel that he has lost his dynamism, has gone too deep into his roots and has become immobile. He is faced with the question of whether what he has is enough. This moment makes him strive for new horizons, leaving the zone of stability in pursuit of expanding his boundaries. Thus, the Two of Pentacles symbolizes the uncertainty of the current moment, imbued with doubt and hesitation.

The Two of Pentacles card symbolizes the continuous hustle and bustle and restlessness of the spirit. It is like acrobatics, keeping balance in the air, constant efforts to find stability in the unfolding events. In it lies the desire to take two opposite positions at the same time, the desire to compromise between the material and spiritual worlds, between two essential but different ways of development.

Thus, the Two of Pentacles card represents a person who is plagued by doubt and indecision, who thinks a lot before taking action. This card speaks of his caution and adaptability, his flexibility in finding compromises and his entrepreneurial spirit in connecting the diverse elements of the world around him. It also emphasizes his ability to find a way out of unstable situations, not remaining passive but acting actively, albeit with some disorder and chaos.

Relationship

A real bag sits against an innocent white ground, while its ghostly double floats against a soft pink sky. This symbolizes fluctuations in personal relationships, which can range from complete indifference and predictable stability to sudden immersion in deep love feelings, idealized dreams, romantic building of air castles and creation of fantastic illusions.

Ropes of delicate white color symbolize not only pure-heartedness, impeccability and fidelity, but also coolness in the relationship, emotional detachment and a tendency to conceal true feelings. In general, the presence of ropes can indicate a strong attachment to a partner, perhaps a meaningful bond between them. The situation may develop in two ways: a person may be faced with the choice of leaving or staying in the relationship. There may be a variety of factors that bind the person to the partner, but at the same time there may be thoughts about the need to start anew, leaving behind existing ties.

A voluminous warm sweater hints that a person craves support, lacks trust and emotional warmth in a relationship. The gray color of the sweater carries an implication of seriousness, as well as feelings of loneliness, emphasizing the lack of sincere closeness and warmth in the couple. That's why thoughts of separation begin to creep into a person's thinking - in search of the very emotional warmth and closeness they need.

The individual feels insecure, hesitant, and as if stuck in one place in his thoughts. Probably, he is no longer so close to his partner, because the doubts that oppress him do not allow him to open up completely. Ropes can also symbolize dependence on the partner, which may have a financial aspect: a person may depend on the material support of his second half. And although the partner himself may not satisfy him fully, remains at the expense of the sense of security and comfort that this connection provides him.

Similarly, the Two of Pentacles can signal constant emotional fluctuations in the relationship: the partners do not cease to get closer and away from each other, their connection is devoid of stability, and the mood of the couple changes as in a kaleidoscope, constantly challenging them to find common ground.

Work and finance

The bright red color of the bag symbolizes a huge craving for possession of material goods, passion for accumulation and satisfaction of material needs. At the same time, fifteen stitches stitched on this bag create an association with the fifteenth Major Arcana - the Devil, which emphasizes unhealthy attachment to material values and possible dependence on them, indicating the degree of their influence on human life.

People strive to achieve more, do not want to stagnate on what has been achieved, have a desire to rise above current circumstances, to seek new ways to expand their horizons and prospects. The Two of Pentacles card may reflect the emergence of additional sources of income, random luck or the opportunity for a temporary part-time job. However, the same card can also portend instability, bringing elements of uncertainty to the financial situation.

In a scenario where a person is contemplating an investment or investment, they may face a lack of experience in a new field and limited capital to feel comfortable investing without having to deny themselves anything. This situation is characterized by constantly moving money from one direction to another, searching for balance and trying to hold positions in different projects or places of work. According to the Two of Pentacles, in such circumstances it is often necessary to conclude contracts, sign agreements and execute documents, which is related to partnership and cooperation.

Occupation

Salespeople, managers, speculators, administrators.

PLACES AND FACILITIES

Stores, currency exchange offices, pawn stores, roads.

Tip

In today's world, it is important to learn how to effectively balance different sources of income, demonstrate adaptability and the ability to quickly switch from one task to another. It is important to learn to make decisions easily, without excessive hesitation, to free oneself from the weight of unnecessary thinking and to act quickly and decisively. The situation requires quickness of action and the ability to find non-standard solutions.

Warning

At the same time, you should not rush into all the hard work at once; it is more important to concentrate your efforts and choose one direction for development. The key is to be able to identify what is really important and to act consistently, following the chosen course. It is important to maintain personal conviction and independence of opinion, not to succumb to the influence of others. Fluctuations and postponing things for later can lead to undesirable consequences and loss of opportunities.

Three of Pentacles

S ymbolism

1. The three mandalas represent emblems of the physical body, mind and soul. Achieving balance between these aspects leads to superior achievement. The orange mandala symbolizes creativity, enthusiasm, the desire for self-realization and the expression of one's uniqueness. The red mandala signifies activity, focus and vigor. Green color is associated with material well-being, reliability, fruitfulness and harmony. The presence of a pentagram on a green mandala symbolizes achieving protection and stability in the material world. Red and orange mandalas are represented in the state of becoming, emphasizing the idea of the need to continue development and move on to spiritual and creative achievements after gaining material stability.

2. A man dressed in green shade is connected by a thread with a link of green mandala, which symbolizes his authorship and investment of male energy, strength, protection, perseverance and activity. The green mandala is the basis and foundation of the whole tapestry. The man is in a position above the women, his view is more spacious and he supports the whole design, emphasizing that the basis of everything should be rationalism and practical approach to life.

3. The girls are dressed in white blouses and skirts of red-orange tones, which harmonizes with the colors of the tapestry and mandalas. One of them is knitting, connecting all three mandalas, which reflects the three necessary qualities to achieve success and abundance symbolized by the tapestry. Knitting with red yarns speaks of favorable fortunes, health, endurance, passion and

perseverance in achieving goals.

4. The tapestry is the embodiment of abundance and prosperity. The energy of perseverance and determination is invested in it by the red mandala. Orange mandala promotes the desire to reach the cherished goal and enjoy the process of achievement. The green mandala symbolizes systematic efforts for growth and progress.

5. The white ball of thread lying on the floor represents the path of destiny, the path out of difficulties, the invisible bond between mother and child. The purity and whiteness of the thread hints that if a person makes efforts to improve the quality of his life, he is able to create for himself a happy and abundant life, by analogy with the creation of a magnificent tapestry from the threads.

6. A strong brick wall symbolizes the strength and reliability of the relationship, protecting them from any manifestations of jealousy, malicious rumors and other unfavorable external influences. It also reflects the stability of family ties and indicates that the building of strong relationships between partners is gradual, each small gesture of attention and care lays a solid foundation for the future.

7. A solid wooden floor symbolizes reliability and stability in a relationship, indicating that the partners have a deep understanding and support for each other. This implies that the foundation of the relationship is stable and can withstand the challenges of life.

8. The ladder symbolizes the common aspirations and goals of the partners, showing that they are both actively working to achieve their desires and go together towards the future. It indicates joint efforts and striving for common success in the relationship.

Total value

The Three of Pentacles symbolizes the transition from an unstable state, represented by the Two of Pentacles, to a more stable one, ensuring the gradual development and implementation of plans. It reflects diligence, predictability and organization. The Three of Pentacles also emphasizes skill and the importance of cooperation in team endeavors and joint projects. The card signifies strengthening positions, achieving balance, working harder and improving skills.

This card shows recognition of efforts on the part of others, can symbolize passing exams and various forms of qualification assessment. It indicates career growth, accumulation of knowledge and skills. The card emphasizes the need to build partnerships, join forces with others to achieve common goals and more successful realization of ideas. It also advises seeking counseling or engaging professionals to advance projects. The card is associated with gaining new experiences, acquiring knowledge, joining certain circles, which contributes to an increase in social status. It represents the accumulation of experience and its improvement.

The Triple of Pentacles depicts an individual deeply absorbed in the process of self-improvement. Such a person works hard, improves his skills and is characterized by practicality. He is able to find a common language in a social environment, to agree with others, to unite in teams to work together. This person gets along well with colleagues and partners both in personal relationships and in the professional sphere. He is focused on joint participation, strives to ensure that everyone makes an equal contribution to the common cause. Responsibility and rejection of arbitrariness is his credo. He approaches every case seriously and thoughtfully. He fairly distributes responsibilities both in the work team and in family life.

Relationship

Mutual respect of partners and their equal investments in the relationship create coziness and comfort in their union. They not only take care of the current well-being of their relationship, but also work together to achieve common goals, and may even accumulate funds for joint plans. The card may also depict joint efforts in hobbies, interests, and in caring for the home, such as home repair and decorating, where both put their energies and creativity.

This card hints at the likelihood of a marriage where the relationship is characterized by maturity and practicality. Both partners try to contribute to the well-being and strengthening of the union, striving to be the best version of themselves for their companion. Their labors and efforts are aimed at improving the quality of the relationship, and they delight each other with notable and meaningful actions.

Work and finance

Stepladder in tarot symbolism is associated with gradual but steady growth in the financial sphere and career advancement. This card does not portend a sharp and dangerous upsurge, because in front of us is not a ladder in the clouds, and modest, but functional stepladder. It also emphasizes the importance of speed and flexibility in solving economic problems. The stepladder symbolically points to favorable prospects in business and various projects, to the possibility of development and achievement of goals.

The white color prevails both on the tapestry itself and on the girls' clothes, symbolizing unity, adherence to tradition, and commitment to a common cause and ideals. The pose of the girls sitting with their backs to each other symbolizes mutual trust and focus on achieving a common successful goal. Tapestry is also associated with financial prosperity and stability, implying that the person this card points to has enough money to ensure a comfortable life and is successful in his professional life. It guarantees profit, availability of orders and flow of clients.

The Triple of Pentacles reflects a person's deep commitment to his work, his passion and pleasure in the process of work, professional growth and improvement of skills. This card shows high efficiency and quality of labor that is performed. It symbolizes a harmonious and cooperative working environment, where everyone is busy with their own work, but ready to support colleagues. The person associated with the Triple of Pentacles is a responsible and disciplined employee. This card symbolizes the achievement of new professional heights, recognition of merit and appropriate payment, as well as demonstrates a high level of expertise and competence in the chosen field.

The tapestry symbolizing marriage speaks of financial prosperity and comfort in the marital relationship. The card portends a long-term and reliable relationship, emphasizing the prosperity and comfort that partners create in their union.

Occupation

Designer, artist, seamstress. A person who is engaged in knitting, creates all kinds of decorative items and interior decorations, costume jewelry design. Architect, builder, consultant, lawyer, diplomat, teacher.

PLACES AND FACILITIES

Home, place of work, workroom, office, study room, workshop.

Tip

To do my own work, improving my professional skills and knowledge, to grow and develop in my chosen field. To work in tandem with colleagues, striving for equal contribution to the common project, avoiding selfish desire to take all successes for oneself. Work tirelessly to improve your skills, build up professional experience. Collaborate with others, actively sharing experience with experts or engaging them for specific tasks.

Warning

It is important to be able to take a break in time, to distract yourself, to lift your eyes from the daily routine. You should not get involved in extraneous projects or involve outside people in your endeavors when it is not the right time for new partnerships and joint endeavors. It is vital to give yourself the opportunity to disengage from work processes, give your body and mind a good rest and recuperate, so that you can look at your tasks from a new angle and return to them with original ideas and clarity of thought.

Four of Pentacles

Symbolism

1. The massive mountain in the background symbolizes the boundary between the woman and the inhabitants of the poor neighborhood. In order to reach a new level of financial development, she needs to let go of her fears and take risks, to free herself from the established beliefs about wealth. It is important to realize the meaninglessness of attachment to a certain amount of money and the need to strive for growth, to reach new heights in self-actualization, to set higher goals. Instead of fearing for the safety of your own fortune, you should look for ways to expand your financial horizons.

2. The brightness of the red dress emphasizes a deep attachment to material possessions and a passionate attitude toward money. This symbol can also indicate potential aggression towards those who, in the woman's opinion, may threaten her financial well-being. Red, associated with the first chakra, Muladhara, represents the desire to feel protected, and the presence of money brings a sense of security.

3. The abundance of jewelry on a woman symbolizes how her material success becomes a shackle that limits her freedom. It is an expression of fear of losing what she has accumulated, fear of losing stability. Thus, the person in the image seems to become a slave to the material goods that hold her in their chains.

4. The woman's head turned to the side with her eyes closed symbolizes her unwillingness to see reality beyond her own wealth. Opening her eyes, she would see poverty and the contrast between herself and others, but prefers to remain in her enclosed

world, ignoring other people's poverty. This indicates conservative views and limited perception, where one is unwilling to recognize the problems of others, focusing only on personal interests.

5. The traditional wearing of valuables in a turban here epitomizes a woman's tendency to keep everything of value to herself without sharing with others.

6. The background behind the woman's back depicts a light blue sky, which symbolizes the lightness and freedom she so desperately needs. In contrast to her, the people walking behind the fence do not feel attached to material things, they seem more free.

7. Mandalas on the wallet carry symbolism: green mandala reflects stability, red - power, yellow - success in financial multiplication, emerald - protection of wealth. The gray color of the wallet symbolizes constancy and a responsible approach to financial management.

8. Earrings with rune Othala emphasizes that the woman is oriented to the traditions and lessons learned from ancestors, particularly in matters of finance. Listening to the advice of the older generation, she may be following the stereotypes and patterns established in childhood, which may influence her financial behavior.

Total value

After a person has achieved some success in the Three of Pentacles, in the Four of Pentacles his ambitions are directed toward maintaining what he has achieved. He fears the loss of accumulated wealth, his reputation and social status. This behavior is also expressed in increasing avarice in relations with colleagues with whom he was on equal terms in the preceding card. According to this card, the desire for all fame and financial rewards to go exclusively to him becomes dominant, and there is no desire to share the results of joint labor with others.

By the Four of Pentacles a person is entirely focused on maintaining his current stable position. The card represents not only keeping control over the available assets, but also the conservation of circumstances, leading to some stagnation. It symbolizes one's ability to protect one's material possessions and income. At the same time, it may foretell the receipt of a valuable gift that has both material and emotional value. The situation described by this card requires clear limits, discipline and organization. It is important to guard your resources, loved ones, personal relationships and beliefs, to give value to what you have and to cherish it.

The individual described by this card adheres to the belief that all material goods have their price and that almost everything in this world is available for purchase. Such a person can work without weekends, living solely in pursuit of financial well-being and material recognition. He shows greed not only in monetary matters, but also in emotional communication, is not inclined to spread compliments and prefers to keep his real views and desires in secret, building around himself an impregnable wall that prevents others from penetrating into his personal space and thoughts.

The person looks extremely cautious and distrustful of people around him, as if at any moment expects a threat from the outside and takes precautions to protect himself. This person shows avarice, and it is not peculiar to him to share anything with others, he keeps his resources exclusively for himself. Extreme caution and intransigence regarding risky actions stem from a deep-seated fear of leaving the confines of the familiar space, which he considers his comfort zone. The character demonstrates a high degree of self-discipline, the ability to maintain composure in various situations and avoid stressful events, which contributes to his psychological resilience.

Relationship

At a wedding reception, orange turbans are a sign of the establishment of a marital bond. This symbol can indicate that a person is getting involved in a serious relationship and that their chosen one has intentions of building a shared future and family.

Othala's hand often symbolizes a family nest, the continuation of family traditions, the possibility of living together and raising offspring. It can indicate a deepening relationship, the presence of strong family ties. People united by this card are often connected not only emotionally, but also by blood ties, for example, common children.

In some marriages and relationships, there is a high degree of calculation and pragmatism. Marriage contracts may be present, and partners may practice equal sharing of expenses, avoiding shared financial and emotional investments. In such relationships, each pays for personal needs on his or her own, and there may be stinginess between partners, not only in monetary terms but also in showing affection. Relationships are often based on habit and a sense of duty, excluding the presence of deep emotional ties. Such a position can be accompanied by jealousy and a sense of possession, when mutual restrictions make the atmosphere in the couple overwhelming. In such relationships, partners may not show interest in each other's personal affairs and emotions, paying little attention to communication.

As far as the emotional sphere is concerned, one can encounter situations where a person is extremely appreciative of his or her partner. Like the girl on the card hugging the purse, the partner may feel deep affection and closeness to his life partner, considering him as an important and integral part of his being. However, outwardly, he may hide his feelings, giving the impression of emotional coldness and detachment. Such people are not used to express their emotions often, believing that it is enough to show them once. In such relationships, partners do not seek change and do not seek new levels of relationship, maintaining the status quo. This card also symbolizes loyalty and devotion, when partners value each other and avoid impulsive actions that can break the established stability and routine in the relationship.

Work and finance

In the financial aspect of the predicted scenario, there is no noticeable progress or expansion of opportunities. The situation is characterized by stability and certainty: everything remains at the same level, without significant changes. Even if there is a need for investments for business development, such as investments in marketing, advertising campaigns, educational courses or services of qualified specialists, the presented person is unlikely to dare to make financial expenditures. He perceives such steps as an exorbitant risk and prefers to stick to a proven, albeit small, but stable source of income, believing that "a tit in hand is better than a crane in the sky".

Reflecting the financial behavior of a person, this card indicates his tendency to hoard. It means not only saving money, but also accumulating

346

various valuables or setting aside funds to achieve certain goals. The card opens up the prospect of inheritance or real estate ownership, emphasizing the overall stability of the person's financial condition. According to the Four of Pentacles, a person can save up money for a future important purchase, while striving to control his expenses and avoid unnecessary spending. This card advises practicing financial discipline, saving and being frugal with one's budget.

Occupation

Bank employee, accountant, cashier, real estate business, real estate agent, rental income, family business.

PLACES AND FACILITIES

Banks, safes, wallets, jewelry boxes, balconies, small rooms.

Tip

Strive to maintain your point of view, strengthen your beliefs. To protect oneself and one's personal property from possible threats. Show firmness and adamancy in your right to possess something. Reduce unnecessary social ties, avoid borrowing, and keep all your resources with you. To lead a life within the limits of one's own financial possibilities, not to spend money on things that have no true value, to strengthen and stabilize one's financial condition.

Warning

Avoid stagnation, do not cling to stability as a lifeline. Excessive staying in the comfort zone and avoiding innovation can hinder personal growth. Do not suppress the desire for achievement and fear to take bold steps. The card also serves as a reminder that controlling behavior towards a partner or loved ones can lead to problems. Too much possession, self-interest and fear of loss often turn against the individual.

Five of Pentacles

Symbolism

1. The image of a woman in tattered clothes expresses not only material need, but also a decline in spiritual strength. It awakens in us compassion and a desire to help. Tattered clothes reflect not only poverty, but also a general decline in vitality, a series of misfortunes and deep feelings of defeat. It is the personification of both financial difficulties and moral suffering. The card illustrates a difficult period in life. The girl squatted on the floor with her head down on her knees, which symbolizes her exhaustion and lack of desire to see anything in front of her, deep fatigue has brought her to the point where there is no strength left to fight and keep any hope.

2. A door closed in front of a person is a metaphor for the impossibility to continue one's path, to achieve something desirable in life. It symbolizes the transition, which is not feasible now, but which in principle can be made if a person decides to act. Keyhole appears as a chance to change something, to open or close for themselves, it is a riddle of opening and closing roads to new opportunities. Everything lies in the hands of man: whether opportunities will remain hidden behind an insurmountable wall or whether he will open the door to the future on his own. The size of the lock and key hints that man has all the resources he needs to move forward, to open the paths to new opportunities that may be waiting for him very close at hand.

3. The key is a symbol of possession, the ability to make choices, the possession of freedom for action, knowledge and the beginning of a new path, opening new horizons, prospects, achieving goals and

realizing desires. The key gives a chance to expand the horizons and move in the direction of future changes. But a person does not want to even look at the key, on which the light falls, he doubts his strength to achieve the ultimate goal, and doubts himself; in addition, he is overwhelmed by fear of the unknown, which may hide behind the door. The light illuminating the key symbolizes the clues from the universe about how to find a way out of a difficult situation, but the person does not perceive these signs, having gone so deep into his worries and problems that he has not even given himself a chance to search for alternative ways and revive hope. This light is a sign of spiritual awakening, which tries to penetrate through the thick clouds of misfortune that envelope man.

4. A pentagram consisting of five mandalas is painted on the door. This ancient symbol of protection and harmony indicates that behind such a door one can find the desire for safety and reliable protection from the hardships of fate. The pentagram acts as a promise of refuge and a guarantee of inviolability for whoever dares to enter.

5. Interpretations of the meaning of the white bracelet are quite diverse. For example, Tony Blair, former Prime Minister of Great Britain, wore a similar bracelet as a symbol of support for the fight against poverty. This is reflected in the context of the map, emphasizing the desire to escape poverty, which is confirmed by his position at the threshold of change, at the door leading to a new level of existence.

6. The girl's crossed arms speak of her reticence and unwillingness to accept outside help. Her distrust of the world is so great that it is as if she is restraining herself, holding her legs, stopping her way forward, because the negative experience of the past has become a heavy burden for her, depriving her of the opportunity to move forward. She ignores opportunities, rejects them, afraid to even acknowledge their existence.

7. Dark shoes symbolize that a person's path was far from easy and light, he passed through difficulties and darkness of life's trials.

8. A sweater of deliberately bright red color, covered with a gloomy marsh shawl, symbolizes that the will to life, energy, passionate desire to fight and dynamism of man is obscured by a veil of despondency and suppressed by the burden of pessimism.

9. The tangle of threads resembling a spider's web and entangled in the girl's hair hints at a jumble of thoughts, overflowing with doubt and uncertainty, and demonstrates how heavy and tangled her musings are.

Total value

After the fortified and impenetrable barrier of the Four of Pentacles, where the person felt safe and secure, suddenly he finds himself all alone, without means of subsistence, destitute and deprived of the usual support. In the Five of Pentacles there is a breakdown of the stable and protected state in which the individual had been. In this card, he has lost everything that seemed to him a reliable support, which he held firmly in the Four of Pentacles. The Five of Pentacles symbolizes obstacles and loss of illusions, it is a difficult life ordeal. It reflects a picture of loss, loss and misfortune, indicates a moral decline and loss of willpower, doubts about their own abilities and favorable fate. This is a time period of decline in activity and a series of failures.

This card depicts an individual who is gripped by fear of life's challenges, who has lost faith in himself, who is gripped by insecurity, whose self-esteem is significantly lowered. He is shown to be shy, indecisive and sympathetic. His will to live is weakened and he does not believe in his abilities or that his life circumstances can improve. His inner energy tends to be minimized. The image of the person represented in this card depicts him as exhausted by the hardships of life, extremely worn out by the incessant unfavorable situation and literally squeezed like a lemon.

Relationship

This card may reflect the hardships of a partnership, where living together causes more pain than joy, but people stay together, bound by force of habit or because they have nowhere to seek solace. It may be that someone is so used to being in the role of patient partner that they have convinced themselves that no one will accept them outside the current union and leaving will bring more suffering. There is a fear of an unknown future and an inability to part with the familiar pain of the past.

A person may find himself in the role of a victim in a relationship where his partner systematically belittles his dignity, underestimates his abilities and talents, ridicules his appearance. This can lead to the fact that a person begins to feel insignificant and helpless, strongly dependent on his partner. In such a situation, financial dependence can also arise, when one partner is completely maintained at the expense of the other, perhaps even living in his house. Sometimes this state of affairs is aggravated by prohibitions on independent earning, which makes one of the partners completely subservient to the other.

The card can also indicate the presence of obstacles that prevent partners from being together - this can be both physical and emotional distance (symbolized by a closed door). It can indicate a deep love between people that is overshadowed by shared suffering. Or a couple separated by circumstances, where both partners long for each other but cannot meet, perhaps because of bureaucratic obstacles such as the inability to obtain a visa. The card may also reflect a lack of finances for living together or an inability to create comfortable living conditions for the two of them.

In the context of loneliness, the card can symbolize despair and the inability to find a way out of this situation. It can be associated with a loss of faith in oneself, in the opposite sex or in the relationship as such. It can represent goodbye and breakup scenarios, when one partner decisively closes the door to the other, and the latter does not know how to resume communication and is tormented by the lack of communication. It can also indicate unrequited love, when one partner's feelings are not echoed by the other.

The card can also express difficulties in reaching agreement and intimacy in a relationship where there is a lack of deep understanding and emotional connection. Closed doors can represent secrets and unexplored facets of a relationship, indicating that partners may be hiding significant secrets from each other. In some cases, one partner may be afraid to open the door to the other's world of secrets, even with the key, because they fear what might be revealed.

Work and finance

It is a significant financial loss and a clear decline in financial well-being. It is a sense of helplessness in the face of the financial difficulties that have arisen, as well as fatigue due to persistent money problems. It is a time of distress, of relentless wandering in search of shelter, a place of refuge. It is a time of deep need and lack of sustenance. The means of living are clearly insufficient, there is no steady income, no steady job. This is an era of forced austerity to the last coin. The loss of social status is accompanied by reduced professional growth, reduced job responsibilities, lack of bonuses and incentives. Freezing of bank accounts, state of bankruptcy, financial loss. These are punitive penalties, struggling with debt and onerous loans. Living beyond one's means leads to waste.

Presence of stagnation in career development. Period of crisis in money matters, difficult time for business and professional activities. Loss of confidence in their own abilities and in the future of the enterprise. Problems arising in the workplace and within the workforce. Downsizing of staff and rising unemployment. Prospects for professional growth and success become inaccessible to the individual.

The atmosphere at work causes anxiety, tension due to upcoming inspections and project deadlines. This card may also indicate that a person works hard, but his remuneration remains low, he does not appreciate his efforts, accepting negligible remuneration. In such a situation, he should immediately reconsider the pricing of the goods or services offered. In addition, the card may signal that the products are not in proper demand, so a large investment in the business at the initial stage may not be justified. You should not invest heavily until you have assessed which aspects of the business are profitable and which are not. You should test the market carefully at the beginning.

Occupation

Social worker, homeless shelter worker, janitor, key maker, door maker, low-cost clothing store worker.

PLACES AND FACILITIES

Homeless shelters, refugee camps, churches, social service agencies, hospitals, nursing homes.

Tip

It is necessary to gain courage and make a choice, to make a bold step towards the unknown, putting aside the fear of possible risks. It is important to strengthen faith in personal abilities, in the fact that there are forces to change the current situation. In addition, it is recommended to show increased attention, because fate provides a chance to change the current state of affairs, and it is extremely important not to wallow in self-defeat and self-doubt, so as not to miss a unique opportunity to get out of difficulties. In order not to be in a hopeless situation, you should actively take the initiative in your own hands, show determination and do not hide from reality, like an ostrich hiding its head in the sand.

Warning

If a person is inactive and continues to wait idly for change, without making efforts to get out of the predicament, the circumstances may escalate significantly and reach an extremely negative state. You should not ignore the opportunities and refuse the support offered. Staying in a state of apathy and despondency for a long time can lead to getting used to such a life, losing the last bits of inspiration and aspiration for self-improvement, which can end in a complete loss of personal growth and regression.

Six of Pentacles

Symbolism

1. The blue mandala is a symbol of the triumph of the spiritual over the material aspects of existence, embodying the pursuit of knowledge and deep wisdom. It also reflects the ability to empathize, implying that a person not only feels the needs of another, but also cannot stand aside without showing participation.
2. Cardinal red mandalas are messengers of compassion for those in need, they emphasize the active energy exchange between people. They hint that energy flows are constantly circulating, avoiding stagnation or depletion for both donor and recipient. In addition, cardinal red mandalas symbolize abundance, indicating that a person has something to offer to the world and something to receive from the world.
3. The warm orange mandala carries a message of a person's desire to bring joy to themselves and those around them, a commitment to share what brings pleasure and to help in whatever way they are able, to improve the overall quality of life.
4. The pastel beige mandala speaks of auspiciousness and equality in energy exchange, while the mandala of the color of peaceful brown speaks of a person's reliable protection in the aspects of financial stability and health, and emphasizes the fact that he feels confident standing on the ground.
5. The green background of the card is a symbol of life in its original form, harmony and perfect balance. It symbolizes stable balance and fair exchange between the parties.
6. The depicted hand on the card is a sign of power, protection and

transfer or reception of energy, mainly financial. Traditionally, the right hand is the giver, the left hand is the receiver. This rule states that those who have such a card, excluded any misunderstandings about debts and responsibilities. Everything is obvious and transparent for them: they know who has to do what, what to give and what to receive.

7. Lemniscata, the symbol of infinity on this card, indicates a fair exchange of energy between people, where no one is left out and does not use the other for selfish purposes. Each participant of interaction appreciates the investments of the partner and respects his contribution to the common cause. Lemniscata here acts as a principle of gratitude, when a person does not take received benefits for granted, but responds with generosity and gratitude for the benefits and services rendered to him.

8. The image of a road on the map foretells the opening of ways to achieve what you want, leading to an increase in wealth and prosperity. It also symbolizes successful career advancement and possible promotion. The road suggests the presence of many alternative ways to improve the personal situation, foreshadowing the imminent opening of promising opportunities. In addition, the road can be a sign of individual search in this world, in the choice of a suitable path of development and profession, and on lemniscate this desire is accompanied by a desire to be useful to society, to seek interaction and feedback from people. Also, the road is often associated with travel and movement; mandalas, which are passed from hand to hand, often symbolize stamps in the passport when crossing borders, obtaining visas and travel abroad. So, if there is a question of a future trip, the card clearly says "yes".

Total value

The Six of Pentacles reveals a path that symbolizes an accessible route that follows the closed opportunities noted in the Five of Pentacles. An individual who has left the restrictions in the Five of Pentacles, finds support, his life is filled with new opportunities, he opens the very door that used to hide him from communication with the outside world. In the context of this card he opens a wide range of prospects, there is a chance for exchange with the world, for receiving and giving. From the map of limitations of the Five of Pentacles he moves into the sphere of the Six of Pentacles, where he finds support, where the world reciprocates, where new horizons and opportunities open up before him.

Six of Pentacles is the arcana of help, support, mutual understanding, it emphasizes the importance of energy exchange in our lives. It reminds us that everything has its price - be it money, time, strength or health. And that it is necessary to understand what you have to give in exchange for what you want to receive. This symbol reminds us that it is important not to let energy stagnate, that accumulated resources should be actively used, invested, given, and new ones will come in return.

This card speaks of revitalization in the financial realm, replenishment of energy reserves, improved health and renewal of other important resources. Opportunities and generous gifts that seemed lost in the Five of Pentacles return in the Six of Pentacles in the form of support and new chances. The card reminds us to treat people the way you would like to be treated. It indicates that it motivates people to pay off debts, give each other financial help and support.

This arcana can represent a person who shares their resources and gives help, driven by self-interest, seeking something of value in return, or ego satisfaction, wanting to have a reason to be proud. The card can also indicate the presence of certain habits in a person, whether it be an addiction to smoking or a craving for a certain person.

The card also describes a mentally generous and generous individual who will not stand aside if someone needs help. This is a person who has an inner harmonious balance. With such a person is easy to find a common language, arrange an exchange of goods or services, make a fair deal. He is responsive and able to sympathize with others.

Relationship

Partners show mutual care and sincere respect for each other's personal views, life values, choices and feelings. They demonstrate complete acceptance of and respect for their partner's individuality. For them, the overall happiness of both participants in the relationship is of paramount importance, not just the well-being of one. There is no selfishness in their interaction; they generously share their feelings, give gifts, advice, care and help. There are no walls between them, they openly discuss all important aspects of life and are well aware of their companion's affairs. The bond between them is exceptionally strong, they perfectly understand and feel each other. When one of the partners is having a hard time, the other shares his worries and is ready to provide support. In such relationships, sometimes personal boundaries are erased, as people become inseparable, and often can no longer distinguish their own thoughts and feelings from others, but at the same time they feel absolutely harmonious and whole in such a unity.

This card can also indicate a relationship based on the financial interests of one of the partners, when one lives at the expense of the other, who maintains him without objection. In certain circumstances, especially if confirmed by other cards in the chart, may symbolize a long-distance relationship where the partners are separated by a literal distance. May also reflect a situation where one partner is paying for the other to travel or come to visit. The mutual support and sharing of responsibilities in such a couple is set up in such a way that both feel fulfilled and not deprived. It is an expression of deep affection and a desire to care for the well-being of one's partner.

Established relationships show strength and people feel a deep mutual affection. The emotional aspect may also reflect not only commitment, but also a great desire to both receive and lavish love. This card may signal that individuals are legally married or will be married in the foreseeable future; like the exchange of mandalas, which symbolize the circulation of energies, the couple exchange rings as a sign of eternal love and affection. For single individuals, this card carries a message: to attract a worthy companion in his fate should be previously honed personal qualities, look inside yourself and work on yourself. The famous expression: "Claim to fit in" fits here, that is, you should start with self-improvement and changes in yourself, if you want to attract good changes in your life.

Work and finance

The road and the lemniscata hint at the need for activity in the financial matter: money should circulate, not accumulate in idleness, for example, under the mattress. They should be invested, spent, thus maintaining their continuous flow, which contributes to the influx of wealth in life in large quantities. The symbolism of the road also suggests that the individual has prospects for income, and the funds are already on the way to him - you just need to stretch out your hand. Additionally, it symbolizes investment in personal development, in their own business and projects, which eventually returns the investment with interest. On this card, businesses and projects are profitable, there is a constant flow of customers, as well as opportunities for partnership and interaction with others.

The mandala image in the form of a money well is a symbol of direct attraction of material prosperity. Its design influences the subconscious mind, causing the desire to earn and multiply wealth. Mandala in the form of a well helps to accelerate the achievement of financial goals, spurring ambition and desire to improve the material state.

Considering this card, we can say that a person has the ability to borrow or take loans, but he is also able to repay them in a timely manner. This forms a kind of endless cycle of financial transactions: take - return. The card can also signal work trips abroad that involve income. According to this card, funds find their way to a person when there is a clear understanding of their purpose - when a person knows what he would like to spend them on. So, if there is a question about the expediency of a large purchase because of the potential need for money in the future, the card seems to suggest: "Make the purchase, the money will come", especially if the purchase brings joy - then the funds are returned quickly. The card also symbolizes various transactions - from simple shopping to buying or selling a house or a car.

This card is a reflection of the financial state achieved by a person due to personal contribution and efforts. It shows that the results in the material sphere did not come by chance, but are the result of directed actions, thoughtful investments and hard work. The received success is a deserved reward for fruitful work and the right strategy of doing business.

Occupation

Traveler, customs officer, volunteer, bank teller, store employee, cashier, tennis player.

PLACES AND FACILITIES

Store, bank, social assistance institutions. Also this card in this deck can indicate places of border crossing, passport control, visa center, registry office.

Tip

Spend effort, finances and energy wisely where positive results can be expected. Don't be afraid to share and avoid stagnation in the energy flow. Seek a healthy exchange of energy in both work processes and relationships. Appreciate the efforts of others and respond with appreciation. It is important to be attentive to both directions and take advantage of opportunities that arise, as even a small chance can open the way to success.

Warning

Urgently review your environment and pay attention to those areas where your resources and efforts are going "unseen". Perhaps this is a futile endeavor that is only draining your resources and energy. On the other hand, this card also encourages you to evaluate whether you are getting as much as you are putting in and emphasizes the importance of maintaining balance.

Seven of Pentacles

Symbolism

1. A situation is formed that begins to gradually unfold and give the first signs of activity. The case, on which a lot of work has been done, is already leaving the initial stage of its development. This is the case in which a lot of effort and hopes have been invested, now it is on the threshold of prosperous growth and blossoming. According to this card, go away doubts about their own abilities, because the first results of labor become obvious. This card also reminds of the importance of enjoying the process, not focusing solely on the end result; it is important to live in the here and now, appreciating every moment on the way to the goal.

2. The earth is a symbol of stability and safety, it is the guardian of all living things and the riches of our world. It symbolizes rebirth, the richness of fertility, the source and abundance of life force. This card emphasizes the importance of patience and waiting for the right time, similar to waiting for fruit to ripen or waiting for a mother to give birth. These processes cannot be rushed; they need time to mature. Just as a tree requires light for strength, so all areas of our lives need the warm glow of attention and care. Just as a child requires care, a relationship requires attention to a partner, and our work, our projects require patience and care for their growth and prosperity.

3. The yellow background and the emitted light from the hands symbolize the bright rays of the sun, representing creative energy, a source of life and warmth. This indicates that the matter or situation under discussion requires active intervention and care, cannot simply be left unattended, expecting it to resolve itself. For

its development it is necessary to invest vitality and create suitable conditions.

4. Mandalas located underground and intertwined with the roots of the plant symbolize hidden resources and opportunities, like seeds that sprout if given a chance and patience to nurture them. These are potentials, hidden from view, undiscovered and not yet manifested in the light, but with great promise. They speak of faith and conviction in one's own strength, in what is not yet visible and cannot be known in advance, faith in one's own talents, projects, in other people, in relationships, and so on. It's about believing that investments of time and effort will lead to deserved results.

5. The colors of the mandalas indicate what needs to be put into the core of the business: The pink mandala indicates the importance of putting love and care into the endeavor. The orange mandala emphasizes the importance of laying true desire and intention from the beginning. The two red mandalas emphasize the need to respond in a timely manner to changes that occur in a business or project, emphasizing that one should not stand back and trust the process to spontaneity, but rather provide support at critical moments, infuse energy and initiate development. The three green mandalas symbolize the expansion and development of a case, they speak of the advancement and growth of a case or situation.

Total value

After the individual in the Six of Pentacles has mastered the art of exchanging benefits with the world around him, having learned the balance of giving and gratitude, he faces the test in the Seven of Pentacles, where he has to give without expecting an instant return. Here he must learn the lesson of faith in his own strength and in the case for which he takes, to learn to see the hidden opportunities that can present him with fate. If he remains persistent, will tirelessly put his heart and soul into his endeavor, carefully patronize him and sincerely believe in success, then, in the end, he will be able to reap a rich harvest of his labor.

The card emphasizes the importance of exercising patience and believing in yourself and the potential of your endeavors. Your project will develop slowly, but steady growth and progress is sure to follow, though not immediately, but surely. According to this map, you need to give enough time to make your efforts effective. Haste is pointless here, but it requires non-stop work and constant investment of energy in the case. The card emphasizes the importance of perseverance in achieving goals and finding joy in the process itself.

This card depicts an extremely unhurried person who approaches each of his affairs with particular scrupulousness and without haste. He finds pleasure in the quiet flow of life, appreciates every moment, does not seek to participate in the endless race and daily hustle and bustle. Such a person masters the art of waiting, he is ready to work hard for many years for his goal, confident that diligence and patience will eventually give the best fruits.

Similarly, the card may indicate a situation in which a person invests a great deal of effort, but the result is a disproportionately small effect. It can also reflect an unnecessary waste of energy and lack of perspective. An example may be a situation when a person expected to receive a bonus, but despite all the work he has done, he has not seen the expected reward. The person invested a lot of effort and the result was disproportionately modest.

Relationship

In the sphere of relationships, this card can symbolize the processes of establishing kinship ties, for example, waiting for an addition to the family, caring for a child, which indicates the close interdependence of partners. It can also predict the likelihood of pregnancy. In addition, the card hints at a relationship in which there is a clear dominant role of one of the partners: this person is both a guardian and a mentor, and the age difference between the partners may be noticeable. The partner who occupies a more powerful position, treats his other half as a fragile creature, wraps him with care and protects him from any troubles and difficulties. This person is inclined to invest his forces and material resources in the well-being of his partner, contributing to his advancement in society, supporting him in career growth, business initiatives, etc., because he is deeply confident in his potential and prospects for success.

This symbol also reveals a gradually growing sense of affection between the partners, indicating that over time their union is becoming stronger and more stable, and the relationship is gaining more maturity. In such a union people experience an increasing love for each other, feelings are not just budding, but actively developing, starting with the first interest, sympathy and attraction, which symbolizes a germinating sprout. But the card also indicates long-lasting, enduring feelings, rooted deep in the ground of their relationship history.

People described by this card are inclined to confirm their affection through actions, surrounding their companion with warmth and attention, sparing no personal resources to create coziness and comfort for the beloved. The card also opens the possibility of such relationships, where the partners are not yet a couple, but exchange signs of attention and hints of sympathy, while none of them does not show determination to make the first step. It is as if they are frozen waiting for the resolution of this uncertainty. The card advises patience and letting the relationship develop naturally, emphasizing the importance of investing mutual attention and care in the couple.

The card may reflect the state of a person who is not yet sure about the need to build a relationship with a particular partner, continuing to observe him or her and assessing the general outlook, trying to understand how important this relationship may be and where it may lead in the future. It hints that one should be prepared to develop the connection slowly, for haste is inappropriate here. The partners may be quite comfortable in the current status of their relationship, which has not yet reached the degree of intimacy necessary to move to intimacy or marriage.

The seeds of feelings are already present in the heart of a person, manifested in a reverent attitude towards the object of their feelings. This card can also indicate a situation when one of the partners is constantly demanding more from the other than he is able to give, trying to adjust him to his own expectations and standards. At the same time, this card can symbolize the desire to motivate the partner to personal growth and moving forward, to develop better qualities and achieve new heights.

Work and finance

This card signals gradual progress in the development of a personal enterprise or project. Career growth is carried out leisurely, with thoughtful attention to each step. It indicates the presence of long-term prospects in the work and financial sphere, the realization of which will require hard and systematic work. In symbolism, mandala cards enclosed in the ground denote the potential for development, which can be utilized by creating the right conditions for their growth. The card motivates one to continue an endeavor despite the lack of immediate results, as it requires considerable effort or investment of resources, but may ultimately prove more successful than one might expect.

At the same time, it may predict that the invested efforts will not bring the expected benefits. It also promises fortunate chance finds, increase of money and other material benefits. According to this card, now it is important to be prudent in financial expenditures, postpone large purchases for a later period. It is important to realistically assess your resources and opportunities to complete what you have started, as it will require considerable time and energy. The card suggests the need for diligent and careful work to achieve professional heights. The success predicted by this card comes after much effort.

Occupation

Gardener, caregiver, nanny, agronomist, farmer, investor.

PLACES AND FACILITIES

Garden, vegetable garden, cottage garden, house yard, house, park, flower pots.

Tip

The most sensible step is to dive into the nuances of the task, carefully analyze every aspect and allow time for the natural evolution of what is happening. The most sensible step would be to immerse yourself in the nuances of the task, carefully analyze each aspect and allow time for the natural development of what is happening. It is important to show resilience and determination in your endeavors. The card instructs to lay a solid, thorough foundation for any activity, based on the understanding that the results directly depend on the quality of the invested efforts and initial resources - the future harvest depends on what was sown.

Warning

It is important to allocate your efforts and time wisely, paying attention to the areas where expenditures do not bring appropriate results. Maybe your efforts resemble the fruitless labor of Sisyphus. There is a risk that the labor may be in vain. The card also serves as a warning: you should not abandon what you have started halfway through and capitulate before the end of the road is reached.

Eight of Pentacles

ymbolism

1. The greenish flame of the wax candle in the girl's hands becomes an emblem of warmth, enthusiasm and deep devotion to matters related to growth and prosperity. Sitting with her back to the observer, the girl demonstrates with her whole appearance that her main attention is directed to the light of the candle, a symbol of prosperity and improvement of personal skills.

2. She carefully gathered the herbs that had yielded in the garden of the Seven of Pentacles and carefully dried them to use in her magical potions. These dried plants are a sign of her ability to approach problems in an unconventional and creative way.

3. A writing pen lying on her desk symbolizes a period of learning, establishing and expanding business relationships. It can also indicate the signing of important documents, agreements, denote literary skill. The pen, located next to the volumes of books, hints at the creative influence of the girl on her environment. Book as a symbol of knowledge and wisdom, and books next to it - four, emphasizing the need to have a clearly organized system of knowledge.

4. The girl's bare feet speak of her desire to feel comfortable while working without discomfort and tightness in her movements. This image emphasizes her need for absolute creative freedom and personal space, as well as indicates the desire for stress relief, unity with the natural elements, thirst for maximum productivity.

5. Owners of high hairstyles often have a stormy temperament, but such people usually do not have many sincere friends, which marks the peculiarity of their character.

6. The workspace becomes an extension of the girl herself, she seems to merge with it, and this space seems to absorb her completely. All her time, her thoughts and her main focus of attention are unwaveringly fixed on the work process, which takes over her completely.

7. The halo of orange-pink and red hues above the girl's head reflects her active work, intense creative process and deep passion for the activity that has completely captured her attention.

8. The changing phases of the Moon are a symbol of passing time, continuity, symbolizing fertility, constant renewal, rebirth, eternity, secret knowledge, changeability, intuition and depth of feeling. It indicates the importance of choosing the best time to act, corresponding to the lunar phase, the ideal day. It also emphasizes that one is ready to work at any time, and that the desired result is achievable by working hard without regretting the time spent. Blue-blue mandalas represent the purity of water as a source of life force, and express the ability to empathize and developed intuition, which is important for competent financial management.

Total value

When an individual has completed the planting of seeds in the context of the Seven of Pentacles, with ambitions to give life to a new plant, he moves on to the stage depicted in the Eight of Pentacles. Now he has not only harvested and prepared the crop for further use, but he is also immersed in painstaking labor: combining herbs, creating elixirs, and drawing up detailed instructions for his creations. This card embodies the essence of routine work and calls for steady labor. Its wisdom is that rigorous labor will eventually lead to cherished achievements, personified by the Nine of Pentacles. But work should be methodical, professing the principles of systematicity and stability, because in front of us - a true workaholic.

The person identified with the Eight of Pentacles has the character of a realist, realizing that the results directly depend on personal effort, and that without initiative success is impossible. He tends to see the essence of problems and avoids illusions such as "I work hard, but there is no money - then I just have no luck". Instead, he recognizes that perhaps it's the wrong approach to work or the wrong field, and is willing to change his tactics and strategy. By refusing to be lazy, he shows himself to be an effective worker. The representative of this card is convinced that the cause of many problems lies in inaction, and that the best solution to any difficult situation will be employment and earning money. He believes that work can banish bad moods and discouragement. This is a card that emphasizes focusing on one's work responsibilities. According to it, a person is improving as a specialist and polishing his skills every day, also believes that true rest lies in changing activities.

The representative personified by this card stands out for his productivity and discipline. He is truly absorbed in his work and is a true professional in his business. He tirelessly improves his professional arsenal, constantly learning and developing. He is characterized by discretion, prudence and prudence. Extremely able to work, this person is able to continue to work even in conditions of illness. He is always open to new knowledge and actively expands the scope of his skills, which makes him an outstanding specialist.

This card illustrates circumstances that emphasize meticulous attention to detail, that require deep analysis and careful attention to detail to achieve goals. These are scenarios where there is a need for patience and the conviction that it is only through one's own efforts that one can build one's own well-being. Here we are not talking about inaction and dreams, not about visualizing desires, but about the willingness to roll up your sleeves and work hard, about reality and a practical approach.

The card emphasizes the need to put in order all of his endeavors. The Eight of Pentacles symbolizes the continuous development of a person and improvement of his skills, it is the moment when after a certain period of time, a person looks back and sees how much he has been transformed and how much his life has changed thanks to steady work.

A person associated with the Eight of Pentacles realizes his full responsibility for his own life and that he has the ability to change it in accordance with his aspirations. Eight of Pentacles is not discouraged in the face of difficulties and does not look for convenient excuses, does not hide behind the pretexts of karmic laws or injustice of fate. This card teaches that the main cause of problems - in idleness. The main tenets of this arcana - the belief that patience and effort can overcome any obstacles, and that it is necessary to work on every aspect of life. Want financial prosperity - work, strive for harmonious relationships - put effort and work on them, not expecting initiative from a partner, want to master a new language - engage regularly. Constancy and systematic - these are the qualities that the Eight of Pentacles emphasizes as the most important. This arcana fosters diligence and dedication.

Relationship

The mortar in this context is an emblem of the feminine, which embodies creative power, while the pestle symbolizes the masculine component. These two elements together represent the process of change and the emergence of new aspects in the relationship between the partners.

Flowers are often used as a means of enhancing the feeling of love and rekindling it. They are a sign that the couple's relationship has the potential to restore harmony and strengthen the sensual connection. However, flowers alone are not able to correct the situation - it is necessary to take active action, turning them into amulets, creating potions from them and so on, which emphasizes that the relationship, as well as the preservation and maintenance of love requires constant work and attention.

This card may reflect hidden feelings, where the individual prefers not to show their emotions, acting from a position of indifference and emotional impregnability. The position of the girl on the card with her back turned may indicate that she faces ignoring or resentment from her partner. This behavior may be part of manipulation, when the partner manages the situation through lack of attention, refuses to communicate. The person may be entirely absorbed in their own affairs, not noticing those around them, and not tolerating distractions from their tasks, completely focused on work or personal accomplishments, and as a result leaving no time for their partner.

The girl in the illustration is seated on a white chair, which emphasizes her stability in the position of emotional coldness and remoteness. Often it can indicate that the individual shows excessive pride and arrogance, which prevents him/her from making contact and initiating warm communication with the partner, being an initiator of reconciliation and resumption of warm relations.

The posture of a person with his legs thrown back indicates his unwillingness to compromise and meet the other person. The diagonal cross on the chair, reminiscent of the Roman symbol of restrictions, hints at the fact that the individual has set rigid boundaries in the relationship, beyond which he does not allow his partner, not allowing him to delve into his personal space, to be aware of his affairs and often present around.

White candle on the card is associated with purity and inner strength, it symbolizes purification and awakening of hope, revival of all the most good and bright in the human soul. This element hints at the fact that there is a possibility that a person can overcome his impregnability and become more open and available for emotional communication.

The presence of the different phases of the Moon in the chart emphasizes the idea of constant change over time, suggesting that things can change dramatically over time, and the person may eventually turn to face their partner, showing a willingness to make changes in the relationship.

This card may indicate the couple's realization of the importance of joint efforts to maintain and develop their relationship. It symbolizes the idea that love is like a fire that needs to be constantly nourished to keep it burning. The partners are ready to take responsibility, take up the axe and go to the forest for fresh wood for their fire. There is an understanding in their relationship that they need to spend time communicating, strengthening their bond and working through any issues that come their way.

The person reflected in this card understands the value of constant investment in a relationship and the need to set aside time for its improvement and growth. She or he realizes that a harmonious and happy relationship requires not only desire but also action - working on oneself and the partnership. This card can also indicate a person's willingness to deal with existing problems in a relationship and a desire to improve its quality.

At the same time, the card can denote a person who does not seek new connections and closes himself off from the possibility of new relationships, preferring to keep a distance and not opening his heart to potential partners.

Work and finance

This card emphasizes that financial success does not come by chance; it requires perseverance and hard work. Funds are earned by diligence and active work. If a person does not work thoughtfully and without much diligence, then the reward will be modest. At the same time, the one who works hard can count on significant rewards. This card emphasizes the importance of an economic approach in both domestic and professional affairs. Organized person is expressed in the fact that he has every object in its place, everything is planned and prepared in detail, the workspace is kept clean, everything necessary is always at hand.

The card emphasizes the possibility of getting a new job, a promising position, the start of interesting projects, as well as the period when you will have to deal with routine tasks. It symbolizes professionalism and deep understanding of one's specialization. Sometimes the card may indicate the need for additional education in order to expand your professional horizons. It promises stable business growth and tangible results of hard work. A continuous flow of clients and orders is also reflected in this card, as well as a brilliant reputation, meticulousness in the details of work, constant attention to work processes.

Purple flowers are a harmonious combination of red and blue, symbolizing a person's willingness to wait peacefully and work methodically to grow their enterprise. Such flowers exude the energy of perseverance and tireless enthusiasm, while reflecting aspirations to reach career heights. Purple is an emblem of greatness, abundance, prosperity and prestige. In the context of career issues, it hints at high quality work performance, appreciation of the uniqueness of their projects and the manifestation of an unconventional approach in their implementation. Also purple emphasizes the desire for consistent and balanced career and financial development, avoiding sudden leaps. The readiness for significant growth is always inherent, and intuitive flair helps to determine where to invest resources and at what point it is best to realize a new idea. In his endeavors, the person strives for excellence and creative problem solving.

Nearby red flowers promote advancement in the professional field, empowerment, which in turn contributes to increased wealth and prosperity.

Pink creates an emotional attachment to one's work and fosters passion for the work, leading to meaningful achievement and high levels of rewarding work satisfaction.

The colors of the blue hue on the desk make it easier to make intuitive decisions regarding financial matters and money management.

Yellow flowers symbolize success and favorable circumstances in career advancement.

Orange blossoms ignite in the soul the desire for new professional heights and encourage efforts in increasing income.

Chamomile in the language of flowers symbolizes not only wealth and love, but also good luck in financial endeavors, representing favorable prospects.

Aloe acts as a protector, guarding against money mistakes and possible threats to income. It plays an important role in protecting savings and financial well-being.

Green candles placed in a space attract money flows and promote success in the business sphere, symbolizing growth, striving forward and general development. The green color of the candle is associated with abundance and helps to find optimal solutions to financial issues.

The chair is not just a support, but also a representation of the position occupied in the work, indicating the presence of a certain status and satisfaction with the position. The chair, as a symbol of height, can talk about career growth, about moving up the ladder. It is also an expression of recognition and respect of colleagues and partners. A chair of white color symbolizes purity, perfection and dedication, indicating a person's desire to achieve ideal results in their work.

Occupation

People who work with their hands, creative professions. Writer, poet, composer, screenwriter, teacher, course instructor, herbalist, jeweler, builder, businessman, office worker.

PLACES AND FACILITIES

Place of work, library, desk, office, workshop.

Tip

Any problem can be defeated if you put your best effort into solving it. Diligence and hard work are the key ingredients for achieving amazing success. It is important not to give up or give up, but to persevere in your pursuit of your goals, because you have the power to make a difference. Focus on your tasks, expand the horizons of your intellect, strive to deepen your professional skills and improve your mastery.

Warning

Sometimes it is important to pause and disengage from the work that has completely consumed your attention. You need to refresh your thoughts, have an epiphany and look around to see if something equally important is slipping away because you are focused on only one goal. Devote enough time to family and friends, because life consists of more than just work. The current moment requires you to pay attention to different aspects of your life, so don't miss out on what's important by focusing on one area.

Nine of Pentacles

Symbolism

1. Wearing a white dress symbolizes popularity and respect from others, as well as appreciation for the results of work and the successful completion of endeavors.

2. The book with potion formulas created in the previous Eight of Pentacles card is now a reliable tool for making potions, reflecting the idea that the effort expended in the Eight of Pentacles turns into real benefits and conveniences in the Nine of Pentacles.

3. Afro hairstyle, forming a round shape, emphasizes the idea of integrity and abundance of thoughts. Mandalas above the head, which the girl reaches for, symbolize the aspiration for a higher level of being and social status. This aspiration can lead to the fact that financial well-being and the ability to present oneself become more important than personal interests. There is a desire to stand out and demonstrate one's accomplishments to others. The character's gaze and gestures are directed upward, indicating unlimited prospects for achievement.

4. The girl's smile expresses her happiness and satisfaction with her achieved position and results.

5. In the practical application of the card, the mandala in the hand is often associated with using the phone for selfies, photos, and stories on social media. The bird perched on the mandala held in the hand emphasizes the desire to share one's achievements with others, and also symbolizes the ease with which achievements and financial prosperity come to a person, implying that communication contributes to success.

Total value

After long and diligent endeavors reflected in the Eight of Pentacles, the Nine of Pentacles card promises the arrival of important achievements, improved financial standing and increased social status. The Nine of Pentacles symbolizes financial good fortune, stable income and profit, wealth, material abundance, upward trajectory in career growth, respect and bonuses for work. This card reflects a sense of satisfaction with one's own performance, the results of hard work. In the Nine of Pentacles, a person feels justly proud of his labor successes, appreciates his own efforts and the activities to which he is devoted.

The person represented in the Nine of Pentacles has a well-organized life, is in a situation of prosperity and comfort, which gives him the opportunity not to exhaust himself with endless work, but to engage in personal interests and hobbies. Such a person is confident in his strength and in his ability to maintain a high standard of living. He behaves like a full-fledged master of his destiny, has a stable and balanced character, is independent and self-sufficient, with high self-esteem. Such a person shows fine taste in clothing, watches his appearance and health, is not stingy on investments in personal development and aesthetic pleasures. He also has a rich life experience and a deep understanding of the world around him.

Relationship

In this relationship there is stability, the atmosphere of harmony and mutual respect comes first. Partners appreciate the joys that life gives them, prioritizing aspects such as attractiveness and sexual compatibility. They also place great importance on respecting personal boundaries. The Nine of Pentacles card depicts a lonely person who feels quite comfortable in such a state, just like the heroes of other Nine of Pentacles cards. Such people do not feel an acute need for constant communication or mutual attention. They form a union of two independent personalities, whose relationship relies on an adult and meaningful approach, excluding dramas and conflicts.

In the context of the Nines, the theme of loneliness is often present. Thus, in the Nine of Swords a person is worried about loneliness, while in the Nine of Pentacles loneliness does not bring him suffering, he finds satisfaction in solitude. He feels pleasure in his independence and does not seek partnership for partnership's sake.

The person sincerely appreciates his partner and their joint future. As the girl on the card looks at the pentacle with reverence, so the man cherishes his relationship, feeling joy at the presence of his partner in his life. He considers his partner a priceless gift of fate. But at the same time does not tolerate restrictions on freedom because of jealousy, not wanting to be in a "golden cage", which is symbolized by the bird sitting on the mandala on the card. The meaning of the card is that there should be trust and space for personal freedom in a relationship; people who follow this principle remain faithful and respectful to each other. The card suggests treating your partner with trust and not restricting their freedom, so the partner will remain close for years to come.

Work and finance

This card symbolizes the blossoming of career and material well-being, indicates purchases of various scales - from small accessories to magnificent objects of art. It indicates a stable and impressive income, as well as the presence of a business that brings significant profit and satisfaction from the process of its conduct.

The color green, filled with associations with nature and harmony, symbolizes growth, freshness and development, bringing with it a sense of calm and peace. It suggests that a person feels confident in their current prosperous state, their business processes are in order, which promotes career and financial growth. Green is also the color of maturity and vitality, indicating a person's maturity in solving serious financial problems and running their own business.

The shade of yellow-green symbolizes freedom of thought and action, reflects energy, creativity and self-expression, as well as openness to the world and a friendly attitude towards people. This color inspires contentment and brings order to thoughts and feelings. Considered a symbol of agriculture and fertility, the yellow-green shade emphasizes that the person represented by this card has freedom in professional actions, is not limited by other people's expectations and has full autonomy in making decisions about his business.

The color red is inextricably linked with vitality, passion, joy, abundance and vitality. The individual indicated by this card has a sincere love for his work and especially appreciates the results of his activity. He not only strives for new heights, but also enjoys demonstrating his successes to others, doing so brightly and visibly.

Orange color is a symbol of ambition, high self-esteem, love of life and joyfulness. It indicates that professional activity brings a person joy and emotional uplift, making every working day like a holiday. The person cannot imagine his life without his favorite work and striving to achieve goals in it. The card emphasizes the importance of work, where there is always room for achievement, which then allows one to feel proud of oneself and one's successes.

The light purple color in the mandala symbolizes the individual's desire to achieve harmony in all aspects of life. It reflects the individual's efforts to find a balance between his inner aspirations and external successes, the world of emotions and real achievements.

The brown color, reminiscent of earth, expresses strong roots, a practical approach to life, and a desire for stability and security. It speaks of a person's reliability, their desire to build a solid foundation for their future and their preference for stability in a changing world.

The image on the card, where everything is covered with herbs, including dried juniper and basil, carries deep symbolism. Juniper is known as a powerful amulet against negative forces and as protection against loss and theft, symbolizing also the desire to materialize desires into reality. Under its influence, one seems to be financially secure, guarding one's accomplishments and resources, and has ample prospects for career advancement and improved financial status.

Famous for its association with areas such as money, love and protection, basil symbolizes the path to abundance and prosperity. The use of basil tincture can have a favorable effect on increasing income and career development, implying that a person is skillfully using all available resources to achieve their financial goals.

Lilac in the culture of many peoples is associated with attracting happiness, creating an atmosphere of harmony and general well-being, which indicates the human desire to create around him favorable conditions for development and growth.

The cauldron in magical traditions represents an instrument of transformation, creating a new reality from the elements mixed in it. This ability to manage work processes, directing energy to achieve the desired result, shows that a person has the ability for shrewd and farsighted planning in financial matters.

Blue candles on the chart are associated with Ajna, which is responsible for intuition and thought processes, implying that one has the ability to intuitively make good financial decisions. Blue is also associated with the patronage of Jupiter, the planet of expansion and business, indicating the potential for development and prosperity in the professional sphere.

Occupation

Blogger, model, presenter, herbalist, beauty salon worker, beauty worker, ecologist, ornithologist, biologist, designer, fashion designer, jeweler.

PLACES AND FACILITIES

Place in nature, park, zoo, beauty salon, fitting room, photo studio.

Tip

It is important not just to notice, but to celebrate any successes, whether they are small or significant. It is important to emphasize every step achieved, to strengthen self-esteem and to stimulate oneself by one's own achievements. To free oneself from imposter syndrome is to realize and value one's knowledge and skills. Be proud of yourself and every victory, regardless of its magnitude. It is important to love what you do on a regular basis, look for the positive aspects in the things you do, and emphasize all the good things that bring you joy.

Warning

Self-confidence in Temperance is healthy, but you also need to be mindful of those around you, the people who inspire and support you. Self-confidence is a good thing, but overconfidence can lead to problems if performance does not meet expectations. Therefore, it is important to assess the situation objectively and avoid unrealistic expectations of yourself and others.

Ten of Pentacles

S ymbolism

1. The illustration shows six figures, which carries the symbolism of universal love, humanity, sympathy and readiness to provide support. It emphasizes that an atmosphere of harmony, understanding and love prevails in a relationship, family or team.

2. The children's outfits are colored in shades of orange, yellow and white, which symbolizes their cheerfulness, bright mood, vigor and also indicates their pure-heartedness and devotion. Playful kids in the background of the image do not care about problems, foreshadowing a calm and joyful future, because children are the embodiment of tomorrow.

3. Dressed in snow-white clothes, the couple demonstrates the strength of their relationship and mutual devotion. They exchange glances, smiles and are in a state of happiness. The girl joining their hands through the mandala symbolizes the inseparability of family ties, emphasizing the sincerity and naivety of the adults' childlike feelings.

4. Abundance of yellow color on the map carries the meaning of warmth of relationships, creates a visual perception of positive space in the dwelling. This color also characterizes a person as enterprising, not inclined to despondency, full of energy and vitality.

5. The garland on the card symbolizes the celebration of fate and prosperity. In its image is the symbolism of connection and unity. The snow-white hue is associated with purity, ideal and fidelity, suggesting that people are united by reliable, loyal ties and aspiration to the ideal. The garland also represents the sequence of

various events in life. Its brightness and festive appearance implies that people are waiting for joyful moments. In addition, it symbolizes the longevity of a relationship.

6. In the image before us is a man with a dog, recognized by the Six of Cups, which symbolizes respect for one's history and recognition of the importance of past life lessons. The man perceives this, considering that the experience of his partner and relatives is also valuable, for the past is the basis for the present, from which, in turn, the future is formed. He realizes that he learns lessons throughout the phases of life, and that these important conclusions deserve special attention.

7. The dog is the embodiment of loyalty, courage and vigilance, it is a symbol of protection and the ability to sacrifice. This indicates that people in a couple, family or team are willing to prioritize each other's interests over their own, and if necessary, will not hesitate to defend their family, property or business interests.

8. The shades of the mandala carry the following meanings: The brown color of the mandala is associated with career prospects, the ability to concentrate and perseverance in achieving goals. The green color of the mandala, on which the girl stands, symbolizes prosperity and welfare, means the ability to continue the family, to create a stable and profitable business or business. A pale purple mandala in the hands of two people speaks of spiritual harmony, important for family unity. It emphasizes that the family is a holistic organism where each member of the family internalizes the experience of others, and in this case the adult is passing wisdom to the younger generation.

Total value

After the person in the Nine of Pentacles has enjoyed solitude, appreciating his successes and achievements, in the Ten of Pentacles he shares these achievements with the people he loves. This is the result of hard work and achievements in past cards, which has allowed him to enjoy a fulfilling life with loved ones. Frames a picture of happiness in the family sphere and a powerful union, represents a warm and kindness-filled home.

The Tree of Sefirot, taken from the Kabbalistic tradition, with its ten circles (sefirot), serves as a universal model of world order. It not only organizes the structure of the universe, but also connects its constituent parts into a single organized complex, reflecting the idea of unity: "everything exists in one, and one is present in everything. According to this philosophy, each element contains a reflection of the entire universe, which hints that the person reflected in this card has a multifaceted personality with a broad outlook, has insight and is able to see the essence of things. It also symbolizes abundance and prosperity at all levels of existence, in all areas of life. When you reach the Ten, you should consider how satisfied you are with what you have achieved and whether you want to remain in this state of prosperity, or whether you want to expand your horizons and start a new cycle to reach even greater heights.

A huge mandala of rich red color symbolizes health, vitality and endurance, being associated with life roots and fundamental energy center of a person. It testifies to his stability, physical health, strong ties with past generations, respect for the traditions of his family and family. The Tree of Life, which is part of this mandala, also emphasizes the importance of family and ancestors as part of the universe that shapes you and which you yourself continue, giving life to new generations. The Tree of Sephiroth carries the knowledge of the human desire for progress and continuation of the species. The red color of the mandala symbolizes passion, love of life, powerful energy, and reflects the fullness of life, beauty, warmth, love and home comfort.

The personality represented on the card feels a deep self-confidence, is proud of his life, of what he has achieved, appreciates the comforts and conveniences he has created. He gives credit to his merits and successes, respects those around him and nature. Recognizing himself as a part of the big world, he shows respect to everything that surrounds him.

Relationship

This card reflects harmonious relationships, strong union, common offspring. In this context, parents act as a worthy example for their children, guide them along the path of life. There is thoroughness and adherence to traditions in the couple, excluding the possibility of a free type of relationship or frivolous behavior. This is an adult and conscious relationship. At the level of feelings it is deep love, mutual respect, absolute understanding of each other, which brings joy on all levels, and entails mature, strong and stable feelings. It is a bond designed to last for many years, and possibly a lifetime, where both partners remain faithful to each other. Reliable feelings and relationships imply the fulfillment of mutual obligations, the couple is in complete harmony, both sexually and emotionally, and in the commonality of goals and aspirations.

The lamp is a symbol of illumination, life-giving power, deep love, aspiration and hope. Kerosene lamps bring a unique coziness to the environment, it indicates that in the relationship of a couple or in the family prevails a very warm and comfortable atmosphere, permeated with the light of mutual love. Staying with your family by the light of the lamp is a sign of unity, coziness and home warmth. There are five lamps on the card, which figuratively indicates the importance of all five human senses. This number tells people to experience life to the fullest, to enjoy each other's company, to decorate their homes with objects that create coziness, to cook appetizing dishes, to fill the house with excellent aromas, and to perform sexual acts with full commitment and understanding.

Work and finance

This card symbolizes a state of prosperity, wealth and financial progress, indicates significant success in business and professional sphere. It reflects favorable circumstances for the development of any endeavor and promises brilliant prospects for the future, because children are a symbol of hope and continuation of the family. It represents confidence in one's material status, the pinnacle of success, extensive wealth and a high level of prosperity. It is the pinnacle of achieved success and financial completeness.

The predominance of the yellow hue in the card indicates the ability of the person to achieve goals in his activities, thanks to skillful diplomatic behavior and excellent skills in interacting with others, which contributes to the growth of entrepreneurship. The card foretells a measured, secure and comfortable life, perhaps indicating an inheritance or participation in a family business. It represents the image of a professional with a high level of skill, who possesses considerable experience and diligence. The card promises impressive and wide-ranging business opportunities, successful investment investments and projects. It also symbolizes favorable working conditions, pleasant and friendly environment in the team. It is a card of expanding professional horizons and the opportunity to pass on your experience to your colleagues, as well as receiving well-deserved bonuses and cash bonuses at work.

Occupation

Family business, big business owner, environmentalist. Esotericist, working with ancestry. Archival worker, a person engaged in the restoration of the family tree, geneticist. Decorator, interior designer.

PLACES AND FACILITIES

Home, family nest, large, beautiful halls, design and decor studios, interior design stores.

Tip

Treat life as a precious gift, cherish your family and friends, as well as your personal achievements and the resources you currently have. Understand what is the foundation of your well-being. Seek to broaden your horizons, expand your entrepreneurial endeavors and improve your living conditions. Show respect for your family members, both older and younger, realizing that everyone is of equal importance. Look for ways to build wealth, discover the beauty in every moment you live, and realize how all aspects of life are intimately connected.

Warning

There is a risk of getting stuck in the established framework and continuing to live in a familiar, cozy world from which you will not seek to get out. It is important to think independently, not to follow someone else's way of life and avoid internalizing negative habits inherent in your family environment. The card also suggests the need to protect the comfort of your home, care for the safety of loved ones and protect the boundaries of your personal space. Pay attention to established life scenarios that may carry potential harm.

Page of Pentacles

Symbolism

1. Traditionally, a mandala is formed of various patterns and symbols, which are selected by a person depending on his personal preferences and aesthetic perception. Everyone brings a piece of their soul into this unique artistic drawing, enriching it with individual meaning and deep significance. The shade of yellow in the drawing indicates that the creator of the project breathed his warmth, cheerfulness and energy into it. This is a reflection of a person's desire to put light emotions and bright energy into his creation. The tone of blue in the mandala symbolizes a person's desire to put into his work the ability to understand the needs of others, his readiness for empathy and the ability to empathize deeply. This indicates that when performing a task, a person strives to take into account the wishes of the client, tries to understand his needs, showing care and understanding both to the partner and to others. Green is associated with growth and development, which emphasizes a person's attitude to improve his skills and expand the capabilities of his business or project. Brown, in turn, is the color of stability and pragmatism, which indicates that a person reliably fulfills his obligations, regularly takes orders and thus improves his skills each time.

2. The shades used in the mandala are also found in the rug woven by nature itself. The girl borrows these qualities directly from nature, drawing inspiration and energy for creativity from there. Nature serves as an invaluable teacher and inspiration for her. She follows the patterns of nature, trying to harmonize with it. What we see on the map is a reference to the principle of mimicry, where the

creation of architectural objects or design borrows forms, structures and processes found in the natural environment.

3. The pants are fastened with a cord that holds them on the body, reminiscent of a root emerging from the soil. This symbolizes the support that a person receives from loved ones, from the native roots, as well as loyalty to their own patterns and skills that serve as a reliable support in life. The practical qualities of the Pagus of Pentacles, his devotion to his own ideals and close people create a sense of stability and security. Orange color portends a positive attitude to the acquisition of new skills, improvement of one's professional skills, and also symbolizes creativity, uniqueness and originality in approaches.

4. The root wrapped around the leg indicates a strong connection with another person or a certain situation, a deep kinship, close interaction and immersion in the essence of what is happening. The girl stands on one leg, while the other remains free, which implies some instability and fluctuation in position. The roots of the mandala, by which she is attached to the mandala carpet on which she stands, indicate a close relationship with the work of her labor, her creativity, for the creation of which she drew inspiration from nature and the earth.

5. Conifers have the property of regeneration and rejuvenation. Reducing the aging processes of our body is achieved through cell regeneration, and the use of products containing pine needles helps not only to restore youth to the body, but also to overcome many diseases. It speaks of a young man or child, characteristic of the image of a pageboy, as well as an adult who retains youthfulness through rejuvenating treatments. The forest is a place where one can get lost and it symbolizes an unpredictable, confusing space. The girl standing with her back to the forest and creating her patterns in the pattern of nature demonstrates that the person represented by this card is capable of bringing order to any chaos, systematizing and organizing disorder.

Total value

The Page of Pentacles is the initial card in the hierarchy of the suit of Pentacles, representing the least experienced member of the suit. However, despite his youth and lack of much life experience, he stands out for his steadfast drive and tireless work ethic, which symbolize his deep connection to the element of Earth. This card speaks of an inherent ability for powerful creativity and a close unity with the natural world. The Pagus of Pentacles appears to us as a model of rationality and practicality, it indicates the possibility of important events or news. And since the suit of Pentacles is associated with the material aspects of life, the news or opportunities it portends are most often related to finances, acquisitions, or the creation of something important.

The person reflected in the Pagus of Pentacles experiences real pleasure in the process of starting new projects, learning skills and creating something new, enthusiastically immersing himself in the peculiarities of his profession. This person is characterized by increased responsibility and reliability. He consistently and confidently takes up the tasks set before him. The Page of Pentacles has the ability to find joy in small things, to appreciate and accept life with all its colors, the ability to pay attention to nuances and constantly work on their own development and improvement of their skills. This character carefully studies the instructions and follows the rules, he is thoughtful about every little thing, realizing that they form the basis of our existence. Therefore, he tirelessly improves in every small aspect of his work, striving to achieve a high level of professionalism. The Page of Pentacles is aware of his abilities and knows how they can be competently used to achieve their goals. He is an exemplary student and a conscientious performer.

Relationship

In relationships that are described through the image of the Pagus of Pentacles, one sees a practical and hard-working approach. For these partners, building and maintaining a relationship is a consistent process that requires attention, effort and time. They take the view that love strengthens over time and that respect, commitment and expressing one's feelings are key in the long term.

Partners who fit the description of the Page of Pentacles believe in the importance of little things and the importance of attention to detail. They tend to show their love through actions, gifts and care, which is their way of showing affection and love. In this relationship, affection and habit play an important role, as symbolized by the roots that the Paddy has grown close to. It can also indicate the length of the relationship and its depth.

The Page of Pentacles values his partner and treats him like a family member - with care and deep respect. In a couple people value the comfort and well-being of each other, trying to create a harmonious and cozy atmosphere. In this case, the physical aspect of the relationship is also important, as the Pagus of Pentacles is associated with the element of Earth, which implies the earthly and sensual side of love.

The Page of Pentacles can add a special touch to the routine, making ordinary evenings memorable with his attention to detail and ability to create a romantic atmosphere. He can be so focused on the relationship that everything else takes a back seat, including socializing with friends and other social aspects of life, which shows the depth of his affection and willingness to invest all his time and energy in his partner.

Work and finance

The carpet symbolizes the level of financial prosperity, which indicates that the financial resources from this card are sufficient for life: funds are not abundant, but they are quite enough for a comfortable existence.

Voluminous pants on a girl signals that she has not yet reached the highest level of skill, but she is making efforts every day to get closer to that level and eventually reach it.

The Pazh, who holds a mandala in his hands and focuses on it, symbolizes the need to receive support and recognition of his work from others. In order to express himself, create and achieve goals, it is important for this person to feel support, believe in himself, especially when his work finds deserved recognition and praise.

The card portends the beginning of new projects and the availability of necessary resources for their realization. The person shown on it makes every effort to work on projects, corrects mistakes, strives for continuous improvement of his skills. This card can also indicate small profits, unexpected opportunities for earning, receiving the first income from a new endeavor. It is associated with the conclusion of contracts and deals.

The Page of Pentacles shows neatness, technical literacy and accuracy in the performance of work, he learns by taking over the experience of others.

Occupation

A painter, a sculptor, it is a tangible work, something you can touch, a naturalist, an ecologist, a landscape designer. A person who is practicing. Creativity according to this card is tangible, which can be touched: it is paintings, sculptures, creation of decorations, jewelry, clothing, etc.

PLACES AND FACILITIES

Park, garden, forest, exhibitions, places for children, playgrounds, kindergartens.

Tip

To focus on one area, tirelessly honing one's skills in that craft. It is important to pay special attention to your chosen field, perfecting every tiny detail. It is also important to boldly demonstrate the results achieved, without fear of sharing your skills with others. Find inspiration in this process and create new things. Special attention should be paid to people with whom you have close ties, show care and responsibility for the relationship, maintain constant contact and be a reliable support.

Warning

There is a danger of becoming so absorbed in one activity that everything else slips away from attention, resulting in a loss of control over the rest of life. It is important to unload oneself, to distract one's gaze in order to restore harmony in the various areas of one's existence. The card warns that the current strong attachment to something or someone may cause obstacles and difficulties in the future.

Knight of Pentacles

S ymbolism

1. He walks leisurely, paying attention to his surroundings, treading barefoot to feel and experience the present moment. He walks, taking pleasure in every movement, feeling the grass caressing his soles, he absorbs the power of the earth and connects with it. He lives in harmony with nature, with the flora around him, with the earth. He realizes that the abundance of his future harvest depends on the amount of seed he sows. His footsteps leave behind grains that herald beautiful sprouts.

2. The Knight of Pentacles distributes mandalas-pentacles on his plot, investing labor to see the fruits of his efforts later. He moves toward his dream unhurriedly, the slowest among the knights. But his progress is deliberate and measured; each step is the result of careful calculation. The mandalas depict eight-pointed lotuses, symbols of solid protection. It is a representation of a person's stable position, an indication that his financial status and income are protected. Mandalas symbolize the merging of the masculine and feminine, promote self-realization and enhance creativity. Red mandalas reflect love and dedication, orange mandalas portend the joy of the coming harvest with a worthy investment of effort. Violet and light purple shades symbolize the desire for harmony, the search for balance between the inner world and external achievements. Brown color of mandalas speaks about the desire for stability and security.

3. The black horse on which he rides is associated with earth, practicality and discipline. This demonstrates the Knight of Pentacles' clear and realistic vision of his path, his disciplined

adherence to the chosen route without deviation. The decorated saddle symbolizes that the person overcomes his path, enjoying each step.

4. The pentagram engraved on its shield indicates a sense of complete security, faith in the future. It is a symbol of the security of the situation, protection of material well-being, protection of relationships and other aspects of life.

Total value

After in-depth attention to detail of the Pagus of Pentacles, which symbolizes the earthly firmament, the Knight of Pentacles appears, combining the elements of earth and air. In his image is seen expansion, expansion of boundaries, he steadily and unhurriedly moving forward, in contrast to the Pazh, which seems to be rooted in one place. Knight of Pentacles symbolizes the desire for success and deserved recognition through hard, consistent and patient work. However, you should pave the way to the cherished goal cautiously, thinking through every step along the way.

In the life position of the Knight of Pentacles everything is calibrated and harmonious, everything goes its own way without fuss and worry. His light-colored robes carry a message of inner harmony and natural connection with the world around him. Knight of Pentacles is comparable to a participant in a marathon: his stamina and determination are combined with the ability to manage their resources in an organized manner and clearly lay the route to the intended goal. He is demanding both to his own activity and to the results. His appearance symbolizes the stabilization of the situation and indicates the duration of the processes. The Knight of Pentacles reflects the reliability and solidity of the situation, indicating a solid foundation for enterprises and endeavors.

Relationship

The participants in the relationship show mutual respect and care, creating a strong alliance. In such an alliance, each partner actively attends to the needs and desires of the other, providing reliable mutual support and the ability to rely on each other in difficult moments. There is an atmosphere of trust between the partners, they strive to work together to improve their relationship, day by day making them stronger and more mature. Their relationship is dominated by mutual understanding, tolerance for each other's weaknesses and reliable support from their partner. An important aspect is the value of quality intimacy and other earthly pleasures that bring pleasure to both.

Such relationships are based on devotion and sincere loyalty to each other. Partners often share common goals, such as saving a certain amount of money or buying real estate. Mutual care is expressed in such small things as the ability to make a relaxing massage, cooking a delicious dinner or taking care of the partner during illness. The emotional background of the relationship is colored by deep affection and sincere feelings for the partner. The Knight of Pentacles symbolizes a person who tries to do everything possible to make his partner comfortable and pleasant in this relationship. The card can also mean that the Knight of Pentacles is ready to woo the object of his feelings for a long time, expressing his care, devotion and attention, sometimes it can last for years.

Sometimes this card hints that one of the partners has decided to go through life alone, as the figure on the card has his back turned and is moving forward without looking back at the past. This can be a sign of routine in a relationship, but it also symbolizes its permanence and reliability.

Work and finance

In his professional activity, he invariably follows the chosen path, without deviating from the intended road. He is not in a hurry, but consistently achieves the tasks set before him, investing in personal development and strengthening his business, so that in the future it will give him abundant fruits. With due care and diligence he approaches his work responsibilities. Knight of Pentacles depicts a man thorough, practical and reliable. He is distinguished by exceptional equanimity and stability. Everything he undertakes, he invariably brings to a logical conclusion, leaving no business unfinished.

He is characterized by accuracy and deep concentration on the task at hand. Just as the character on the card draws strength from the earth, so the Knight of Pentacles feels a surge of energy when actively engaged in business, finding his calling in work. His gaze is fixed on the future, where he seeks to bring the fruits of his labor. He often possesses a variety of important skills, which become his support in life and help him in his professional activities.

This card symbolizes dedication and hard work, and also emphasizes that results will not come immediately, but they are sure to show up over time, even though the process will progress slowly. It emphasizes the importance of prudence and frugality in financial matters and business activities. The card also predicts contracts and various agreements. It may also refer to real estate, land and movable property such as automobiles and cattle. It is also a symbol of stability in work, where a person can work in the same place for many years, gradually moving up the career ladder. The Knight of Pentacles is a serious and responsible worker with professional skills and a high level of craftsmanship that he has developed since the time of the Pagus of Pentacles.

Occupation

Farmer, manager, cab driver, mechanic, financier, equestrian person, agriculture.

PLACES AND FACILITIES

Forests, parks, fields, outdoor places, racetracks, stables.

Tip

It is important not to rush to conclusions and avoid haste in changing circumstances. It is worth listening carefully to your inner feelings in order to understand which path will be the most correct and favorable. It is necessary to consciously and consistently move towards the goal, acquiring the qualities of a true marathon runner. You will have to realize that there are no instant solutions and that will require persistence and patience. In this situation, it is necessary to show not only patience, but also perseverance.

Warning

The likelihood of difficulties arises from the tendency to delay decision-making, which can lead to missed favorable opportunities. Opportunities can disappear much faster than a person is able to recognize and take advantage of them. The present moment requires concentration and activity rather than a relaxed and slow progression, with a keen eye on the world around us. Procrastination may not be so useful in the current environment.

Queen of Pentacles

S ymbolism

1. On the head of the Queen of Pentacles there is a turban of green color, which not only performs a practical function, storing jewelry and money, but also has a deep meaning. The turban serves as a reliable protection for the third eye, which symbolizes intuitive vision and protects from outside influences on thoughts. This explains why the person associated with this Tarot card has a mindset of abundance and growth. He shields himself from other people's thoughts of lack and scarcity, maintaining his confidence in the richness of the world.

2. The crown, decorated with leaves resembling horns, creates an association with fertility gods from various mythologies. This crown symbolizes the crown of prosperity, reflecting a state of complete well-being when one possesses everything one has ever desired. The Queen of Pentacles radiates the energy of abundance, and everything it touches is filled with the desire for life and development. The six green leaves on the crown emphasize harmony and integrity of life positions, indicating that one is sovereign in the management of one's resources, relying on inner comfort and intuition for investment or spending.

3. The Queen's closed eyes indicate her total immersion in a state of wealth, and the green shadows on her eyelids emphasize her vision of the world as a place full of opportunities to increase wealth. She holds the Pentacle without strain, without clenching it too tightly, unlike the character of the Four of Pentacles. Holding it aloft, she recognizes her right to own and control her own wealth, convinced that financial security is an integral part of who she is.

4. The pillow on which she rests symbolizes not only coziness and comfort, but also an auspicious position in life. The red color of the pillow is associated with the root chakra - Muladhara, which is responsible for our physical health, vital energy and the basis of stability.

5. The upholstered armchair in which the Queen is comfortably seated reflects her state of prosperity, wealth and peace of mind. The beige color of its upholstery is associated with nature and emphasizes the feeling of security, harmony and stability in life.

6. The green tree spread over the Queen of Pentacles emphasizes her connection to nature and a way of life consistent with natural cycles and rhythms. This tree, being a symbol of living, growing and blossoming nature, reflects the Queen's being surrounded by abundance and her inner harmony with that abundance. She feels part of nature and the family circle, which is the source of her strength and well-being.

7. The Queen's luxurious dress, made of quality fabrics, speaks of her predilection for high quality and value. She prefers something that lasts long while emphasizing her status, preferences and taste. The beige and brown hues of the dress reinforce the association with nature, earth and stability. A person like her has the ability to use resources wisely and sparingly, preferring to emphasize elegant and unobtrusive things in her appearance.

8. The Queen's jewelry and mehendi on her hands in the form of grains emphasize her focus on abundance and prosperity. Mehendi can symbolize wealth, harvest and renewal. The arrangement of patterns on both hands may reflect her ability to act (hands as a symbol of action and control) in a way that attracts and multiplies prosperity both within herself and in the material world.

9. The coniferous forest in the background may indicate that the Queen has the ability to see order in chaos and to manage that chaos, creating harmony and structure out of it. The fact that the forest is vague and unclear may indicate that the Queen of Pentacles prefers to distance herself from situations that lack

clarity and order, and not get unnecessarily involved.

Total value

After the Knight of Pentacles has worked hard scattering seeds on the ground, the caring Queen of Pentacles continues this work, watching the plants grow and develop. The element of water is strongly present, symbolizing deep attention to her situation, the ability to care for the fruits of her labors and the preservation of the resources that have been gained through hard work.

In the view of the Queen of Pentacles, comfortable conditions and high quality of life are valued. She would rather buy one expensive and high-quality item than several cheaper, but of questionable quality. In her house reigns order: glasses stand in certain places, linens are always smooth and neatly folded, cosmetics orderly laid out in special organizers. Her home reflects cleanliness and comfort, surrounded by quality furniture and filled with the aroma of delicious food.

The person reflected in the Queen of Pentacles has stability and success in life, has enough money for a comfortable existence. She has the ability to earn and effectively manage her life, prefers order and timeliness in all aspects of his existence. Such a person cares about the livability of his home, is self-sufficient, looks at the world with the eyes of a realist. This Queen of Pentacles is characterized by experience and wisdom, provides a strong material base and order in her environment.

The person who personifies the Queen of Pentacles is characterized by security and practical approach to life. She not only knows how to manage her finances, but is willing to share her abundance with others, doing so out of the fullness of her heart, realizing that there are plenty of opportunities in the world. She has no thoughts of lack of money, she believes that finances are something that can be created from a variety of sources, that there are many ways to achieve wealth and prosperity in life. The image of the Queen of Pentacles can be recognized in the image of a mother, spouse, homeowner or business owner.

Relationship

The Queen of Pentacles often reflects the image of a married lady or wife, indicating a relationship that is characterized by longevity and strength. In such a union, the partners are not necessarily officially married, but their bond is so close that they perceive each other as close relatives. The card may denote blood ties. Mehendi bracelets in the iconography of this card symbolize prosperity and success in family life. These relationships are characterized by reliability, where trust between partners is strong and unquestioned. This relationship expresses maturity and stability, with an emphasis on loyalty and devotion. The partners value each other highly and strive to create an atmosphere of coziness and comfort in the relationship, where one can rely unconditionally on the support of the companion. In such a union, partners realize that feelings are subject to change and are not the basis for cardinal decisions. Mutual respect, comfort and support are the main pillars of their union.

The Queen of Pentacles also symbolizes commitment to traditional values in relationships and the partners' unwavering confidence in their choices. The card speaks of deep and constant emotions, of strong attachment that unites people. In such a relationship, partners show unconditional devotion and are ready to do everything possible for the well-being of the other, paying special attention to material security and financial stability in the couple. Important aspects for them are comfort, home coziness, prosperity and general prosperity, which indicates their desire for a secure and happy life together.

On the negative side, the Queen of Pentacles can reveal a tendency to mercantilism in relationships, when the main emphasis is placed on the benefits and practical interests of the partners. The card can also reflect a tendency to jealousy and possessiveness, which entails the danger of losing sight of the true feelings and emotional connection between partners. In the pursuit of material comfort and coziness, the couple may lose sight of the depth and sincerity of their relationship.

Work and finance

Based on this card, it can be argued that the person's financial situation is extremely stable and secure. He has access to a vast amount of resources, a stable and well-paid job, and the likelihood of passive income, income from investment activities, stocks or bonds; he may also be investing in jewelry. The Queen of Pentacles embodies wisdom in the management of finances and other resources, she has an inherent confidence and competence in these matters, and is in her elemental environment.

Her ability to deeply understand the intricacies of financial transactions comes to the fore because the Queen of Pentacles possesses characteristics of the element of water, common to all queen cards, which gives her special insight and intuition in monetary matters. One who associates with this card lives in a state of prosperity and complete material satisfaction. This symbolizes success in the professional sphere, career growth, financial well-being, comfort and abundance. Such a person demonstrates high qualification in business and economic matters. Consequently, the current situation requires a conscious approach and skilled management of both finances and work processes.

Occupation

Business owner, banker, financier, accountant, civil servant, landscaper, florist, manufacturer of quality and expensive goods, housewife, beautician, florist.

PLACES AND FACILITIES

Home, places in nature, forests, place of work, government agencies.

Tip

It is necessary to dive deeply into the basis of what is happening. It is important to comprehend what actions contribute to the favorable development of the situation, its prosperity and growth. It is necessary to be prudent in managing your assets, to use them competently. The approach to the situation should be as practical as possible, pragmatism and patience are most important. The view of circumstances should be realistic.

Warning

Sometimes overprotection of circumstances or a person can lead to undesirable consequences. Excessive pedantry and slowness can act as obstacles to the achievement of a goal. Excessive austerity and precaution may prove to be an obstacle to progress in the development of a given situation.

King of Pentacles

Symbolism

1. His hair is silver-gray, which emphasizes the depth of his experience and the sharpness of his mind. His beard is also gray and much longer, indicating not only his experience, but also his tendency to traditional values and conservatism in some views.

2. His clothes are chosen with a bias towards maximum naturalness and harmony with nature. The green sweater symbolizes not just growth and prosperity, but also the power of life, the fertility of the land, of which he is the patron. The gray color of his garment carries shades of restraint, poise and harmony of the inner and outer world.

3. The library surrounding him is a separate universe, full of strict rules and orderliness. It is a symbol of a huge luggage of knowledge and rich life experience, reflecting his high intellectuality, extensive erudition and comprehensive knowledge. It indicates that the King of Pentacles is able to find a solution to even the most intricate problem, never finding himself in a dead end.

4. Wolf, always vigilant and cautious, symbolizes in the King of Pentacles inner fortitude, insight and nobility of spirit, as well as unbending loyalty. His fur is colored in shades of brown and gray, which speaks of a deep connection with the natural elements and inherent instincts of man, which he perfectly controlled. The gray color also emphasizes his ability to make decisions with strength and firmness, especially when it comes to maintaining loyalty and promises.

5. The space around him is overflowing with red color, which clearly indicates the presence of the element of fire in him. This is a

reflection of his steadfastness, leadership qualities both in the business sphere and in family relations. King of Pentacles - a true lord of his business and home, always consistent in his material aspirations.

6. A beige chair, soft and cozy like that of the Queen of Pentacles, also symbolizes the desire for comfort and the desire for a prestigious position in society, at work and in the family. This color is associated with natural harmony, speaking of security, tranquility and reliability.

7. Accentuating comfort and coziness, the pillow emphasizes his confident and strong position in any situation. In addition, the red color of the pillow is associated with the root chakra Muladhara, which symbolizes the basis of stability, health and vital energy, which is nourished from the earth force.

8. The King is depicted happy and laughing, looking at his family or far away, seeing the realization of his dreams. He holds the pentacle lightly and casually, showing no fear of loss and confidence in his own abilities and wealth, being in a state of material and spiritual abundance.

Total value

The King of Pentacles combines the powerful energies of earth and flame. After the Queen of Pentacles' careful stewardship of resources and their conscious investment, the King of Pentacles, with the power of the fire element, seeks to expand and increase his possessions and influence. He is a leader in the field of economics and material well-being, personifying power and prosperity.

The King of Pentacles card can represent various circumstances related to business, business management, government agencies, large-scale companies, financial affairs, work, home life and family values. It symbolizes authority and esteem in society, among colleagues, household, emphasizing responsibility and striving for excellence in all endeavors. It reflects career growth, achievement, dominance in the workplace, as well as abundance and material abundance. The King of Pentacles utilizes his experience and wisdom to manage finances and strategically expand his influence.

This person has a high social rank and a burning desire to engage in the launch of profitable initiatives, create new jobs, contribute to the growth of wealth and strengthen their position in this status. King of Pentacles is characterized by the seriousness of intentions, he is not in a hurry, but his actions are always very deliberate and reliable. If he takes for something, then necessarily perform it at the highest level. He always has plenty of money, and he knows exactly how to maintain his financial well-being. In his philosophy of life, funds are always available and can be acquired at any time. He is excellent in understanding the financial currents and mechanisms.

This person is also unwavering in his promises and words: if he promised, he will certainly fulfill them. He is adamant in his decisions, pragmatic, sees everything very clearly and realistically. For him, career and work is always a priority, he is a true master of his craft, knowing it to the last detail. The King of Pentacles portends a clear structure and orderliness in any situation.

Relationship

This union is characterized by reliability and solidity. The King of Pentacles is a devoted family man who adheres to traditional family values and represents a conservative marriage union. This King is steadfastly concerned with the well-being and reliability of the family structure. His endeavors are aimed at ensuring that the home is always filled with abundance and that the family is not in need of anything. He protects and defends the interests of his family and his companion. This relationship is imbued with seriousness and maturity. The sensual side includes both the passion characteristic of the fire element and the deep respect and affection characteristic of the earth element. Earth has the ability to love deeply and over a long period of time. This is a long-term, stable relationship in which partners truly appreciate and respect each other.

There may also be an element of jealousy and a sense of ownership in the relationship. Partners in this union show loyalty and confidence in their life partner. This union can be characterized as patriarchal, where the man often acts as the head of the family. King of Pentacles demonstrates his feelings not so much with words, but with deeds and obvious concern for the well-being of his family. In his behavior there is restraint and adherence to conservative views.

Work and finance

Financial prosperity, sustainability, security for the future - these are the key characteristics of this state. What is meant here is a stable and high income, which is ensured thanks to the ability to earn well. The personality represented by this card does not avoid taking on additional obligations and responsibilities in pursuit of large incomes. It indicates the achievement of high social status, possession of a prestigious position and is a sign of a true master and professional in his work. It also traces rapid career advancement, rise, business expansion and increased income.

The King of Pentacles behaves like a true financial strategist: he wisely manages his assets, invests wisely and works purposefully to strengthen his capital, implementing a step-by-step financial development. If he encounters difficulties, he does not panic or fall into despair, but changes tactics in a measured and thoughtful manner, adapting to new circumstances. His determination and steadfastness resemble the steadfastness of flint: it is difficult to throw him off balance or make him retreat in the face of failure. He will withstand any trials and confidently continue on his way to the intended goal.

Occupation

Businessman, owner of a garden, field, agronomist, supplier, real estate work, investor, engineer, builder, mechanic, financier, producer, store owner with expensive, quality goods or their manufacturer.

PLACES AND FACILITIES

Offices, libraries, stewards' offices, state offices.

Tip

It is necessary to take a sensible and logically sound approach to the tasks at hand. It is important to be competent in managing your assets and actively seek opportunities to increase them. It is necessary to pay due attention to career development, strengthening of home and family relations. It is important to take responsibility, to show yourself as a reliable and practical person who can be relied on in any circumstances. Expanding your knowledge in the field of finance will also contribute to overall success.

Warning

One should not be too stagnant and adhere to outdated tenets in a changing environment. Excessive conservatism and intransigence in decisions can be harmful. It is important to be open to other opinions and not allow the desire for stability to become a limiting framework. Do not pay excessive attention to minutiae and avoid necessary changes by remaining excessively immobile.

AFTERWORD

This book describes each of the Light Seer tarot cards as fully as possible, but of course we may not have seen in it what you may see. Therefore, when studying this deck, be sure to keep your notes, as it is quite possible that it is you who will be able to find the true meaning of certain cards.

Milton Keynes UK
Ingram Content Group UK Ltd.
UKHW010700140324
439439UK00016B/1912

9 798224 934157